TOGETHER
WE CAN

PETER BAINES OAM

TOGETHER WE CAN

33 MARATHONS IN 26 DAYS
A RUN TO REMEMBER SO WE NEVER FORGET

MAJOR STREET

"This inspiring book chronicles the author's incredible mental and physical journey, pushing beyond limits to raise funds and awareness for an incredibly worthy cause. It's a powerful reminder of how determination and purpose can turn personal struggle into meaningful impact. A breathtaking story from a truly extraordinary human being."

Paul Reid, Managing Director, Panasonic Australia

"Inspiring stories of endurance are one thing. Remarkable stories of service and commitment are another. When you combine both together, it truly is extraordinary. Peter Baines, his stories and impact, are something quite special."

Darren Hill, behavioural scientist; Executive Director and Co-Founder, Pragmatic Thinking

"This is a story of endurance, courage and perseverance that ends in a story of inspiration."

Peter Costello AC, Former Treasurer

"I've coached a lot of runners over the years, but working with Pete has been a highlight. He's one of the humblest blokes I've ever met. His grit, consistency and quiet determination are unmatched. What Pete achieved over 1400 kilometres and 26 days running across Thailand wasn't just about physical endurance. He battled heat, fatigue, and serious wear and tear, and kept showing up. What made the difference was the purpose driving him: the work of Hands Across the Water, and the strength of the team behind him. It's proof that when you combine heart, mission and community, you can go well beyond what you thought possible."

Matty Abel, running coach

"An incredible story of resilience, determination and making an impact. It's a great reminder that alone we can go far but together we can go further!"

Jess Fox OAM, six-time Olympian and Olympic champion

"There are few who walk their talk the way Peter Baines does. Having been deeply inspired by his mission, commitment and passion over the years, I can't wait to see the impact of this special book."

Michael McQueen, Multi-award winning speaker and author

"This is a must-read for all. I have often said, 'We need more Peter Baines in the world'. He is too humble to accept that kind of praise, but after reading *Together We Can*, you'll understand exactly why I say it.

"This book is more than a recount of a 1400-kilometre run in 26 days across Thailand; it is a story of true purpose, perspective, pain, people and connection. Peter brings us onto the road with him, step by step and struggle by struggle to the point that you feel you are running beside him through the messy, beautiful, painful, hard, gratifying and electrifying moments.

"He writes with a raw honesty that gives us a glimpse of what it means to push beyond comfort, to embrace fear and uncertainty, and to find growth through sacrifice.

"It is a huge lesson to all: we grow outside the comfort zone. You do not truly understand your limits until you test them. This book is relatable to all people from all walks of life. We all face hard things, and everyone's 'hard' looks different.

"Peter reminds us that while we cannot help everyone, we can help someone – that the path to impact doesn't start with perfection but with intent. When we do these hard things for the right reasons, we are not just changing lives; we are changing ourselves along the way.

"*Together We Can* will leave you deeply moved, inspired, and undeniably changed.

"Together we can, together we will, together we did."

Domonique Doyle, sports psychologist

"*Together We Can* isn't just the story of an extraordinary endurance feat; it's a raw, honest, and deeply human account of what's possible. Peter Baines reminds us that leadership isn't about comfort, it's about commitment, courage, and continuing to move forward, even when it's hard. If you want to know what you're capable of, read this book."

Dale Beaumont, Founder & CEO of Business Blueprint®

"Peter Baines is an extraordinary Australian who has changed the destiny of so many children living in poverty, often without a family. He has given hope when previously these children had nothing to live for."

Dr Ross Walker, consultant cardiologist, author and media presenter

"Having known Peter Baines for more than 18 years, I've witnessed his unwavering resilience and determination to go beyond the norm – always for the benefit of the children and communities in Thailand, to which he has become bonded for life.

"What began in response to the 2004 tsunami has grown into a life-changing legacy, now supporting over 400 children through Hands Across the Water.

"*Together We Can* is a powerful reminder of what's possible when compassion meets action. Peter's story is both moving and inspiring – a testament to the impact of courageous leadership and the difference one person can make when driven by purpose."

Kay Spencer, Chairperson of NARTA International and the Chair of Hands

"Peter Baines tells the story of an extraordinary life – his own. When you meet Peter, you encounter a man of quiet strength, humility and dignity. He is a serious man who does not take himself too seriously but takes his work with the utmost seriousness. His accomplishments arise from a singular driving force: a deep, unwavering commitment to be of service. This story will move you to tears and stir courage in your heart."

Colin James, international speaker and bestselling author

"Peter is a man of few words, but he makes every one of them count. His writing, like his leadership, is thoughtful, authentic, and impossible to ignore."

Steve Carroll, Founder, Digital Live

"Not all superheros wear capes; some wear yellow Hokas. Peter Baines writes much like he lives his life – with authenticity, humour and a touching vulnerability. His writing style displays humility and modesty, yet his achievements in his humanitarian work and on his recent running odyssey are nothing short of incredible and inspiring."

Andrew Klein, Professional MC

To the love of my life, CT, thank you for believing in me.
And to those who didn't think they could but tried anyway.

Also by Peter Baines
Hands Across the Water
Doing Good by Doing Good
Leadership Matters

"The most effective way to do it is to do it."
– Amelia Earhart

The crew

Claire Baines (CT): Hands CEO, Marketing Guru, Runner (with a daily increase in load), Problem-solver, Wife

Chris Thomas (CT's dad): Captain on the Road

Wendy Thomas (CT's mum): Head Chef

Greg Wallace: Runner

Julie (Jules) Wallace (Greg's wife): Runner Support

Claire Oliver: Medic

Am: Tour Manager

Squid: Mothership Driver

Bew: Support Vehicle Driver

Mae Thiew: Guardian Angel and Cycle Support

Rod Reid: Film Crew

Finn Beaumont: Film Crew

Kelsey Baines (Peter's daughter): Runner

Jack Baines (Peter's son): Runner

First published in 2025 by Major Street Publishing Pty Ltd
info@majorstreet.com.au | majorstreet.com.au

© Peter Baines 2025
The moral rights of the author have been asserted.

 A catalogue record for this book is available from the National Library of Australia

Printed book ISBN: 978-1-923186-35-4
Ebook ISBN: 978-1-923186-36-1

All rights reserved. Except as permitted under *The Australian Copyright Act 1968* (for example, a fair dealing for the purposes of study, research, criticism or review), no part of this book may be reproduced, stored in a retrieval system, communicated or transmitted in any form – electronic, mechanical, photocopying, recording, or otherwise – or by any means without prior written permission. All inquiries should be made to the publisher.

This book is published for personal and educational use only. It may not be used, in whole or in part, for the training of artificial intelligence (AI) systems without the express written permission of Major Street Publishing.

Cover photo by Finnegan Beaumont
Cover design by Typography Studio
Internal design by Production Works

10 9 8 7 6 5 4 3 2 1

Disclaimer: The material in this publication is in the nature of general comment only, and neither purports nor intends to be advice. Readers should not act on the basis of any matter in this publication without considering (and if appropriate taking) professional advice with due regard to their own particular circumstances. The author and publisher expressly disclaim all and any liability to any person, whether a purchaser of this publication or not, in respect of anything and the consequences of anything done or omitted to be done by any such person in reliance, whether whole or partial, upon the whole or any part of the contents of this publication.

Contents

Foreword ... 1

Part 1: We can't change what's happened ... 5
1. Over before it started ... 7
2. The pathway to Thailand ... 17
3. Why start a charity? ... 26
4. It's a marathon, not a sprint ... 33
5. Broken beds ... 43

Part II: It has to be something big ... 55
6. The idea of the run ... 57
7. Assembling the team ... 67
8. Hope is not a plan ... 76
9. The three outcomes ... 82
10. Now, where did I put those running shoes? ... 90
11. Warm up or wake-up call? ... 101
12. Comparison is the thief of joy ... 109

Part III: We can change what happens next ... 115
13. The ceremony and the send-off ... 117
14. Finding our feet ... 127
15. All in a day's work ... 135

16 Injury hits the run	144
Behind every step: a crew's-eye view – Jules Wallace	148
17 I can, I can	154
18 The hardest day	162
Behind every step: a crew's-eye view – Chris Thomas	173
19 Kilometres mattered	175
20 Passing milestones	179
21 The final nights	183
Behind every step: a crew's-eye view – Kelsey Baines	189
22 Mae Thiew bids farewell	195
Behind every step: a crew's-eye view – Rod Reid	199
23 Finished with the marathons	204
Behind every step: a crew's-eye view – Jack Baines	210
24 The final day	213
Behind every step: a crew's-eye view – Greg Wallace	223
25 The darkness of succeeding	225
26 Reflections from the bike	231
27 The three outcomes revisited	236
28 Every day is a gift	247
29 The moments – oh, so many moments	253
Behind every step: a crew's-eye view – CT	257
Acknowledgements: Without you, it doesn't happen	275
About the author	285
Appendix: The numbers as they stack up	289

Foreword

When Peter Baines speaks, people listen – not because he commands attention but because his words carry the weight of lived experience, the humility of a man who has faced both triumph and tragedy, and the steady conviction of someone who leads for purpose.

Together We Can is a compelling book because it challenges us to pause and reflect on what each of us have the capacity to do *if* we are courageous enough to accept Peter's challenge. You will walk away changed after reading this book.

Peter has never been one to observe life from a safe distance. Whether serving as a forensic investigator in the New South Wales Police, leading global recovery efforts after unimaginable disasters or founding Hands Across the Water – one of the Asia-Pacific's most respected and effective social enterprises – Peter steps into the chaos, not away from it. And every time, he leads with courage, compassion and an unwavering belief in humanity.

Together We Can is more than a recounting of moments. It reflects values: integrity, resilience, empathy. Peter takes us into the darkest corners of human experience, yet instead of despair, he finds light. Instead of paralysis, he finds purpose. His stories are not simply about survival; they are about service. Whether he's recounting the horrors of the tsunami in Thailand or a misdiagnosed infection that almost claimed his life, Peter doesn't dwell in sympathy; he delivers insight.

What distinguishes Peter is his rare ability to "have a go". He says yes to the unknown. He commits to the mission before he has the map. That's not blind optimism; it's informed, values-driven leadership. It's a belief that doing the right thing will always point the way forward, even when the path is unclear.

But Peter's journey isn't his alone. At the centre of his story is his wife, CT – his partner, his compass, his constant. Her presence is more than a quiet influence; it is foundational. Their shared life on their beloved Capertee Valley farm is not just home; it's the grounding force behind Peter's strength, clarity and drive. Their bond is a powerful reminder that behind many great leaders is a deeper love that keeps them steady.

Family pulses through *Together We Can* like a heartbeat, as does friendship.

I count myself privileged to be one of Peter's friends, someone who has witnessed Peter's journey up close and felt the warmth of his loyalty and the integrity of his word and actions.

Peter is also a serial social entrepreneur, though labels don't do justice to what he's built. Through Hands Across the Water, Hands Group and Hands Experiences, he has reimagined what it means to give. He has created models that are as commercially sound as they are compassionate, that replace dependence with dignity and charity with choice. He hasn't just raised funds; he's raised standards.

What defines Peter most, though, is not the scale of his projects or the depth of his impact; it's how he shows up. Consistently. Quietly. Fully. He is a champion of humanity.

Together We Can is, at its core, an invitation: to do more, to feel more, to lead with heart and to never underestimate the power of one committed individual – and those who choose to stand beside them.

So, to you, the reader: be ready to be moved. Be ready to be challenged. And most of all, be reminded – profoundly – of what really matters.

Because Peter Baines doesn't just show us what's possible. He reminds us that when we lead with love, conviction and courage, together, we can.

Garry Browne AM

PART I
WE CAN'T CHANGE WHAT'S HAPPENED

1

Over before it started

It was 12 November 2024, less than three weeks before I was to start the Run to Remember: 1400 kilometres over 26 days, which I had spent over two years planning and training for. For the third day in a row, I was sitting in the emergency department of a hospital in the Central West region of New South Wales. I had bumped my leg against a tree stump while running in Thailand three weeks prior, and it was now severely infected.

It was all so innocuous. At the time of walking into the tree, I didn't even think it had broken the skin. I had continued to run and had put in 50 kilometres over the ensuing days, but eventually I realised I needed something more than Betadine to treat the wound. I headed to the local pharmacist, who confirmed it was a nasty infection that needed antibiotics, but without a script he couldn't help me. I rushed next door to my GP, but as I was going in the front door he was heading out the back door, the surgery closed for the weekend. As it happened, I already had an appointment scheduled for the following Tuesday to get a final medical and blood work done for the run. Rather than find another doctor at lunchtime on a Saturday, I convinced myself that the infection could wait until Tuesday when I returned from the farm.

My wife Claire and I split our time between our house at Terrigal on the Central Coast of New South Wales and our farm, "The Crown", which is located within the Capertee Valley. "Where is that?" is the standard response from almost everyone I meet; it is located between Lithgow and Mudgee, about three and a half hours' drive from Terrigal via the Blue Mountains and two and a half hours from Sydney Airport. The Capertee Valley's claim to fame is that it is the widest canyon in the world, one kilometre wider than the Grand Canyon (although not nearly as deep). Our farm consists of 100 acres, about a dozen head of Hereford cattle, a few horses and spectacular views of the escarpment. Without a neighbour in sight, it is a piece of paradise. It connects us to the land and serves us and our families well as a place to decompress and create meaningful shared experiences – be that enjoying a long lunch under the decades-old white box gum tree or working on a broken fence together. We're still awestruck by the colours of the setting sun on the escarpment – it never gets old. I must have hundreds of photos of the same escarpment with the same setting sun, but I still feel compelled to capture its beauty.

As the run approached and the weekends slipped by, I needed to spend time on the farm slashing paddocks, given I would be away for over a month. There is always something to do on the farm, and I love being away from computers and phones and out doing something physical. Having just returned from a week-long leadership program that I had been running in Thailand, and with two weekends until the run, it was time to fire up the tractor. I drove straight to the farm from the GP's surgery and spent the afternoon slashing paddocks until fading light forced me inside. I remember feeling pretty ginger getting off the tractor and that my leg was feeling sorer than it had previously at the site of the infection. Sunday morning was pretty much a rinse and repeat of Saturday afternoon, but each time I climbed down off the tractor my leg was sorer than the previous time. I had the injury covered in a pretty substantial dressing and was wearing jeans, so I couldn't see anything, but I could certainly feel it.

I headed inside around 6 p.m. Claire – or CT, as she is also known – had arrived from Sydney to help get the farm ready for our dogsitters, who would move in for the duration of the run. I lay down on the lounge. I was starting to feel a bit crook. I had flashbacks to my childhood, when falling off the skateboard or bike and getting grazes would inevitably end up with a rushed trip to the doctor for a prescription of Amoxil to fight septicaemia, which was on its way. It would turn ugly within hours: I would start vomiting and my glands would swell in reaction to the infection. You could almost set your watch by it. I would end up being sick for a few unpleasant days. For whatever reason, I seemed to have grown out of it by adulthood, but lying on the lounge I started to wonder if that might be what was going on with my leg.

CT had been cooking dinner, and as I hobbled to the dinner table I think it caught her by surprise how quickly things had escalated. I couldn't even eat. She said, "Do you think you should go to hospital?" I confirmed that I did, which I think shocked her. I knew that the deterioration even just from lunchtime until dinner meant that this couldn't wait until my doctor's appointment on Tuesday. I needed to take action now.

Arriving at the hospital, I limped into the emergency room, where there was a gallery of injured representing a cross-section of society. There was a young bloke who had come off his motorbike and severed his lip, which was pretty nasty; there were the distressed parents of a newborn who wouldn't settle; there was a woman representing the ugliness of domestic violence; and in the corner there was a bloke who looked as though he had been drinking since Thursday. It reminded me of my early days in the police force, when I spent plenty of time in the ER with victims and offenders. To be honest, seeing the injured, I wondered if I would end up just being sent home given what else they had to deal with.

When my name was called, I hobbled over to be assessed and felt somewhat embarrassed at the size of my wound. I said to the triage nurse that I was concerned about the infection, making sure she understood that I wasn't worried about the pain or the size of the injury but the colour and swelling around the site. Her response was a little surprising: "So am I". I had thought maybe I was being a little overdramatic about it all, but apparently not.

I had a cannula inserted into my arm to administer antibiotics and was advised that although I could leave the hospital that evening, I was to return twice a day for the next several days to receive further antibiotics intravenously. I was given pain relief, but the greatest relief was that I had gone to the hospital and not waited any longer. If only I had arrived at the GP's surgery 15 minutes earlier on Saturday, I would have been a good day and a half ahead of treating the infection, but I assumed that things would turn around quickly from here.

Drawing on my old forensics days, I took photos of the wound every day to record improvement and see the reduction in the inflammation, but to my surprise, I didn't see any real change for the better. I had marked the extremities of the swelling with a black marker so the treating doctor could see the original size of the infection and any progress made, but the infection moved outside the borders of the black ink.

So, after three days of treatment, scans and X-rays at the hospital, here I was in a consult room with the treating doctor – the third different doctor I had seen since I arrived on Sunday night. He spent a good long time looking at the wound, reading my patient notes and discussing the injury with me. While I hadn't seen the progress I was expecting, I assumed it was just taking a few more days to get under control. I certainly wasn't expecting what he had to say next.

"Peter, I don't think you appreciate the seriousness of the situation. We have been treating this injury with intravenous antibiotics now for three days and there has been no improvement, if anything, I think it is worse. My real concern is that, due to the proximity of the injury to the bone, the infection may have spread to the bone. If that is the case, that is quite serious, and treatment would involve you receiving antibiotics intravenously via a PICC (peripherally inserted central catheter) line straight into a vein for up to several weeks. I know this is not the news you wanted to hear." He went on to tell me that they would be growing a culture of the wound and taking further scans. If indeed there was an infection in the bone, I would need to be transferred to a larger hospital for a surgical consult.

The doctor left the room, and I sat in a state of complete numbness. How could such an innocuous injury turn into an infection that could end this two-year plan just weeks before I was to fly to Thailand to start what was to be possibly the biggest undertaking of my life? Over the last month or so, I had been so risk-averse to anything that could possibly stop me from running in December. On the November leadership program, I visited an elephant sanctuary where there was the opportunity to get right up close and wash the elephants, and even get in the river with them. It is an incredible experience to be so close to these magnificent animals, but I didn't want to get too close and run the risk of my foot getting under theirs. But here I was potentially about to miss the run from an injury the size of a 50 cent piece. *This can't be happening.* I thought. *Surely not.*

I requested a transfer to a hospital closer to home in Terrigal. The doctor agreed to the transfer across to Gosford Hospital, which was a much larger hospital, but told me I should proceed directly to the pharmacist upon leaving the consult room to have two antibiotics scripts filled and commence taking the additional medication. He prepared the discharge papers and transfer notes, had the cannula removed from my arm and gave me the two scripts for additional antibiotics, bringing it to three different antibiotics I would be taking to try and stop the spread of the infection.

I left the hospital and sat in my car, not really able to comprehend that the run could be over. *What do I do?* I thought. *How do I unwind this? Do I put it off for 12 months?* I sat there for several minutes in a state of disbelief. I could feel tears welling up as I imagined the conversation with those who had invested so much in this campaign. My biggest fear in taking on this run was letting down those who mattered most – those who had supported me, advocated for me and donated on my behalf – and here it was, my greatest fear about to be realised, and for what sounded like such an incredibly lame excuse.

I headed straight to the local pharmacy, presented the two scripts and received the two new medications. I immediately took a course, as instructed by the doctor. I drove the three hours home and took another course of the new medication, then started getting ready to drive to Sydney to attend a fundraising event for the run. Prior to leaving home, I received a message from my daughter-in-law, who is a nurse and specialises in wound treatment. She asked what medication I was on. I sent her the names of the two new medications, then I started driving to Sydney. Not long after I set off, I received a message from her saying I must have written the names incorrectly because I wouldn't have been prescribed these medications, but I couldn't check them now that I was on my way to Sydney. I thought I had copied them down correctly, but I decided to check when I returned home much later that night and send her a copy of the packet.

I attended the fundraising event, not letting on that the run was now in doubt. Arriving home from Sydney at 11.30 p.m., I checked the names of the medication against what I sent her and found that I had written them correctly. To remove any confusion, I sent her a photo of the front of each packet.

At 6 a.m. the next day, I was on my way to Gosford Hospital when my daughter-in-law called me and said, "Pete, where are you? Do not take any more of that medication. You need to get yourself to hospital immediately, but do not drive. You have been prescribed the incorrect medication". I knew she was concerned because it was the first time she had ever rung me.

I arrived at the Gosford Hospital emergency department and advised the triage nurse that I needed a cannula to resume the IV of the antibiotics, and I asked her why I was on the medication I had been prescribed. Her response was, "You wouldn't be on that medication". I presented the discharge papers prepared by the treating doctor, which listed the medication, and she said, "That must be a typing error. You wouldn't be on that medication". I pulled the drugs out of my bag and showed them to her. She said, "How many have you taken? Come with me, we're going in to see the doctor".

The first treating doctor at Gosford Hospital took my vitals and, without showing any obvious outward concern, discussed with me the process I had been through to receive the medication. I recounted the story to him and confirmed that I didn't now or at any time in the past suffer from high blood pressure (because one of the medications I had been prescribed was for high blood pressure). He said that was obvious given my level of fitness and my heart rate of 41 beats per minute. This was three or four points below my normal resting heart rate, so the medication was certainly doing its job – it just wasn't the job I needed done.

The doctor went to consult with the head of the emergency department. A short time later, they returned together. After a similar conversation and a review of the discharge papers and the medication I had in my hand, the ED head said, "This is a mistake. He shouldn't have been prescribed that medication. We need to speak to the treating doctor".

The doctor who had prescribed the incorrect medication was horrified and deeply apologetic. It turned out that instead of prescribing me an antibiotic, he had mistakenly prescribed me heart medication that is used to treat people with high blood pressure. The dose of this particular drug was 50 milligrams every 24 hours. I had been prescribed 100 milligrams three times a day – six times the correct dosage. My resting heart rate prior to taking the medication was 45 beats per minute, which is pretty low. I had been recording various data points in relation to my body in the lead up to the run, and I could see that my *average* heart rate for the 24 hours I was on the incorrect medication was 41 beats per minute, meaning that during the night, when I was at rest, it had dropped into the 30s if not lower.

Later, I was contacted by the medical director of the hospital where the incorrect prescription had been made. His frank admission was that if I had continued to take the medication and gone to bed for a second night, or if I hadn't been in as good physical shape, it may have resulted in a very grave and serious outcome. My daughter-in-law was more direct: a second night on that dosage and I may not have woken up.

With a new medical plan established, my previously prescribed medication replaced and my CT scans reviewed, the doctors at Gosford Hospital agreed that there was no bone infection and I could be discharged to continue treatment at home.

I returned home, grateful that the mistake had been detected early and no real ongoing damage had been caused. After all, we all make mistakes, and I genuinely believe it wasn't due to a lack of care by the treating doctor. Still, I'd had a close call – not through risky behaviour on my behalf, not through ignorance or disregard of the advice from medical professionals, but because I followed the advice of a medical professional. That's not supposed to happen. I couldn't shake the thought that just one more night taking those drugs and I might not have woken up. CT was still at the farm, so I was home alone, reliving forensic jobs I had attended where someone had died in their bed and been found several days later after missing appointments. It was always upsetting to know how long people – the elderly in particular – could lie dead in their home and not be missed. I kept imagining the horror and impact it would have had on CT arriving home and finding me dead in our bed.

I was struggling to comprehend my situation. It was now 17 days until I was due to fly to Thailand to start this run that I had thought about every night since the idea was first spoken about in September 2022. The journey so far had been relatively smooth. I had experienced iliotibial band (ITB) issues in my right leg and a tear in my popliteus, a muscle that runs behind the knee, but given where I had started from and my training load, I was pretty happy. Now, though, not only was there the risk of this infection spreading to my tibia, I was lucky to be alive given the cocktail of drugs I had been prescribed. After two years of planning, the Run to Remember now felt very much in doubt.

2

The pathway to Thailand

Growing up, I wasn't a standout student or athlete. I wasn't one of the kids marked to go on and do big things. I was very much middle of the road in everything I did. There was nothing remarkable about my childhood. Mum and Dad lived in a classic loveless marriage, and given the ill feelings that still existed 40 years after they separated, I have to wonder if there was ever a time when they were really in love. Dad worked long hours, and perhaps that was more about being out of the house than about income generation. Our holidays were spent at my grandparents' house every year, and we never left the state of New South Wales as a family, let alone travelled overseas. Come to think of it, I can't remember going on more than one family holiday where they actually paid for accommodation and we didn't just stay with my grandparents. I guess they did the best they could with what they had at the time.

Joining the New South Wales Police as a 19-year-old wasn't a childhood dream, but it clearly appealed, as I ended up spending

23 years there. I worked in uniform in General Duties for the first four years, starting at Merrylands before moving to Cabramatta. I grew tired of dealing with drunks and domestics – or, in lots of cases, domestics involving drunks – and knew there was more on offer.

I moved into what would become the Forensic Services Group during a time of significant change in how true science was integrated into the role of the crime scene examiner, and the role was being glorified by the proliferation of crime-scene shows on television such as *CSI* (which still runs today). The work we did in the Crime Scene Unit, as in any job in any industry, was filled with the mundane, but it also offered cases that I remember 30 years on. There were cases that turned on the collection and interpretation of the forensic evidence, resulting in the successful prosecution of heinous felons who may otherwise have escaped punishment. There are several cases I was involved in where there were no witnesses, electronic evidence or admissions, but there was forensic evidence at the scene that revealed a picture that, without collection and interpretation, would have gone unseen.

I commenced my time in forensics working out of the Sydney Police Centre, servicing the busy areas of the city of Sydney, the eastern suburbs and the inner west. The areas covered included people living in the wealthiest harbour and beachside suburbs as well as people living in public housing and sleeping rough on the streets. It ensured the work was varied and, if nothing else, constant. It involved the full range of things you would expect: murders, armed robberies of high-end jewellery stores, arsons, drug overdoses, suspicious deaths and suicides by all different methods. Working in the centre of Sydney also meant that we had access to all the specialist resources that we needed as the circumstances dictated.

Things were different when I relocated to Tamworth in the north-west of New South Wales as a crime scene investigator servicing a large chunk of the north-west of the state. There, I really developed my craft. The jobs were as varied in the bush as they had been in Sydney – there remained the domestic homicides, suicides and drug- and alcohol-related violence – but the drug investigations changed: rather than clandestine labs in rented houses on family-filled streets, we were investigating and collecting evidence from cannabis crops which were measured in acres. There were also way more fatal vehicle collisions due to the high speed of drivers on country roads, as well as fatal farming accidents, plane and helicopter crashes, and other crimes I didn't see in Sydney, including the theft of cattle. It was a different world working in the bush.

I committed to a minimum of three years living and working in Tamworth, but I ended up spending ten years there. During that time, my first wife Nicole and I had our three kids Lachie, Kelsey and Jack. It was a comfortable and easy life, and I could have settled in and seen out the rest of my career there, but the idea of working "on call" every second week for the next 20 years held little appeal.

I moved through and up the ranks within the Forensic Services Group to reach the rank of Inspector by the age of 36. It wasn't that I was a standout; it was more the case that I put myself in the position for opportunities as they presented themselves. I would apply for different opportunities because if I didn't apply, I couldn't be considered. To complement what I was doing inside work, I applied myself outside and studied forensic science and then law at university, graduating from both.

Being a crime scene investigator exposes you to a side of life that occurs under the cover of darkness or behind closed doors – the ugly side of humanity that many others don't see and are probably happy to keep that way. Attending scenes of death on a weekly basis, I bore witness to loneliness, addiction, greed and violence in my community and what happens when the demands on mental health services far outstrip supply.

Some of the saddest scenes I attended were not the ones that made the news. They were the elderly who were found in an advanced state of decomposition, having passed away some weeks prior and neither found nor missed. They were the deaths within housing estates where neighbours were uncomfortably close yet, for all intents and purposes, miles apart. They were the suicides – the teenagers who took their lives as a result of unrelenting bullying, and those who couldn't find their way out of debt, addiction or guilt for some past deed. And they were those who died from a broken heart – having lived for 50, 60 or 70 years with "the one", when that person left, so too did the will to live.

The level of cruelty and control that people are capable of inflicting on others was never more evident than in the domestic violence incidents I encountered. At one point I can only assume there was love and trust in these relationships, but for a myriad of reasons it was replaced by anger and violence, bringing families to their knees and inflicting scars, seen and unseen, that would never completely heal. As uniformed police working in the western suburbs of Sydney, I was often part of the car crews responding to these incidents; as a forensic crime scene examiner, I only became involved once they reached a fatal end. I used to wonder why the hatred had to get so bad, why time could not have been called on the relationship and assets shared with an acknowledgement that "we tried, but it didn't work out".

Bring religion into the mix and the debate about whose God is right and whose is wrong and the violence escalates to a whole different level, involving communities and countries diametrically opposed to one another.

The Bali Bombings of 2002 were just over a year after 9/11, and given the proximity to Australia and the love affair Australians have with Bali, it changed the way we viewed the world and, certainly, the way we went about international travel. The response to the bombings involved the investigation of the scene, the criminal investigation into those responsible and the identification of the 202 victims, 88 of whom were Australian. I was involved in the forensic identification of those who died. The task of identifying bodies during a mass fatality incident is never easy – in this case, the stakes were too high to get it wrong, but the trauma to the bodies exposed to the explosions and subsequent fires made the task difficult.

It is universally accepted by the vast majority of developed countries to ensure consistency in process and procedure when it comes to the identification of bodies following mass fatality incidents. The disaster victim identification (DVI) process, regardless of the cause of death, involves a postmortem examination of the deceased with the purpose of collecting samples from the body to forensically compare against "antemortem samples" – information about the person prior to their death provided by their family. The three main identifiers are dental, fingerprints and DNA. The postmortem information gathered includes dental X-rays and the collection of fingerprints and a sample of DNA, such as a segment of bone from the deceased. The DNA is extracted from the bone by scientists in a laboratory. These samples are then compared to the antemortem samples, such as a history of dental work previously undertaken and physical items known to have belonged to the deceased that may reveal fingerprints or DNA, such as a hairbrush or a toothbrush. When all the information is gathered, it is then up to the forensic specialists to undertake a comparative analysis of the evidence to find a match and positively identify the body.

The work of identifying and repatriating a loved one back to their family is hugely significant. Without the positive identification, without the return of the body, there is no burial or cremation, and the family is caught in a state of uncertainty and unable to move through their grief. However, while it is a relatively straightforward application of forensic science, complexity comes from the number of bodies and samples. That makes the process slow, which goes against the desires and expectations of those who have lost a loved one.

My deployment into Bali in response to the bombings was a defining moment in my career – not for the contribution that I made over there, as it wasn't profound or prolonged, but because it positioned me as one of Australia's senior forensic leaders. The relationships I established and, to a degree, the credibility and reputation that came from working over there meant that if something significant happened within the Asia–Pacific region, I stood a good chance of being involved.

Just over two years after Bali, an earthquake off the Indonesian coastline on 26 December 2004 would trigger a tsunami that would result in what is still, at the time of writing, the largest loss of life resulting from a natural disaster in the 21st century: best estimates put the number of lives lost somewhere between 250,000 and 300,000, the vast majority of which were in Indonesia. In Thailand, as the torrent of water ravaged the coastline, 5395 lives were lost, including both Thai nationals and foreign tourists. The forensic work to identify and repatriate those who lost their lives lasted over 12 months. I was deployed on several occasions into the disaster-stricken region to lead both the Australian and international teams. On my first deployment, I travelled to Thailand as the sole New South Wales Police representative, and I couldn't have imagined how profound the impact would be on my life.

The work that I did in Thailand was as part of an international team of people who utilised their specific skills to identify the bodies of those who had died. As was the case in Bali, the forensic work was complex not because of the science involved but because of the sheer volume of pieces of evidence that were collected as part of the DVI protocols. In Bali, there were 202 victims; in Thailand, there were 5395 bodies recovered that required identification. From each of those bodies recovered, up to a dozen pieces of evidence were collected, totalling an estimated 60,000 pieces of evidence.

At times it can be easy to read those numbers and not appreciate that each of those individuals represented a loved one lost: a mother, a daughter, a husband, a wife, an aunty or uncle.

While our work in Bali was in response to a terrorist attack undertaken with the ultimate aim of claiming lives and instilling fear, our work in Thailand was a humanitarian response to a natural disaster. There was a distinct difference in the feeling of the two responses. Bali carried with it that edge of fear for the safety of those on the ground: was another attack imminent, a second phase planned to hit the first responders? Thailand had none of that edge.

The work I did in Thailand and the time I spent away from home came at a cost. While I was there on the ground identifying those who had died and reuniting them with their families, I was away from my family. However, I was able to reconcile this personal conflict knowing the time away from home, while it felt agonisingly long at times, was in reality measured only in months, and the work we were doing as a forensic community would have a profound effect on the families of those lost for the rest of their lives.

What I remember most of my deployments to Thailand was the connection to individuals. I remember carrying the frozen bodies of young children in my arms, knowing it was the last time they would likely be held that way. I remember unzipping the body bags that contained children and feeling the need to move their hair out of their eyes, knowing it served no purpose other than to make me feel somewhat better.

I met a mother who lost her three children and made the 12-hour journey to the site I worked at to collect the bodies of her children on three separate occasions. She kept coming until she had no more family left. On each occasion she travelled to our site, she displayed a level of grace, dignity and gratitude that will stay with me forever. She had to have been at the lowest point of her life, but all she could do was thank us for the work we had done.

I remember the warmth and gratitude conveyed in hugs from strangers I was meeting for the first time, people who had lost someone dear to them. We couldn't deliver what they desperately wanted – they would never see that person alive again – but we could deliver their loved one's body to be buried according to their faith and beliefs.

I met a grandfather beset by survivor's guilt. He had run from the tsunami with a grandchild holding each of his hands. He reached a tree as a torrent of water descended upon them, and he had a decision to make. He knew that he must save himself if either of his grandchildren were to have any hope of surviving. He also knew he couldn't climb the tree with both of them. Which grandchild would he take up the tree with him, and which would he let go of? How do you make that decision? How do you decide who lives and who dies? He and the grandchild he chose survived – battered, bruised and cut with lifelong scars. The grandchild that he let go of was washed away and died.

I met this grandfather many times during return trips to Thailand in the years after working there as part of my forensic duties. The decision he was forced to make that day broke him, and how could it not? There was nothing I could offer this man, no words or reason that made sense. His story has stayed with me with great clarity, and I have shared it hundreds of times. We all face challenges and are forced to make difficult decisions, and after making those decisions we then need to live with the outcome.

These interactions shaped me and the time I spent in Thailand, and not just during my tours as a forensic specialist: they laid the groundwork for the work that would serve as food for my soul in the years that followed.

3

Why start a charity?

There is an assumption that starting Hands Across the Water was a reaction to what I had seen and done in Thailand, that in some way I felt compelled to act, to right the wrongs. Perhaps that is true in part, but it's not the full picture. When people ask me why I started Hands, my answer is, "Because I realised I couldn't change what had happened to the kids, but I felt I could change what happened next". I didn't know how at first, but I felt I had the capacity to do something that could bring positive change into the lives of the survivors. Then again, perhaps there is something deeper that has driven me to continue 20 years on from my initial commitment, something that others have suspected but I've never completely acknowledged myself. Was the impact of my work in Thailand greater than I have given it credit for in me setting up and continuing Hands?

The bodies of the tsunami victims were relocated south from Wat Yan Yao, the temple in the town of Takua Pa, to Tha Chat Chai, just on the other side of the Sarasin Bridge that links mainland Thailand to the island of Phuket. The bodies were stored on makeshift shelves in refrigerated shipping containers, awaiting examination and identification. The Thai army was deployed to the site, and their key role was to move the bodies from the shipping containers to the examination area for the forensic specialists to perform autopsies and gather postmortem samples and information that would ultimately lead to their positive identification and return to their families. Towards the end of my time in Thailand, though, many of the soldiers had been released from their duties, allowing them to return home to their families after many months away. The task of moving the bodies had fallen then upon the forensic specialists working at the site.

Cracking open the steel doors to the shipping containers was never subtle – their weight, and the locking mechanism that created a seal between the outside temperatures in the mid-30s and minus eight inside, required an almost aggressive action to leverage them open. Therein were the bodies of those yet to be reunited with their families, lying in a temporary state of namelessness. Regardless of who they had been in life, how they had lived, how well they were known and what fortune they might have amassed, at that time they were each known only by a number on tags attached to their wrist and the outside of the bright blue or white plastic body bag in which they lay. The name they had been given at birth and known by ever since was a mystery. Our sole purpose for being in Thailand was to change that – to identify those bodies and return their identities, and in so doing return their dignity, allowing their repatriation to their families so they could be buried according to their wishes, beliefs and customs.

The smell inside each of the shipping containers was different to the smell of the decomposed bodies we confronted on the grounds of Wat Yan Yao. A combination of suspended decomposition and disinfectant, it represented death. Who was within each body bag was unknown. Was this a father from Germany who had died desperately trying to save the lives of his children? Was this a local Thai grandmother who had succumbed quickly to the force of the water, unable to swim and lacking any real chance of survival? Was this a young boy who, minutes prior to the arrival of the torrent of water, had been playing tag in the hotel pool with his sister? I encountered all of these people and many more. While their bodies were yet to be identified, their lives and stories unknown by those of us who had the job of identifying them, it wasn't hard to imagine the circumstances that led them to the shipping container. It wasn't hard to imagine the fear and terror that had come upon each of them in their final moments of struggle and fight. That wasn't necessarily a good thing, not when day after day we needed to work to return their identities and dignity.

You had some idea of what was within each body bag by the size and shape, by how much of the bag was occupied by the body within. Whether it was an adult of large proportions or a child was obvious. Lifting down the body of a frozen adult male of larger propositions was always difficult and clumsy. The bags were slippery and heavy, and the floor was covered in ice. However, in some strange way, the relative ease of moving the body of a child was harder. The adults' bodies were placed on a trolley to be moved throughout the site. The children's bodies were carried. Placing them down on the examination table and unzipping the bag, it was often the innocence in their face that hit hardest. It was the absence of the wrinkles that represent a life lived. It was their small hands and features, which had years of growing left that would never occur. I would move the hair out of their eyes, and I did all I could not to imagine the loss of my own child, not to imagine too deeply this child's life up to the events of 26 December 2004, or what they would miss as a result.

There was a balance to find and a very thin line to tread. It was important to recognise that every child we carried through the site had a parent and family. Some of them might also be in one of the shipping containers; some might be elsewhere in Thailand or might have returned to the country they came from, broken and destroyed by the loss of their child. Each of the adults too had someone, somewhere, who would miss them for the rest of their lives. So, showing dignity and respect to every individual was not in question and came without compromise. However, investing in their lives or imagining their final minutes, or the loss that would be felt by those left behind, wasn't necessarily going to serve us well in the long term.

The impact this time had on my life and those close to me, both positive and negative, is inescapable. I didn't believe at the time and am not entirely sure now, either, 20 years on, that it was the exposure to the loss suffered by so many that was the impetus for starting the charity. What I do know is that, but for a chance meeting with a group of kids, my life could very much have returned to something resembling what it had been prior to 2004. I was always going to be a changed person – you couldn't see what I had seen and do what I had done and not be changed – but I could have returned to a version of my life that was only slightly different. Perhaps I was a little damaged, but life could have resumed as close to normal as possible. But meeting a group of kids who were then living in a tent in the grounds of a temple, having all lost their families and homes, would set my life on a trajectory that was unimaginable even by those with the wildest of imaginations.

Within a few short months of this meeting, I had established the charity Hands Across the Water. Within a few years, I had resigned from the only job I had ever known. I was then travelling the world, speaking at conferences and raising hundreds of thousands of dollars to support those kids I had met in that tent and others like them.

Setting up Hands and setting about raising money was never meant to be anything other than a short-term commitment. All I needed to do was raise enough money to contribute to the building of a home. Because surely, once those kids were out of the tent and had a home to live in, all their problems would be solved. I couldn't have been more wrong or naive, but perhaps that naivety served everyone well, because if I had understood the commitment I was making, who knows if I would have travelled that path.

As time passed after the events of Boxing Day 2004, the number of people who concerned themselves with the struggles of the children left without parents diminished. Events closer to home, charities working to address matters that felt more relevant or personal, took their attention and captured their wallets. But as the success of Hands grew, so too did the reliance upon our assistance. The more successful we became in raising funds, the more children and communities in need we could support; but the more opportunities we created, the more funds we needed to generate to sustain them. It felt like I was caught in a loop without end. Yet, seeing the positive outcomes from the work we were doing, how do you stop? How do you say, "I've done enough," when you know there is so much more that can be done?

The model that came to define our work at Hands was seeking to provide return to those who supported us. I never wanted to generate funds based on pity or guilt, and we never have.

Perhaps those who have marketing degrees and work in the charity sector will say I would do better by tapping into guilt and sadness, but it's just not something we are about. I wanted the entire process to be positive, and I always wanted the kids we support to be reflected in an accurate way, which is positively. The positive experience needed to work both ways: if we could return meaningful value to those who supported us, if we could create a perception in our supporters' minds and a reality that they were getting more in return than they were contributing, we would have a level of sustainability that was bankable. We also had to ensure the funds we were generating and entrusted to use wisely by our donors and supporters were, in fact, used in the most prudent way possible.

The evolution of Hands and the work we have done resembles the growth and maturity of a foundation that started in the aftermath of a disaster with a desire to help and now creates real, meaningful, generational change. After we addressed the immediate needs for safe and loving homes, and access to nutritious meals and healthcare, we invested in education. Initially, that meant ensuring all children from all the homes we were supporting were attending school. Then, it meant creating access to tertiary education for those who wished to continue their studies. It started with one student, Game, enrolling at university to study law, and as the younger kids started leaving school, the numbers enrolling in and completing university degrees grew. Game, our first university graduate, is now studying for his PhD, having already completed his masters degree. He was the first, but we have recently celebrated our 50th student graduating.

The students who are graduating are etching out their own lives. They can be found in different countries across the globe, working in the hotel industry, marketing and PR, advertising, and a range of other industries. The joy I share with the supporters of Hands is in seeing these once dependent kids become independent, creating a life where they are not reliant on others to support them but are now capable of supporting their own children when that time comes.

The growth of Hands from an individual wanting to make a difference to the lives of some kids in the aftermath of the tsunami to what is now, and has been for many years, the largest contributing Australasian charity to Thailand shows the good that comes from the collective contribution of many.

4

It's a marathon, not a sprint

Think about your favourite charity, the one that is closest to your heart. You might have a deep connection to it or simply donate once a year. It may be part of the very fabric of your soul or just one that you feel is making a real difference. No matter the charity or the level of your connection, what would you say is its ultimate measure of success? What would your emotions be if it ceased to exist? Ultimately, that is what most charities should be working towards: the time when their services are no longer required. The need has been met, the cure has been found, the homeless are all housed and the hungry have full bellies. The race has been run. Until that time arises, there remains work to be done.

Hands was established in 2005 with the single focus of building a home for the kids that were left without parents or carers as a result of the Boxing Day tsunami. If we had not taken on any additional projects or elected to support any future children, we could have closed our doors after ten years. The need had been identified and met: house needed, house built. If only it was as simple as that. Travelling to Thailand for the official ceremony and opening of the first home at Baan Tharn Namchai in Phang Nga, I believed the job was done and that would be the end of my charity contribution to Thailand. Leaving that day, I realised the job had just begun and the building of the home didn't come close to meeting the needs of the kids or the community.

When I returned from the opening of the first home with a newfound awareness of the job before me, my focus was to set up the charity in accordance with the rules and regulations governing such entities and build a team that would connect with and support the future direction. Without knowing it at the time, "together we can" would be the only way future success could be achieved. I had started the operations in Australia, I was the one sharing the stories and raising the funds, but growth would only come from building a team who shared in the vision.

Within 12 months of the opening of what was supposed to be the home to solve the problem and end the need, there was indeed the need for a second home. It was now a couple of years on from the devastation of the tsunami, but the number of kids who had been taken in by Khun Rotjana, the director of Baan Tharn Namchai, had doubled. The girls were sleeping two or three to a bed, and the boys were sleeping on mattresses on the ground in the hallways. The obvious question was, "Where are these kids coming from?" The reason for the influx was something that I saw occur in the various crisis and disaster locations I worked at throughout the world. I spent time working in Bali, Thailand, Saudi Arabia, Japan and, of course, Australia after various disasters, and I saw the same thing each time. In the immediate aftermath of the event, lots of people and organisations responded to the needs of the people affected.

Corporates donated, governments committed funding and support, and charities asked for support and delivered services. They were there before the dust settled, the water receded or the flames went out. They provided the locals with the essential care and support needed to get through the initial days and weeks following the disaster. However, as the smoke cleared, the water dried out and the outside world moved on, either to focus on the next crisis or simply because the stories from this crisis had been told, communities were left on their own. Their problems hadn't gone away just because the world chose to look in a different direction. The houses that were destroyed by fire or floods weren't rebuilt in the weeks or even months that followed. The children who lost their parents didn't get them back, and of course they never will. But while we can't change what happened, we can all change what happens next.

> **While we can't change what happened, we can all change what happens next.**

As the number of kids continued to grow at Baan Tharn Namchai, Hands committed to build them a second, much larger home that would cater for future growth and provide them with the best we could. The second home was officially opened in 2009 and became the centre for what now is best described as a village. There are the residential homes, learning areas, soccer fields, a basketball court, a music room, an art room and spaces for the kids to be kids. We recognise that when all things are equal, the best place for kids is within a family, even when that family is not the traditional one. When that option doesn't exist for any number of reasons and the kids need a short- or long-term safe option, Baan Tharn Namchai provides that solution. And we like to make it feel like a home, just a really big one.

The commitment to Baan Tharn Namchai was locked in and the change to the lives of the kids was significant. We also offered certainty to Khun Rotjana and her staff in relation to future funding. The costs of feeding and caring for 100-plus kids and maintaining the infrastructure to support them are huge. Also, all of the staff that were present 24 hours a day needed to be paid. I know that we created peace of mind for Khun Rotjana that she could count on the funds we were generating to support her kids and the staff.

Almost 20 years since we opened the doors, we still receive requests from local government agencies to provide care and support to children for whom they see no viable alternative. An example of the ongoing need is Andy*, our youngest and most recent addition to the home. She was born to a drug-addicted mother, her father unknown. Government welfare staff determined that Andy's mum was incapable of providing a safe level of care for the immediate future. At the request of government staff, we have accepted Andy into our home and will care for her for what we hope is a short term. The ultimate goal is that her mum receives the treatment she needs to remove drugs from her life and care for her child, and that the two are reunited. Right now, with an addiction battle and facing criminal prosecution for crimes that support her drug habit, it is not looking as though a reunion between the two is likely, at least in the short term. Andy would certainly not be the first child to come to us under those conditions and for their mother or father to simply disappear and never return.

---

* Not her real name.

Through the first five years of operation we enjoyed considerable growth and support. It's not hard to achieve growth when you're starting from zero, but we started a couple of initiatives that would set us up for success and that continue to this day.

In 2007, I spoke at a conference in San Francisco for an organisation called NARTA. This conference was a life-changing experience for so many people. I left with a cheque for $250,000, a new chairman for the board of Hands in Kay Spencer, the CEO at the time of NARTA, and, importantly, the long-term support of a business community on a level I could never have imagined. The commitment from NARTA to Hands in 2007 has remained to this day, and their total contribution since then to the work we do has surpassed $10 million.

If there was one greater gift to come from the NARTA conference than their support of our work, it was the enduring friendship and support from Kay Spencer. She became, and remains, one of the most valued and trusted people in my life. Without her, Hands would not be what it is, and I would not be the person I am. There are many children in Thailand who enjoy a life of choice and a bright future today thanks to Kay and NARTA.

NARTA's contribution and support was a defining time for us that might only be surpassed in significance and magnitude by our charity bike rides in Thailand. "I'm going to ride from Bangkok to Khao Lak and raise $10,000 for the kids," said Brigid Gibson, a supporter of Hands. My response was, "Can I ride with you?" Neither of us were bike riders, owned a bike or particularly liked the idea of cycling, but it seemed like a good idea at the time. Our first bike ride was in 2009 – we opened the second home at Baan Tharn Namchai at the end of it. Seventeen riders rode 800 kilometres over eight days. Each rider raised $10,000, so in total we raised about $170,000. We did it again the year after, doubling the number of riders to 34, and by 2011 we were offering the choice of two rides: the first left in early January and the second left two days after completion of the first. In 2013, I led our first "corporate ride", a private ride for a business group. The growth of the rides has been nothing short of astonishing. With the exception of the COVID-19 years, we have hosted a couple of hundred people every year across several rides, raising well in excess of $1 million a year, just from the bike rides, for the work that we do.

Before I go on, let me make it clear that our bike rides are not really for bike riders – they are for people looking for an experience that will leave an indelible impression upon their lives, and it just happens to be on the back of a bike. The vast majority of our riders who turn up year after year only ride to train for our charity bike rides. It is the depth of the shared experience that brings them back. It is the creation of new friends, the reunion of friendships, and while it might appear to be an opportunity to do something for someone else, it quickly becomes clear that this is time well spent on personal growth. It is food for your soul. The fundraising is for the kids; the ride is for personal enjoyment.

The rides have brought thousands of people into the Hands community – riders, family and supporters of those riders, and those who donate. For some, the ride is a one-off event. They may have heard me speak about the ride at a conference and decided it was something they would like to do. For some, it sits on a bucket list to be ticked off when the time is right. We had two riders in 2023 who told me they first heard me speak at a conference ten years prior and made a commitment to one another that when the time was right, they would do the ride – it just took ten years before the time was right. Then there are those who return annually. One of our most loyal riders is Frank

Newton, a business leader in the real estate industry. Frankie first saw me speak at a conference in 2010 in Phuket. He supported two of his staff to ride in that first year after the conference, and in 2012 he participated in his first ride. With the exception of the COVID-19 years he has never missed a year, and he has personally raised hundreds of thousands of dollars for the kids we support. Then there are Carol and George Spence from New Zealand, who see it as their personal mission not only to ride but to bring along family and friends. They keep returning with friends and family because this is a community, rich in heart and soul, to which they belong. They see the kids we support grow, and they can hand-on-heart testify as to where their funds have gone and the difference they have made. Individually, we can't achieve this outcome, but together we can.

The individual riders come for the personal experience, but the success of the business rides comes down to those who advocate for the rides on our behalf. They have seen the value created and understand the value of bringing people together for a meaningful shared experience. We have two business leaders in Dale Beaumont and Steve Carroll who have brought in riders through their respective business communities – Business Blueprint and Digital Live, respectively. Both Dale and Steve are incredible advocates for the virtues of the rides. They see not just the personal reward and benefit for the individuals but, importantly, commercial benefit for those who ride. The rides build strong and enduring relationships, which are fundamental for business growth.

Prior to the disruption by COVID-19 to all things we took for granted, I was working on some initiatives at Hands that would generate income through commercial activities, creating future pathways and employment not just for our kids but for the broader community. Additionally and importantly, they would reduce our reliance on donations, which were predominately coming out of Australia. We had three exciting initiatives that were in their early stages of conception: a hospitality training centre, an agricultural learning centre and a digital learning centre. The intent was that these centres would provide educational opportunities for the kids, with a focus on those that directly led to employment. However, the digital learning centre opened during the months leading up to COVID-19, and momentum and support from our partners who could no longer travel to the centre was lost.

Hands was severely impacted by the pandemic and the shutting down of international travel, as it rendered us unable to host our annual fundraising bike rides in Thailand. The public rides and the corporate rides were crucial, together bringing us 70% of our annual income. We just hadn't planned for such an important part of our income to be taken away – I think it's fair to say no one saw that coming! As we came out of COVID-19 and the impact it had on our operations, our initial focus was on the recovery of the income we lost through the cancellation of our international rides. We had managed to sustain Hands throughout the pandemic: all the staff remained in employment and the kids continued to receive support for their development and education. While this was certainly a positive position to be in, it had drained our cash reserves and put pressure on the organisation. As global travel restrictions lifted, we looked at how we did business at Hands and how we could strengthen our response to such a dramatic disruption to business.

For many years we had been using one service provider to deliver the rides, and when any business relies on one partner only to deliver such an integral part of its operations and income generation, it can develop an unhealthy dependence.

Facing up to this, I commented to CT one day, "We should do this ourselves". We should run the tour operations, own the bikes and own the business side of the rides, not just the charity income, and not be so dependent on someone else, particularly when they were motivated by profit for themselves while we were trying to generate financial support for the homes. Not for the first time – nor the last, no doubt – I made a statement without too much thought that snowballed. Her response was, "Why don't we?" In that moment, Hands Experiences Thailand (HET) was born.

HET is a social enterprise based in Thailand that serves as a commercial income-generating entity, the profits from which flow back into the Hands Across the Water foundation. We'd had the exact same model operating in Australia since 2011 under HATW Pty Ltd (or Hands Group), so why wouldn't it work? HET was established to become the tour operator for our annual bike rides in Thailand, therein removing the friction that can exist working with a partner who has different objectives. Rather than working with a for-profit, whose ultimate aim is to make a profit for themselves, HET would be service-focused first and foremost, with profit flowing back to the foundation. This would give us total control of the operations and our own destiny. Another benefit, which would prove incredibly important, was the pathway it would create to job opportunities for the kids from our homes who may choose to become involved in the business. They could work within the tourism industry, travelling through Thailand, knowing the work they did was bringing funds and support to the home they had grown up in. We now have a number of former students from both Baan Tharn Namchai and Baan Home Hug (which we'll meet in the next chapter) employed by HET as full-time staff. HET now provides day tours to tourists in Khao Lak and beyond, with the profits returning to the kids we started this whole journey for.

HET is still in its formative years, and like any new business, it takes time. But the goals we set for HET and the very reason for its existence have already been met. The level of service we are able to offer our riders has exceeded that previously offered by the commercial tour companies. Pathways exist for our kids, who see this as a career option, and when it comes to profit and loss, it is washing its own face.

The work that we have done in Thailand has expanded across different areas while continuing to create brighter futures for those we support. From what I see, there is no shortage of opportunities to have a positive impact on communities within Thailand, and I see that continuing for years to come.

Broken beds

In the north-east of Thailand, there is a town you have likely never heard of called Yasothon, which is an hour's drive from Ubon Ratchathani, a city you have also likely never heard of. In Yasothon is Baan Home Hug, a home for sick children in need. The home was established several decades ago by a fierce, diminutive woman called Mae Thiew, who would come to play an instrumental role in expanding our charity's influence beyond those affected by the tsunami.

In 2010, I was working with a Thai-born Australian on a project when she mentioned Baan Home Hug and its director, Mae Thiew. She asked if I knew of her and the work she did with children, many of whom were living with HIV. I hadn't, but I was interested in learning more. I learnt of the work she did caring for children and the challenges she faced due to the remote location of the home, and the impact she had on raising both awareness and funds to provide for the children in her care. As I know all too well, if your charity doesn't have visibility, if people can't see you or hear from you, it is tough to raise money, regardless of the importance of your work.

I travelled to Ubon Ratchathani for the first time that year. It is a reasonably large city that serves a population of around 200,000 in the city proper and close to 2 million in the broader province. It hosts a base for the Royal Thai Air Force and has six universities. However, you will not find it on any tourists' lists. I hired a car and headed out to Yasothon to meet Mae Thiew, who came with such a reputation that I felt a sense of awe as I travelled to meet her for the first time.

Baan Home Hug was not an easy place to find. The turnoff to the property was on the main road heading into town, so there was pressure as I looked for it with cars passing at around 100 kilometres per hour. It would have been easy to drive straight past and not know it. Towards the end of a narrow dirt road there was a large concrete wall that surrounded the entrance to the home and imposing steel gates. It was a real contrast to the look and feel of Baan Tharn Namchai in the south. It almost had the feeling of hiding from the outside world.

The first meeting with Mae Thiew, someone who would come to have a presence in my life like few others, would make sense in retrospect once I got to know her. I was offered the customary pleasantries that you come to expect from such a meeting in Thailand. There was a welcome exchange of kind words and the offering of food and water. I was given a tour of the home, and the kids performed a dance – a gesture that I see offered to many visitors to our homes. Mae Thiew was dressed in normal street clothes, as opposed to the beautiful bright orange robes that she now wears. Her hair was tied back in two pig tails, which I would come to learn was part of her individual "branding" – it was one of the things that she was known for throughout Thailand.

She seemed to be wearing more layers of clothing than the temperature required, and I did wonder if her health was an issue for her.

Baan Home Hug sat on a couple of acres of land among soaring native trees, which created a connection to nature but also added to the mystique of the home. As I walked throughout the property on my first guided tour, I was concerned, saddened and then moved to take action by what I saw. The home was devoid of the colour, noise and warmth of Baan Tharn Namchai. This wasn't a reflection on the kids, the staff or Mae Thiew, but Baan Home Hug just had the feeling of understanding struggle and facing it every single day. You could see it all too well. The paint was peeling or faded, windows were broken, and there was evidence of water damage to the roof causing flooding during the rains. If the state of the buildings represented the overall health of operations at Baan Home Hug, then things were dire.

As I was guided around the home, it was clear that it had been built on the back of good economic foundations and support, but I wondered how long it had been since such support – and more importantly, the certainty of future support – had existed. The current conditions weren't the result of a lack of care or love but of competing priorities and a lack of access to resources. It's hard to allocate money and resources to paint walls and fix broken windows when kids are sick and dying.

If there was one thing that made me feel I simply couldn't leave that day without a commitment to do something, it was the beds the kids were sleeping in. The kids were sleeping on hospital beds that had been discarded from the local public hospital because of the condition they were in. To fully appreciate this, you have to understand that Yasothon Hospital is not well funded, so the fact that it had decided the beds were no longer suitable for their needs was telling. Not only that, but the very fact the kids were sleeping in hospital beds, with their sterile, cold appearance, no doubt conveyed to them the subconscious message that they were sick. If the overall feeling of the home was of struggle, then this room had the feeling of defeat. The contrast between Baan Home Hug and Baan Tharn Namchai was huge, and it couldn't go unchanged now that I had seen it.

As I walked around the home, it was clear to me that I wasn't deliberately being shown the worst or the best of the home to manufacture a response. I wasn't being lobbied or guilted into a feeling. I was simply seeing life as it was at Baan Home Hug. I am not even sure they understood the contrast between Baan Home Hug and Baan Tharn Namchai, and I certainly wasn't openly sharing any emotions or thoughts about their situation. It wasn't for me to judge based on a one-hour tour; how could I know the depth of their struggle? It was my job to listen and learn first, and then, if welcomed, take action. I didn't have the answers, but I had plenty of questions.

After the tour of the home, we had a sit-down meeting, which provided a chance for Mae Thiew to learn a little about me and for me to learn more about her. This meeting was facilitated by a mutual acquaintance, because Mae Thiew's English wasn't at the level required to allow us a productive and meaningful meeting, and my Thai consisted of "hello" and "thank you", both of which I had already used. One thing I have come to learn over my years of knowing Mae Thiew is that she is the master of many things, but hiding her emotions is not one of them. I am not partnering with her in a game of poker any time soon. As the meeting progressed, it became clear to me that she had formed an opinion of me – or, probably more to the point, of what I represented: a middle-aged western man entering her home, the home which provided a safe place for kids who have seen and experienced the worst of society, with allusions of bringing change to her life. The disdain in her was obvious. I didn't need to understand Thai to know others like me had arrived at her home, made judgements, formed opinions and left without ever returning. Why should she expect I would be different? She didn't owe me gratitude for my visit or feel the need to apologise for anything that I might have seen and not liked.

As the meeting progressed, she learnt of the work I had done in Phang Nga, the province where Baan Tharn Namchai is located, and I built a level of credibility in her eyes by having done what I said I would do and returning when I'd said I would return. Her mood softened, and she looked at me not with judgement but with an invitation to be different to those who had come before.

One of the biggest disappointments that you need to rise above, working in this sector, is when people commit to do something, then don't. People visit our homes, meet the kids and promise to return, promise to support, promise to give, and then quietly disappear back to their lives without fulfilling that promise. No doubt what I was seeing in Mae Thiew was what I have learnt to develop: a level of scepticism when grand promises are made. I now judge people by their actions rather than their words and promises that may go unfilled. (I think these days we call it "ghosting".) I have found it healthier to be pleasantly surprised than genuinely disappointed. I haven't mastered the art, though, that's for sure.

I left Mae Thiew and Baan Home Hug without any promises or commitments. I offered nothing more than my appreciation for sharing an insight into the lives of the kids and the home. I did say I would return, but that is what everyone says.

In the year after our first meeting, I made a number of trips to north-east Thailand to meet with Mae Thiew and better understand the work she was doing and what she needed. We also spent time getting to know one another. Trust – for both of us and those we represented – was incredibly important and would take time. Through time spent together and a mutually shared desire to support those in need, we formed an alliance and trust that to this day feels unbreakable.

It would take time to learn the scale of the challenges before Mae Thiew. I didn't have all the answers to all the problems – the complexity of the situation ran deep, and money alone was not the answer. A partnership, a commitment – that was what was needed here.

In those early days, I formed a task force of volunteers who would travel to Baan Home Hug and invest time and skills into righting some of the wrongs. First to go were those broken-down hospital beds. Next was the leaking roof, and nothing brightens a place more than a fresh coat of paint. The task force put gutters on roofs and added water storage tanks beneath the ground. It repaired what was broken and replaced what was beyond repair. With each paint stroke, with each turn of the Allen key in assembling a new bed, there was a message to Mae Thiew and the kids that we were committed. When we said we would return, that is what we did. When we said we cared, we acted. Very quickly, the kids formed bonds with our volunteers who were returning year on year. The kids became their apprentices, they became friends, and our presence became something they could count on.

I learnt that Mae Thiew had devoted her life to the support of the children in her care. Leaving university, she forwent a life in Bangkok and relocated to support these children who seemed to be unwanted and forgotten by those who should have cared the most. Establishing a safe home that provided for the children became her calling in life, and she rose to that calling.

Many of the children she provided care for were sick with a lifelong illness, including HIV and significant learning and development issues – illnesses that created a burden on their mothers to which I suspect many couldn't see a solution; Baan Home Hug began as a temporary option to see them through a difficult time, but more often than not, children would be left in Mae Thiew's care and the parents would simply disappear, never to return.

By agreeing to love and care for these children when no one else would, and finding a way to meet their medical, physical and spiritual needs, the demands placed upon her increased. Now, those working in government, at local hospitals and in police stations had somewhere to take the children that others simply rejected. The better a job she did of caring for the children, the more children she was sent to care for, and the more the demands of caring for the children increased. What didn't match the demands was the funding needed to support the increased number of children.

She was (and remains) of the mindset of saying "yes" to taking on a child if Baan Home Hug was their last viable option, even when the means of supporting them put an increased strain on her resources. In the years before we met, the situation became so critical that she would consistently be forced to choose which of the children in need of lifesaving HIV medicine would receive it and which would not; she didn't have enough to provide for all and was forced to decide who desperately needed the medicine that day and who seemed strong enough to miss out. The problem with that is HIV builds a resistance to the drugs if you don't take them consistently. What do you do when the number of dying children is greater than the number of pills you can administer? How do you effectively decide who lives and who dies?

Mae Thiew told me once that over the 24 years she had operated Baan Home Hug, she had buried 1027 children. A good number of those children may not have passed away if she'd had the medicine that was required. Hands Across the Water and the supporters that make up this wonderful organisation have been able to bring an end to this alarming child mortality rate. In 2011 and 2012, Hands committed to meet all of the operational and medical costs for all of the children at Baan Home Hug, and something remarkable happened: the children stopped dying. And that's the way it should be. We can't help everyone, but we can all help someone. At the time of writing we have been supporting Mae Thiew and the children of Baan Home Hug for 15 years, and I have had the privilege of witnessing the change and, indeed, the growth of the kids who I first met back in 2010. Many have grown and moved on to live independent lives, carving out their own futures with their own families, and that is the measure of success for us and me personally – not the dollars we raise or the number of kids we provide homes for but creating brighter futures for those we support, seeing them live lives of choice.

A small number of those kids we met more than a decade ago remain in our lives and are closer to us than ever. Am was a young girl when I met her in my early years at Baan Home Hug. I don't know if a photo exists of her where she is not smiling. Her smile changes her face completely, and it also changes yours, because when you see it you can't help but smile. Am studied hard at school, and her caring nature with the younger children was as genuine as it was obvious. Through the emotional support and guidance of Mae Thiew, and the financial backing of Hands,

Am enrolled in and graduated from university. She entered the workforce through an internship with a hotel partner of ours, but her position at the hotel quickly disappeared, a victim of the global pandemic. She returned to Baan Home Hug and took on a role teaching the younger kids. She had gone from the student to the master. However, in the years after COVID-19 and during the formative years of HET, CT could see that Am was not necessarily thriving in her role at Baan Home Hug. Many of the girls she had grown up with had left, and returning to teach the younger kids wasn't really her first choice. CT spent time understanding what Am wanted for herself, and then, in consultation with Mae Thiew, suggested that Am leave Home Hug for a time and take a six-month internship with HET down in Khao Lak to see if it was a job she might enjoy. For Am, it meant leaving behind all that she knew and taking a risk, but embodying the concept that to find growth we have to leave comfort behind, she took up the option. We provided Am with a job, a new home, an income and an opportunity to return to study for her tour guide licence, but more importantly, she was given the opportunity to build another family in addition to the one she would always have at Baan Home Hug. At Baan Nam Khem on the coast of the Andaman Sea, this beautiful young lady thrived, and that infectious smile of hers returned. Her new HET family consisted of Nunn, his wife Nicha and her new, adopted big brother Squid. To watch the support and love the team has for one another shows a measure of success that we never could have dreamt of.

To find growth we have to leave comfort behind.

When I first met Mae Thiew, she looked the same as those around her. There was a presence and aura about her, but nothing beyond that. Some years after our initial meeting and commitment to work together to support the children in her care, there was an event that would change her. Two of the children within her care were sexually assaulted at school, and there seemed to be little care to redress this crime. Mae Thiew was overcome with grief, anger and desire for retribution for the two kids. The only way she could see to address and manage her feelings was to go deeper into her religious beliefs and the teachings offered by Buddhism. As her grief and anger continued to manifest, she went deeper into the peace she found within those teachings. In time she became physically and spiritually changed as a person. Gone were the street clothes, replaced by the bright orange robes of a Buddhist monk, the colour of the setting sun. The robes transformed her physical appearance, and immersing herself in the teachings and philosophy of Buddhism brought calmness to her mind and soothed her anger. Her transformation into a monk would be one from which she would not return.

However, the change had no impact on her appetite to take on adventures and challenges. Within 12 months of us meeting and her learning of the charity rides we were doing, she was reserving a bike for herself and riding the 800 kilometres with us. Seldom a year passes when she doesn't ride with us, and her presence on the road is a gift to our riders. To spend the time with her that the rides avail is truly a unique experience – for me it is a learning experience each time. Equally as special are those mornings with a 4.30 a.m. or 5 a.m. start in Yasothon when we are afforded the truly unique privilege to walk with Mae Thiew through the community, through the early morning markets, where she receives offerings in the form of food from the community. It is such a rare privilege to be afforded the opportunity to do this, and it is certainly not something that can be booked with your travel agent.

Mae Thiew is like no one I have met before or since. Her singular focus in pursuing opportunities that enrich the lives of the children in her care is laser sharp. If there is something she can do that might lead to greater awareness and support for the children in her care, she will do it.

As you will come to discover, Mae Thiew would decide to join me on the Run to Remember. She wasn't invited, she just decided. With scant detail about the run other than the start and finish points, she decided that it warranted her presence and devotion for almost a month. It is hard for me to articulate the depth of gratitude I have for her.

PART II
IT HAS TO BE SOMETHING BIG

6

The idea of the run

I knew that I wanted to do something big to mark the 20th anniversary of the tsunami. There would a number of desired outcomes, but it had to be big. Big to stand out in Thailand and raise awareness of who we were and what we had done, but also big for me. To do something terrifyingly huge, it has to be for yourself. The occasion and the impact on my life, both positive and negative, and the impact on those around me deserved something significant.

CT and I had talked about doing something big without really knowing what. These discussions started in 2022, as we knew the time between the discussions and the anniversary would pass quickly and we didn't want to miss the opportunity. We both felt that at the ten-year anniversary, as a charity, we didn't seize the moment – not publicly, at least, and definitely not within Thailand. From a charity point of view, we didn't miss the boat completely, as we had two sold-out bike rides in January 2015, each with 50 riders, and raised over $1 million just from that campaign. However, there was an opportunity to tell the story of why we continued to operate and why that was important ten years on. That was the opportunity we missed, and we committed to not making the same mistake for the 20-year anniversary, knowing that would be the last time people would seriously consider the impact of that event.

After my time working in Thailand through 2005, I'd returned to the New South Wales Police, and to be honest, I felt a bit lost. Where was I going to find the kind of motivation and stimulation that I had experienced working in Thailand, leading the international teams in what was and remains the world's largest identification effort? It was timely, then, when an opportunity presented itself to undertake a 12-month secondment with the National Institute of Forensic Science on a highly classified project for Interpol in the field of counterterrorism. To be more specific, it was in the area of chemical, biological, radiological and nuclear (CBRN) threats and trends. I would spend 12 months researching and analysing CBRN threats and trends on a global scale and what we should do as an international forensic science community to prepare for them. I would spend time at the headquarters of Interpol in Lyon, France, sharing my findings and presenting to the international community. I would then go on to spend time working with the United Nations Office on Drugs (UNODC) Regional Office for Southeast Asia and the Pacific, developing capabilities around counterterrorism. The 12 months turned into two and a half years.

The thing with threats is that there needs to be both intent and capability for the threat to have substance. If I said, "I am going to blow up a plane," that would be an illegal threat, but in the counterterrorism world I was in, it wouldn't be considered a genuine threat if I didn't have the capability to act on it.

Likewise, having the capability without the intent would not amount to a threat.

Can you see the connection to the Run to Remember? Let me illustrate with another example.

Developing capability can take time, depending on what you are seeking to achieve. If I want to master the ability to speak fluent Thai, that will take considerable time, but the intent is something I can arrive at almost instantly. The most decisive moment in committing to the Run to Remember was not when I reached a certain level of fitness or capability – it was when I formed the intent. It was always going to matter more what I was willing to do than what I was capable of doing. Because, really, when do you know that you have sufficient training, strength and stamina to put the equivalent of 33 marathons back to back in 26 days? The only time I would know I had the capability would be in those final days; the rest of it would be achieved through my intent and willingness as opposed to any perceived or realised capabilities. The question to ask ourselves is, "How much more can we achieve if we focus more on intent than perceived abilities?"

The idea of running from Baan Home Hug to Baan Tharn Namchai came to me as I lay in bed waiting to drift off to sleep. Some of my best and worst thinking is done in that time – some nights I delight in the uninterrupted thinking time as my mind bounces from one idea to the next, and other nights it is a curse as I want the noise to stop.

I sat on the idea of the run for a few weeks, wanting to make sure it had time to drift around in the vacuum that exists inside my head. Each time my head hit the pillow in those first weeks, I visualised and conceptualised the run. After a few weeks, I knew the litmus test would be CT's immediate reaction when I shared the idea with her. If she was on board then the rest would sort itself out. If she had the belief in me, then I would find the belief in myself as well. If her initial response was to dismiss it for one of the many reasons that one could dismiss such an adventure – the main one being that I didn't consider myself an endurance athlete… or an athlete at all, come to think of it – then I may not have pursued it.

Her immediate and enthusiastic response to the idea – which at that time amounted to running from Baan Home Hug to Baan Tharn Namchai to finish on Boxing Day, with no other detail – was possibly the earliest defining moment that set this train in motion. It could have died an immediate death but for her support. Instead, she gave it life in the form of her response: "I believe in you". Is there a more empowering statement than that from someone whose opinion matters most? I think not.

A search on Google Maps showed that the distance from Baan Home Hug to Baan Tharn Namchai was 1320 kilometres, and a simple division of that number of kilometres with the number of days I had to run, which was looking like 26 days, was a smidge over 50 kilometres a day. I had done that more than a few times running ultramarathons, so I knew I had the distance in me for one day at least. Besides, the ultras had thousands of metres of elevation in them, whereas this run would be flat. However, it wasn't lost on me that I would be required to back up the first day of 50 kilometres with 25 additional days of the same, and all in the heat and humidity of Thailand. It felt big, it felt scary and it felt intimidating, and even perhaps out of reach – and for those very reasons it felt like the right thing to do. It if didn't feel scary, then it wasn't big enough. This scared the shit out of me!

I think one of the attractions for me in doing the run was that I was anything but certain of my ability to complete it. We could have circumnavigated Thailand on a bike and, but for an accident,

I know I could achieve that: my longest solo effort on a bike is 276 kilometres in a day, with several trips over 250 kilometres, so covering a lot of distance on a bike, given enough time, doesn't faze me. Running the type of distance I was proposing, though… well, that was a different story, and the uncertainty, the doubt that would exist in my mind and others', made it all the more enticing. I would be 57 when I set off on this run; did I really have it in me? There was only one way to find out, and as soon as it became a public conversation, there was no turning back.

The caveat that came from CT was, "You will need to train properly if you are going to do this, though". Indeed, if I was going to do this then I needed to become a runner.

When do you "become a runner"? It's a funny thing attaching a label to yourself that in some way defines who you are – or, perhaps more importantly, who you want to be seen or known as. For the last 20 years I have consistently struggled to come up with a label for myself to answer the question, "So, what do you do?" When I was with the police, the answer was easy: I was a forensic investigator with the New South Wales Police. But ever since I left that, I haven't felt comfortable defining who I am.

I have spoken at conferences for the last 20 years, sometimes amassing more than 100 keynotes a year, but never do I define myself as a speaker, and hell will freeze over before you ever hear me define myself as a "motivational speaker". For whatever reason, I cringe at the thought of such a label; perhaps it feels arrogant to me. So, if I am not a speaker, what am I? CT and I run Wildnest, a high-end glamping retreat, but that is not who I am either. I have led 41 long-distance charity bike rides in Thailand ranging from 500 to 1600 kilometres each, but I certainly don't call myself a cyclist. We raise Hereford cattle on our farmstead property, and while I would love to call myself a cattle breeder, that would be bordering on the criminal offence of "false pretences", because when I say we breed cattle, what I mean is that we have cattle in a paddock, and through the calving season (whenever that might be) we welcome in new additions that we contribute nothing towards other than ensuring there is grass in the paddock and water in the trough. So, when I am forced to give some type of answer as to what I do, typically it is, "I work for a charity".

So, what about calling myself a runner? No, it would be rather ostentatious of me to consider myself a runner. Surely that label is for those who do it well, those who are good at it.

If I am not sure if I can legitimately call myself a runner now, then there is certainly no time in the past when that label has applied. I have always, through school and beyond, been engaged in some type of sport or activity, with probably the first decade of having kids being when time devoted to exercise of some description was absent. I would go for a run in spits and spurts, usually prompted by a desire to drop a few kilograms, which would sneak up on me. But it was never something I took on with a plan, a goal or consistency.

In 2004 I decided I would take on the Sydney Half-Marathon. I ran around the block a few times in my training and preparation, and with a level of naivety bordering on arrogance, I assumed that I had the base fitness to get me through. Where I thought that base fitness came from, I am not sure. That run created a couple of memorable moments that stay with me today.

The route took the runners under the Sydney Harbour Bridge, through the streets of the city and out and around Mrs Macquarie's Chair, located on the edge of Sydney Harbour and the Royal Botanic Garden, and then looped back through the city to the finish line. As the route headed back through the city, those of us running the half-marathon passed the marathon runners heading out. I distinctly recall looking at those tackling the full marathon distance in a state of awe and disbelief that they could run that far.

The second memorable moment wasn't as pleasant. The run started well and things went swimmingly until the last two kilometres. I had stopped at a water station along the route and grabbed a half-full cup of water, believing that was all I needed. I remember having this strange sensation as I approached the finish line of moving so slowly and people passing me like I was standing still. I came into the final kilometre, and next thing I knew I was on the ground. I remember trying to get up and someone, in the most supportive way, preventing me from doing so. I know I said to them, "Just let me finish, I can see the finish line". I draw a blank from there until I regained some level of consciousness in the back of an ambulance and thought to myself, "Holy shit, I have had a heart attack". I was admitted to Royal Prince Alfred Hospital and diagnosed with severe dehydration that had led to the onset of mild kidney failure.

I was admitted overnight and spent my hospital stay lying in my sweaty running gear (absent my shoes) for the next 36 hours until I was discharged with follow-up appointments booked with my local doctor. I had blood tests ordered and was sent home. Not long after arriving home, the doctor called, having received my blood-test results, and advised I needed to be readmitted to hospital immediately.

So, that was my first half-marathon. Things didn't necessarily go according to plan, but the fact was that I didn't have a race plan, hadn't done the training that was warranted, certainly didn't have the base fitness I thought and got the kick in the arse I well and truly deserved. Importantly, I learnt that as a world-champion sweater, if I was going to embark on any type of exercise beyond an hour's duration then I needed a plan to prevent getting into such a state of dehydration again.

I returned to the Sydney Half-Marathon in 2005 and completed it this time, armed with gels that I had tied to my running shorts, managing to cross the line feeling strong and having loved the experience.

Running would be in and out of my life over the next few years and then kind of disappeared – or, let's say, took a break – for several years as it was replaced by the bike tours in Thailand. The problem was that I didn't complement the annual bike ride in January with sustained riding and training back home, so come November I would head to the local gym for a few spin classes to get me bike fit in time for the next ride.

As a result of personal changes in my life and time that I had on my hands during 2011, I fell in love with road cycling. I purchased myself a decent road bike as a treat from the sales of my first book, and I was on that thing at every opportunity. I was living in Freshwater in Sydney's Northern Beaches region at the time and that bike, much to the dismay of my building manager, lived in my living room and not in the bike locker with all the other bikes – didn't she understand that my bike was so above those down there?!

I would ride incessantly. My favourite ride was from Freshwater north to Ku-ring-gai Chase National Park through Church Point, along McCarrs Creek Road and out to West Head. Every meeting I had in the city was confirmed subject to my ability to find a post-ride shower so that I could ride in. It wasn't just about the joy of being on the bike, which became easier the stronger I got and therefore more enjoyable, but the route to the city. I was riding from the Northern Beaches through the north shore of

Sydney and then over the Harbour Bridge. Sydney has to have one of if not the most beautiful city harbours in the world, and I defy anyone to walk or cycle across the bridge and not be impressed by the beauty of the harbour. Even today, 15 years on, whenever I am in the city I try to squeeze into the day a run that takes me across the bridge and back.

Riding my bike continued to be a major part of my life, and it is what brought CT and I together in the early days: we met on a Hands ride, and for the next 12 months we were riding buddies until it became more. After our wedding in 2015, we continued to ride the Northern Beaches until less and less time was spent on the bike.

In 2018, I put together a group of mates to walk the Kokoda Trail. It would be my second time, and I knew from the first time the only way to make that experience better was to go in a good physical condition. It was through training for Kokoda that I found myself returning to running. During Kokoda, one of the boys talked about ultra running and mentioned that his wife was running Ultra-Trail Australia in May 2019. I had never heard of the sport before, but it seemed like a good goal to aim for and something to work towards beyond the annual bike rides in January with Hands. If it hadn't been for that first trail run in May 2019, running 50 kilometres through the bush with massive elevation, I doubt that the Run to Remember would have ever been a consideration.

So, as I did a few more ultras, what I obviously didn't know at the time was that I was building a base that the thought of the Run to Remember could originate from. I figured if I could do 50 kilometres then how much harder could 60 be? Besides, as I have already noted, there wasn't the elevation to contend with in Thailand. I didn't underestimate the challenge of the run that

I was proposing, but to be honest, I just couldn't have appreciated the scale of it.

I seem to have this ability to decide to do something and then commit to it without truly appreciating what I am committing to. After giving evidence during an arson trial in my early forensics days, I thought it would be a good idea to study law. I found an entryway through the University of Sydney Law Extension Committee, enrolled in the next intake and spent the following six years studying law while I worked full-time and studied a four-year forensic science course through Canberra Institute of Technology. I enjoyed riding in helicopters, so I went ahead and got my helicopter pilot's licence. And here I was now, at the age of 57, deciding that I should be an endurance athlete and run 1400 kilometres. At least I gave this a couple of weeks' thought before I committed to it. What could possibly go wrong?

7

Assembling the team

Once I decided to do the Run to Remember, one thing was clear: I couldn't do it alone. There was a team to build to make it happen.

Claire Baines (CT): Hands CEO, Marketing Guru, Runner, Problem-solver, Wife
In the lead-up to the run, I repeatedly said that no one person has ever supported me more in anything I have ever done than CT.

CT's role as CEO of Hands Group, looking after five different entities across Australia, New Zealand and Thailand, is incredibly demanding. She leads the team at Hands and has built a great culture, exploring every opportunity to enrich the lives of not just the kids and communities we support in Thailand but the team she leads across the various groups.

Even without the run, 2024 was always going to be big. The economic climate was difficult for an international charity operating in Australia, but thanks to our amazing community of supporters, we managed to find a way. In the first half of the year,

CT's focus was on the bigger picture of developing a marketing and PR campaign that would capitalise on the attention that would be focused on Thailand during that time. But, of course, she also had the daily operations and leadership responsibilities she holds as the CEO of Hands Group, which are far-reaching and incredibly demanding.

In the final couple of months before the run, CT's attention and focus was directed more deliberately on all things related to the run. Her background as the leader of the events team for a large national corporate meant that if there was an Olympic event for preparing an event run sheet, she would have podiumed. CT's focus on the logistics of the run coincided with my withdrawal from the logistics. I had worked out the route and attended to the logistics at a macro level; it was now time for me to step aside and let the professionals take over. My focus turned instead to physical preparation, and CT enabled me to focus on the physical while she assumed control of everything else.

Chris Thomas (CT's dad): Captain on the Road

Next in my sights were Chris and Wendy, CT's parents. I am blessed to have such amazing in-laws who I genuinely look forward to spending time with. Chris is very level-headed, and we have taken on many projects together on the farm with neither of us having a clue but always finding our way. Wendy has such a caring soul and lives a life devoid of drama. If they both agreed to come on the journey, I was confident we could build around that core team. Of course, coming to Thailand to support the run would mean personal sacrifice and expense. Being with us on the road for the entire duration meant not only a month away from home but choosing the Run over being with family in Australia on Christmas Day, a not-insignificant commitment.

I made sure they knew that the option of flying home to be with the grandkids for Christmas was definitely on the table.

Chris, or "Father", readily accepted and embraced the run when I first put it to him, and I can't think of another person in my circle who I would have wanted to do the job Chris did. He is logical and finds solutions to problems, and I have experienced this working with him on the farm. I asked Chris to be the chief navigator, responsible for all changes to the route, including finding solutions when we hit roadblocks – literal and metaphorical – and driving the main support vehicle. All of these roles were incredibly essential to the safe execution of each day.

He also held a role we hoped he wouldn't have to perform. In planning the run, we developed communication protocols for when difficult decisions needed to be made. I was clear to the team in the lead-up that I didn't need language or actions that endorsed or supported any negative thoughts or whinging on my behalf. The absolute last thing I needed during really difficult times was someone in the team saying, "You've done enough, call it quits". The message to the team was to be kind but do what they needed to do to ensure I kept heading back out onto the road, even when I might not want to. It was their job to remember that the pain of quitting would last forever, while the pain or discomfort I felt on the road would pass. However, we needed to consider whose job it would be to speak to me if things were unravelling and becoming potentially dangerous to my long-term health. We identified a number of situations that would signal things not being where they needed to be, which included my inability or refusal to take on food or water over a sustained period of time, inability to urinate, medical symptoms suggesting a serious problem, or running back-to-back 15-minute kilometres. I knew I could easily walk a kilometre in ten minutes, so back-to-back 15-minute kilometres would be a sure sign of a problem. The protocol we put in place was that if any of these situations occurred, the people to talk to me about it would be Chris and Claire, our medic. Their goal was ultimately to keep me on the road – to fix me up and send me back out – but they were the ones who had the authority to pull me off the road if need be. We agreed that the strategy would be first to give me a warning: that if I didn't drink more, eat more or urinate more, then I was risking being removed from the road.

Wendy Thomas (CT's mum): Head Chef

Wendy was less enthusiastic to come initially, but not because she was hesitant about supporting us – I had outlined a clear role for Chris but hadn't articulated as clearly what Wendy's role would be, and she was worried she would be in the way or just baggage to the tour.

They say an army marches on its stomach. Arriving into Thailand as part of the forward party, Wendy would support CT to set up the Mothership – a motorhome we would hire for the tour, complete with bathroom, kitchen and capacity for six to sleep – and source all the necessities that we envisaged using over the month. We planned to take a good quantity of food and other essentials into Thailand, as it was important for me to have a diet that was familiar and I was comfortable with.

With the schedule requiring a 4.30 a.m. wake-up call each day, getting breakfast from any of the hotels was just never going to be an option – unless you are in a big hotel at a major tourist location, you will struggle to get a hotel to serve you breakfast before 7 a.m. in any hotel in Thailand, and the breakfast you would get often offers little choice and substance. So, the plan was that Wendy would prepare breakfast for the crew, and indeed the majority of food we consumed during the day, besides dinner. Of course, this meant that Wendy would need to be up at 4.30 a.m. each morning, and her day would be no less arduous than anyone else's.

Greg Wallace: Runner

After my core team of CT and her parents was assembled, the next call was to Greg. He had ridden with CT and I on a Hands ride right back in 2011. Since that time, he and his beautiful wife Jules had attended and supported all of our events. In 2018, Greg, Jules and the family took that support to another level when he committed to run while we rest of us rode the route. With his family by his side, he ran for eight days, completing some 670 kilometres. When I decided to do the Run to Remember, Greg was the only person I really considered inviting to do the run with me – it felt in some way disrespectful of Greg's effort in 2018 not to invite him to join me.

The call to Greg went along these lines:

"Hi, mate. I have a bit of a crazy idea and wanted to see if you wanted to join me?"

"I'm in."

"You don't know what the idea is yet."

"It doesn't matter, I'm in."

I then shared the concept of the run with him, and after a call from Greg to Jules, we had both of them locked in.

Of the hundreds of training runs I did in the lead-up to the run, I can't think of many that I didn't do alone. I don't run with a regular group – given the travel that I do, it doesn't make a lot of sense to – and there is no regular or consistent time that I run. I am certainly not a morning runner – unless I am in Thailand, where the time difference of three to four hours often has me awake at 4 a.m., and there is no better time to head out for a run on the roads in Thailand. This unpredictability to my training made planning to run with someone else difficult.

I did have concerns around what it would be like to run with Greg given his experience and history of long runs, which includes completing the 240-kilometre Coast to Kosci several times and many other runs measured in the hundreds of kilometres. I didn't know what each day would bring and how Greg would approach the run. I just wasn't sure what his strategy would be – or his level of patience! I was always going to be much slower than him and not have the in-built endurance. However, given the pedigree he had built up over the years, I also knew my experience, and my chance of a successful finish, would be enhanced by his presence.

Julie Wallace: Runner Support

If Greg responded to my invitation with childlike enthusiasm, from all reports Jules wasn't far behind. You secure one and you get both.

In the lead-up, I suspected that Jules would be there as Greg's support person and we would almost operate two independent teams. I didn't know if Greg would run with me or ahead, so I wasn't sure how Jules's role would play out, but I knew that they had done this so many times in different formats and they knew what they were doing.

Claire Oliver: Medic

The team was now four and a half confirmed plus me. (The half was Wendy, who was still to be convinced we needed her and she wasn't going to be a passenger for 26 days.) Next on the list was medical support. Fortunately for me, I had connected with two beautiful souls from the healthcare industry while speaking at a conference. Claire and Tracey signed up for our 2023 ride in Thailand, and then, upon hearing of the run, both eagerly volunteered to join. Ultimately, Tracey would need to miss the trip due to a new job, but Claire was in. Again, I offered the option of joining for half or leaving to be home for Christmas, but Claire was in for the full show. Her personal commitment to the run was huge. We all had family who we were travelling with, but Claire was traveling solo, which meant not being with her family for Christmas and also missing her husband Craig's birthday.

Am: Tour Manager

The Australian team was all locked in, but it was always the case that we would have support from our team in Thailand.

As mentioned earlier, Am had joined the Hands Experiences Thailand team from Baan Home Hug and went on to become a licensed tour guide. As she was on staff at HET, it always made sense that she would join us as part of the tour. She speaks wonderful English, which was an asset.

Even before we kicked off the tour, Am showed her worth by booking the hotels and restaurants each night for dinner. I mapped out the route in the months leading up to the run, and I spent hours upon hours trying to find hotels for us in the most remote locations throughout Thailand. You would think a simple Google search would give you all the options you might need, right? Wrong. In many of the small villages, the hotels – or "resorts" as they call themselves, using the label with poetic licence – don't depend on visiting tourists or those looking for accommodation online. Somehow though they exist just nicely, thank you, without the need to pay a tech company to list their whereabouts. A Google listing is considered unnecessary, as is a website or even an email address. I employed the best of my forensic investigative skills and arrived at a hotel option for all 26 nights on the tour. I presented it to Am and requested she actually speak on the phone with each hotel to confirm they did in fact exist and operated as a lodging for travellers, and if they could host our team of eleven on the night we passed through their town.

On top of that, Am would need to find a dinner option for us in each of those towns. If you assumed the dinner option would be one and the same as the accommodation, then you would go hungry. The vast majority of the dinners she organised were held off site, and I don't how she found some of these places – they were not in restaurant guides, and most weren't even on Google, but find them she did.

Squid: Mothership Driver

Squid is another member of the HET team and joined as a full-time staff member in early 2024. He is a driver and bike mechanic for the bike tours, along with undertaking other assorted duties. When we decided to hire the Mothership, the options were to supply our own driver or hire one of the rental company's. Having Squid on staff, it made sense to send him up to Bangkok to be certified in the use of the vehicle by the company and be our driver. Navigating the Mothership through 1400 kilometres of roads in Thailand was not a job I was envious of, especially manoeuvring through the cities.

Bew: Support Vehicle Driver

Bew is one of the students from Baan Tharn Namchai who went on to university with the support of Hands. He graduated in social welfare studies and then returned to work at Baan Tharn Namchai caring for the younger children. He would be a late inclusion to the tour when we realised we needed another driver. Ford Thailand had sponsored the tour with the loan of two vehicles, which were invaluable. Chris would drive one that would remain with me the entire time, and the second vehicle would drive ahead to check the route and be a general-purpose vehicle, conveying the team and sourcing supplies as needed. How I thought we could do the tour without Bew driving, I am not sure.

8

Hope is not a plan

Two years out from the run, I was rationalising how I could make the distance and what the training would look like. What existed two years out and would remain ever present until the final days in December was the fear of quitting. Right from the time I decided to do the run, I knew that once I started, if I didn't finish for whatever reason, the pain of quitting would remain with me forever. It would burn away inside me – I knew this based on my history. There is nothing that guarantees failure more than quitting. I don't underestimate the power of this fear that drove me through the run in Thailand. I think I had built up the fear of quitting so much that I just could never contemplate it.

There are a number of times in my life that I recall with great clarity when I have given up. They remain with me as sad reminders of times of weakness and lack of conviction, and I carry each of them with me.

I enrolled at the University of Wollongong out of school, not because I had a desire to study there or a career in mind that necessitated it, but simply because I got the marks and was the first in the family to have the option. It wasn't as though I was blessed with choice when it came to what I would study: the options were an arts degree or an arts degree. Yes, I just barely scraped in. I selected subjects that I thought offered some direction or hope of a future career, but within months I had handed in my student card, clear this was neither the time nor the place for me.

My regret about the decision to leave isn't that I wish I had obtained an arts degree – even reflecting now, decades on, I am not sure how that would have served me – but that I started something and didn't finish it. In the years that followed, I would return to university and successfully complete studies in forensic science and law, but still, the burn that I feel from quitting the arts degree hurts.

My first marriage lasted longer than my time at Wollongong and would produce three amazing kids, but that too, upon reflection, was something that I quit without sufficient fight or work. Perhaps our lives had gone in directions that meant we would be happier moving on than staying together, but I have always felt I could have worked harder at something so important before pulling the pin. That's another big regret: not working harder before calling time.

Not finishing a 320-kilometre bike ride also sits with me. There is a bike ride held once a year that loops twice around Lake Taupo in New Zealand. Each loop is around 160 kilometres, and I have ridden the single loop a couple of times. The ride offers single, double and even multiple loops around the lake. I decided that I wanted to achieve the 320 kilometres in a day.

Setting off not much after midnight, a group of riders headed out into the darkness, completing the majority of the first loop before the sun came up and getting back to the start/finish line in time to start the second loop as the main field headed off on their first. I completed the first loop somewhere in the middle of the pack. The first loop was done, but during the back end of the first loop I couldn't shake a lower back pain that seemed to be getting worse as the ride went on. I would stop and stretch it out and get back on my bike, but my pace was slowing, the time left on the bike was getting longer and the projected finish time got further and further away.

I accept that the source of my back pain was not being diligent enough in my bike set-up. Unpacking my bike the day before, after the flight across the Tasman, and guessing the right height of the seat post wouldn't have been an issue for a 100-kilometre ride, but for 320 kilometres it had become somewhat important. But the damage was done. I accepted that today was not the day for two loops and rationalised that if I was going to pull out of the ride, I may as well do it sooner rather than later, as each additional pedal stroke was taking me further out of town.

Withdrawing from the ride mattered to nobody but me. Few people knew, and even fewer really gave a shit. It's egotistical to think that anyone would have cared if I had finished the two loops – it just wasn't anything of significance. So, why do I carry the burden of guilt at pulling out of the ride? Because I said I was going to do it and then didn't.

The lesson for me is that the pain of enduring and completing is less than the pain of quitting and then carrying that with me.

Going into the Run to Remember, I worried about the impact of not completing it. I knew that this was a one-time opportunity, and I couldn't take it as a learning experience for next time because there would be no next time. I didn't want to consider options; I didn't want a Plan B; I didn't want to have alternatives and back-up plans. I wanted to complete the run, all

1320 kilometres of it, and finish on 26 December 2024. I needed those around me on the run to understand their goal had to be to keep me on the road, not to entertain my complaining and not to offer any shortcuts or alternative options.

The question I asked myself was whether such rigidity in the plan and the lack of alternative options would create a bigger risk of overall failure. Did my lack of willingness to bend on the distance and time ratio set me up for failure, or did the certainty assist me in reaching my end goal?

As I considered this, and as the planning started to take shape, I reached out to a mate of mine, Dr Sean Richardson, who works with elite athletes and has a history of endurance sport himself. I posed the idea of the run and what I was looking to do. One of things he strongly encouraged me to do was to consider what I was setting myself up for. The model I presented had zero options other than success or failure. Either I ran the full distance and made it to the end on Boxing Day, or I failed. He counselled me to consider something equally as hard but with breakage points along the way. Why did I need to run that distance? Why couldn't I run a marathon a day for 26 days? That was still hugely significant. The other thing he strongly encouraged me to consider during the initial planning stage was to start earlier than 1 December: "Why not give yourself another week or two?"

The thing is, long before the wheels were set in motion, I felt the need to run the entire distance, and I had little appetite to extend the time away from home, not just for me but for the crew. Sean wasn't the only one to suggest that I didn't need to run every kilometre from Baan Home Hug to Baan Tharn Namchai. Years on, nobody would care – the story of the run would stand alone, and it didn't need the risk of failure I was building into it. But it mattered to me. The idea of covering the same distance but only running a marathon a day and then driving to the next start point never sat well with me. I was all in.

As the planning of the run took shape, I revisited the 1320-kilometre route that Google had given me. It was the quickest and most direct route between point A and point B. The problem was that it utilised the main roads carrying freight and regular traffic throughout Thailand and towards the border towns. A few years previously, I had joined a mate in a run from Canberra to Sydney over six days. and the route we had taken was the most direct, with 90% of the running spent on the main highway that links Canberra and Sydney and is the thoroughfare for heavy vehicles moving freight from Melbourne to all destinations up the east coast of Australia. It was a horrible experience. There was nothing pleasant about it: I couldn't hear myself think and I was constantly being pushed back by the wind of the heavy trucks. I wouldn't entertain the thought of a similar run again. It would invite a level of danger into the run that just wasn't necessary, and it wasn't the way I wanted to spend a month on the road in Thailand, that was for sure.

So, there was no way I would take the highway route. The tradeoff, though, was that moving away from the highway increased the kilometres – only one or two here and there, but by the time I had finished routing the run using the software Komoot, I had added 91 kilometres to the run, which was another day and a half to two days of running based on the original plan. I wouldn't compromise with getting off the highway, which meant increasing the daily distance from 50 kilometres to 60 kilometres on average. That was achievable, I hoped.

In the early planning stages, I toyed with breaking up the run into two daily efforts: leave early in the morning and run the first 30 or 40 kilometres, and then get off the road and into the Mothership for a rest before getting back out onto the road after the heat of the day had passed to complete the final 20 to 30 kilometres. I was pretty focused on this plan and had seen other long-distance athletes do the same when they weren't chasing a time record. Although it would be winter in Thailand during the run in December, I knew I would still be experiencing temperatures in the high 30s during the hottest part of the day.

As soon as I undertook my first decent training run on the roads in Thailand, I knew the plan of running in two efforts over the day, broken by several hours off the road, was not the model I wanted. I couldn't imagine having to find the motivation twice in one day, or 56 times over the course of the run, to get out and start again. By the end of the training run, I was firm that when we left each morning of the Run to Remember, we would run until we were finished.

The time between committing to do the run and the actual run passed pretty slowly at first – it was over two years, and that felt like a lot at first. In the first six to nine months, not a lot happened. I thought about it on a daily basis, but from a planning or training point of view there was no real action taken. After all I had plenty of time.

9

The three outcomes

There would be three clear objectives for the run:

1. to raise awareness of Hands in Thailand
2. to raise $1 million
3. to undertake something epic on a personal level in acknowledgement of the 20 years since the tsunami.

1. Raising awareness

Several years prior to the run, I was invited to a dinner at the residence of the Australian Ambassador to Thailand to speak to a dozen leading Australian business representatives about the work of Hands and what we had achieved in Thailand. During his introduction to my presentation, then Ambassador Paul Robilliard advised the attendees that I was the founder of what was, and had been for many years, the largest contributing Australian charity to Thailand. It wasn't something that I had been aware of, and I asked Paul if I could quote him on that, which he agreed to. However, despite this, it is not too much of an exaggeration to say we were unknown in Thailand to basically everyone except those who had benefited from the fundraising and support that we had brought to the country. There was next to zero brand awareness of Hands Across the Water in Thailand, despite the charity having operated in the country for two decades, raising 1 billion Thai baht in the process.

The limited knowledge of our presence within Thailand can be attributed to a couple of things. The first is that as an Australian charity, set up by an Australian, we were considered by many businesses we sought support from to be a "foreign charity", and their preference was to direct funds to charities within Thailand. The fact that the only country that benefited from the funds raised by our charity work was Thailand didn't seem to count for much. The other reason for the lack of awareness within Thailand was the fact that the bulk of the heavy lifting when it came to raising funds was done outside of Thailand, largely within Australia and New Zealand.

When I considered the route of the run, I wanted to bring awareness to the run in the hope that it would then raise awareness in the country of the work that we were doing and, importantly, the work we had already done. One of the main initiatives to raise awareness was to build an event that encouraged engagement and provided us with a platform to promote the work of Hands, and not simply rely on the media interest that might exist around me running through the country. We decided to host a fun run in Bangkok. It would be open to all, and the design of the event was based on participation rather than making it too difficult to compete in (or organise, for that matter).

The event in Bangkok would be a three- or nine-kilometre circuit around one of the main parks. The date for the event was Sunday 15 December, during the Run to Remember. It was one of two potential Sundays we could have chosen, the other being the week prior on 8 December. As the run would take place in Bangkok, either date meant that we would be commuting to Bangkok to participate and then returning to pick up the Run to Remember from where we left off the previous day. Ultimately, we chose 15 December for two reasons. The first was that turning up with 900 kilometres of the Run to Remember under my belt rather than 480 felt a bit more credible and also gave us more time on the road to build momentum and public awareness. The second reason was that I thought it would feel better psychologically to finish the run in Bangkok and then drive south to meet the Run to Remember route, rather than turning around and driving north knowing that it would be another week of running before I was back at the same point.

2. Fundraising

As quickly as CT said yes to the Run to Remember, we arrived at the fundraising amount. "What are you thinking for a fundraising target?" CT asked. "I was thinking half a mill, maybe a mill?" I replied. "I reckon shoot for a mill," she responded, and that's how we came up with the fundraising goal. However, the run was always going to be about so much more than just raising money, whatever figure we attached to it.

There was no science behind the target of $1 million. It was big enough to be daunting and yet conceivably within our reach. If it doesn't scare you then it's probably not big enough – a bit like the run itself, which was certainly big enough to scare me but not totally out of reach. I have been fundraising in some way since October 2005, when this wonderful journey started, but this was different. It was a pretty big goal, and 2024 certainly wasn't a great year to be raising money in Australia for an offshore charity:

there was a cost-of-living crisis going on, and donating to charity is always a discretionary spend. When things are tight, it is the discretionary spend that is the first to go, and this is as true for a household as it is in business in my experience.

The other challenge was the story around the 20th anniversary of the Boxing Day tsunami. Clearly, we were no longer raising funds for the first generation of kids who found themselves without parents as a direct result of the tsunami. That had been our raison d'etre, but our mandate had changed significantly over time. However, getting that story across to someone who has made up their mind about what Hands does is challenging. Then, of course, there was the roadblock at corporate level that "sorry, we don't support international charities". None of these obstacles were new to me, and I had been dealing with them in some way for the past 20 years. This time, though, the goal was big, and I needed to go outside of our community of wonderful supporters.

Some 12 months out from the start of the run, I got onto writing sponsorship proposals. I didn't want to miss the budget allocations for the following year from sponsorship managers within businesses that I believed we could have an alignment with. I didn't just write a generic proposal and send it out to a mailing list of businesses – I honestly believe that each submission I put forward I tied in a specific way to the business I was writing to. I laboured over those documents for days, believing before I sent the first one that I had return value to offer. I must have prepared and sent close to 100 submissions, if not more. Of those 100 submissions, 90 I never got a response or acknowledgement from, five said they weren't interested and the other five opened a conversation that may have resulted in free product. It was hugely deflating not even to get a response from 90% of the submissions I had prepared, but that just meant I would need to work harder. I understood that the number of people who are asking for support at any one time is huge, and the response I got just meant my case wasn't compelling enough. I needed to own that and move on.

While the Australian market was proving incredibly difficult to crack – even to open a conversation, let alone secure funding – we were enjoying greater success in Thailand thanks to the relationships, belief and tenacity of one of our Thai directors.

By December of 2024, we had over $300,000 banked, and while I was stoked to have this amount of money prior to the run commencing, I didn't have a measure of if this was good, great or behind where we should be. I did know that it added a wee bit of pressure during the month of November, when I couldn't run and the entire project was in jeopardy. I wondered what the response from the donors would be if the run was called off.

I think I was scarred by some of the responses I had received back in 2014 when Hands had been asked to manage the donations that flooded in for baby Gammy, a Thai baby born with Down syndrome who was caught up in a surrogacy debacle. We were asked to manage the $250,000 donated and be the conduit between the family and the donors, who were from across the globe. I recall that when we advised the public that Gammy did not have any heart issues, as was originally suspected and reported before we became involved, I received a number of abusive notices from people demanding their $10 donation be returned. I had thought it was news to celebrate, but obviously not.

I wrote some thoughts down at different points in the lead-up to the run, not knowing how I would feel or what might be different as time passed. It's interesting to reflect on what I was feeling 18 months out from the run – the main concern I documented then was the ability to raise the money, not doing the actual run:

It's six months on from the announcement of the run to CT and 18 months out from the start. During the last six months I have started speaking about it to different people. The more oxygen the idea gets, the more real it becomes. I remain really excited for the next 18 months and then the first 26 days of December. I find myself increasingly thinking about the run and imaging and visualising the days on the road. When I have been over in Thailand over the last six months, and I have spent probably six weeks on the ground in the first six months of 2023, I am reminded of how hot it will be during the day.

If there has been a change in mindset it is around the fundraising that is possible. 2023 has been a hard year for the charity. With the rise in interest rates hurting a lot of families, a lack of business confidence and the deferral of discretionary spend by many organisations the first six months has been tougher than we expected. We went into the back end of 2022 with the belief that with the end of the pandemic and the return to travel, we would recover from the challenging years of 2020 to 2022. But that has not been the case and we are not where we hoped or expected to be.

Whilst the run is still 18 months away, I wonder where the economy will be in 12 months. What will consumer confidence be like and will there be access to the type of sponsorship I was hoping? Right now, that feels unlikely.

3. My personal challenge

A big part of my personal reason for taking this on was the commitment to suffer out on the road. It felt right that if we were going to ask people to donate that I should do something that was worthy of their support. I also thought of the privileged life that I lead in comparison to the kids that we support. I can never understand the struggle they will face around loss, identity and hardship. A 26-day run wasn't going to give me that insight or come close to their lifetimes of challenge, but I hoped it would demonstrate to the kids the level of care I had for them and the sacrifice I was prepared to make.

What wasn't lost on me was the opportunity this event presented for personal growth. In my late 50s, life could be extremely comfortable should that be my choice. Our farm and the glamping tents certainly present the opportunity to be "farm fit" with all the physical work involved, but the run presented a challenge the likes of which I had never done before and would likely never do again. The training alone would be hugely beneficial, and while my body felt strong and capable of the training load, it felt incumbent upon me to pursue the opportunity. Run while you can, because the opportunity won't be there forever.

I spoke at a conference in Perth during the training for the run where Emma Carey was also a speaker. Emma was in Switzerland and skydiving for the first time when her parachute tangled and she hit the ground, sustaining permanent, life-altering injuries but lucky to survive at all. One of Emma's sayings is, "If you can, you should". That certainly rang true for me: I could attempt this run, and therefore I should. I seldom ponder opportunities long before taking action. I think and then act before allowing all the reasons why not to do something to manifest and leave me with regret over the missed opportunity. From the moment I committed to the run and gained CT's endorsement, it felt right, and that drove my actions from that moment forward.

The three outcomes

A framed photo with the below quote has hung in the various houses I have lived in since I purchased it in 2010:

> "All men dream, but not equally. Those who dream by night in the dusty recesses of their minds, wake in the day to find that it was vanity: but the dreamers of the day are dangerous men, for they may act on their dreams with open eyes, to make them possible."
>
> – T. E. Lawrence

More than once this daytime dreaming has changed the direction of my life, and through the run it would change it again.

10

Now, where did I put those running shoes?

The good news was that I had two years to train. The bad news was I had two years to train. The training at the level that would be needed was new to me, and it had to be sustained. Having a long lead time presented the risk of mental and physical fatigue, burnout, injury, complacency and perhaps even boredom.

I realised during this training period just how hard it was to get back to where I used to be when I was five or ten years younger than what I was in my mid – OK, late – 50s. The work I was doing out there on the road didn't produce the same results in the same time – I had to work harder and longer to achieve the results that I was looking for. I think the scientific term for it is "getting old". It also taught me patience. I needed to just trust that the changes I was looking for would eventually come if I remained consistent and committed.

It was Father's Day, 3 September 2023, when the training began. I had completed a 50-kilometre trail run in the Blue

Mountains in May as part of Ultra-Trail Australia, but there hadn't been a lot to talk about since then. I wasn't a regular runner; I just trained when I had something to run for. While I had completed more than half a dozen ultramarathons since my first in May 2019, I had only ever run one road marathon. It was actually a few weeks after my first ultra, when we were on holidays in Banff, Canada, and they happened to have their annual marathon on the weekend we were there. While it was a really relaxed event in a stunning location, it didn't ignite a passion in me to do another marathon. I love trail running and the relaxed nature of ultras much more; there is something about being immersed in nature on those trail runs which completely changes the experience from running on the road. Being surrounded by the bush is so much more enjoyable than running on bitumen with cars zipping by.

If I am completely honest, the only ultra that I really committed to 100% from a training perspective was the UTA100. It was during the COVID-19 years, and as I was locked down at the farm I spent the majority of my time training for the 100-kilometre run. Our farm in the Capertee Valley is surrounded by national parks and offers runs of varying distances that were ideal for my training. There was plenty of elevation, and with all of my travel having come to a complete stop, along with all of my speaking work, it seemed like a good use of my time to run through the bush. The training was going well, only for the run to be cancelled a few weeks prior due to a landslide in the Blue Mountains National Park.

For every ultra I had actually run, I had fronted up on race morning knowing that I could have done more: I could have trained harder, put in more kilometres on the road and made other sacrifices. However, I also knew I would get through – it was just going to take longer than if I had trained harder, and it would probably hurt more than it should. Committing to the Run to Remember, though, I was determined not to stand at Baan Home Hug on 1 December wishing I had done more training and knowing on a deep level I hadn't given it my all. This was too big and too much relied on the outcome for me to be anything other than fully locked in and engaged on all levels. Besides, this wasn't just about me – there would be a team who would sacrifice the month of December to be with me in Thailand. If nothing else, I owed it to each and every one of them to train and prepare as best I could.

One of the changes that I made was giving up alcohol from February 2024 until the run was over. CT and I spent a couple of weeks snowboarding and touring through Japan with her mum and dad that month, and I decided that our last meal in Japan would be my last drink until the run was over. Giving up the drink wasn't a huge thing for me as I have never been a regular or big drinker, and there were two reasons to do it. The first was that I never wanted to miss a training run the morning after a night out because I had woken up feeling less than 100%. That didn't mean that I trained every morning, but it meant I never missed the opportunity because of the effects of alcohol. The second reason was probably more a mental one: if abstaining from alcohol for a year gave me even 1% benefit then it was worth it. It also allowed me to stand there on 1 December knowing I had done all that I could to be the best I could be.

For the first eight months after committing to the run, I ran often, and I signed up for as many ultras as I could between then and the run. My thinking was that the ultras would give me the distance of 50 kilometres plus, and the elevation would just be a bonus. There wasn't a plan beyond that, and certainly no science was involved in my training. I just ran with increasing frequency and looked to build more distance. Upon reflection, I wasn't "training", I was just running, and I would come to appreciate the difference very quickly.

One of the first events I signed up for was the Buffalo Stampede in Bright, Victoria. The appeal was that I could enter a 10-kilometre run on the Friday night, a 20-kilometre run on the Saturday morning and a 42-kilometre run on the Sunday morning. All of these were trail runs, and by completing the Grand Slam – as the three events were known – I would cover 3275 metres in elevation across the 72 kilometres. I hadn't done back-to-back events before, and it felt like a nice, soft entry.

CT and I made a weekend of the trip to Bright with our two dogs, Burton and Frankie, and CT's parents. The three events together weren't all that huge from a kilometres point of view, but the combined elevation certainly was new for my legs, and they let me know it. The last run on the Sunday, around the 30-kilometre mark, I experienced a pain in the outside of my right knee, which was new – I hadn't suffered from knee pain previously. The strange thing was that it only hurt when I ran downhill. It got to the point where I couldn't run downhill, and it became quite painful even to walk. I marched on to the finish line and considered the weekend a huge success, even with the injury, which I assumed was a one-off and would disappear as quickly as it arrived.

The next decent run I had planned was to run the last day of the corporate bike ride that I was leading in Thailand in April. It was a five-day ride from Hua Hin to Baan Tharn Namchai, and the last day would leave from the Cliff & River Jungle Resort to Baan Tharn Namchai. It was a 56-kilometre journey and had a hill at the 11-kilometre mark that is famous on our rides: it is four kilometres on the upside and seven kilometres on the downside.

Our first-time riders often get themselves tied up in knots worrying about the hill, but like a lot of things, it is nowhere near as bad as we imagine it to be. I considered running this last day for a few reasons: if I got the job done, it would give me confidence that the run at the end of the year was possible; it would allow me to promote the run through our community and rattle the tin for fundraising; and it would replicate what I imagined the final day of the Run to Remember would look like. CT was on the ride with me along with 68 other riders from our Business Blueprint community, who had been riding wth us since 2013. The plan was that I would get up at 3.30 a.m. and commence the run, hoping to arrive into Baan Tharn Namchai at around a similar time as CT and the other riders.

April in the south of Thailand can have the hottest daily temperatures of the year and an equally high level of humidity. As we approached the ride, I actually started to have concerns about running the final day. For the first time in the lead-up to a run, I was concerned about my health and what the implications might be of running 56 kilometres in the heat after four days cycling in those temperatures. Would my body be stronger from the four days of cycling, or would I suffering from muscle fatigue and reduced energy levels? If I wasn't able to complete the distance, I knew it would severely impact my confidence and my belief in my ability to get the run done in December. Saying that, I also didn't want to push too hard in the heat and risk damage that I couldn't come back from. I didn't share my concerns with CT, or anyone for that matter, but it was certainly weighing on my mind the closer I got to the ride.

Arriving in Bangkok, we enjoyed Songkran – a festival of water fights that takes over Thailand for a few days, celebrating their New Year – before heading to Hua Hin and getting on the bike. There is no question it was hot and the humidity was high, as expected, but I had been there during hotter times. I worried less as the final day of the ride drew closer, and on the fourth and final day of riding for me I found myself drafting behind as many riders as I could for the entire day – over the four days I rode 400 kilometres, so it seemed fair that on the final day on the bike I could be a passenger. Nobody seemed to mind too much, although I did move between various riding packs so as not to be too conspicuous.

With the alarm set for 3.30 a.m. it was always going to be a restless sleep. My kit was all laid out and I had squirrelled some food away from the previous night for breakfast. I was set to go. The plan was that CT would drive one of the support vehicles for the first hour or so before returning to the hotel to pack up the room, then she would jump on the bike with the other riders for the final day. Joining me for the run would be some of the older boys from Baan Tharn Namchai, who would drive the support vehicle with the drinks and food that I would need for the day, and Game, who was going to run the first couple of hours with me.

I was standing in the foyer of the hotel at 4 a.m., ready to run, and it was already hot! The plan was for the car crew to drive to the seven-kilometre mark and wait for me there with a drink. As I ran along the road, the darkness broken only by the light from my headlamp, I was sweating up a treat, and before I even arrived at the seven-kilometre mark I could hear the sound of my shoes sloshing with the perspiration after just 45 minutes of running. I had two spare shirts to change into but no other shorts, socks or shoes. This was clearly my first big mistake and lesson from the run. At the end of the day, that's what this was all about: simulating the run so I could learn from and avoid as many mistakes as possible come December.

I found a rhythm, stopping every three to five kilometres to take on fluids; it was hot and humid, and I was sweating like a champion, so I needed to keep the fluids up. My concerns about the safety of running in these temperatures didn't play out, and I just found myself focused on the run itself. The run progressed without too many issues, except when the niggle in my knee from the Buffalo Stampede – which had turned out to be an iliotibial band (ITB) issue – returned at around the 38-kilometre mark, making things most uncomfortable.

While I ran, I was expecting the riders from the tour to come past me. I was looking forward to seeing them, knowing they would bring a truckload of enthusiasm, and after a good seven hours alone on the road I was looking forward to some motivation. In the end, I heard the riders before I saw them. The first group was pushing the pedals pretty hard, and I heard their cheers as they spotted me on the road ahead. It was such a buzz to hear them, and without question it lifted my spirits and gave me a bit more go in the legs. As they whipped past me, shouting words of encouragement, I felt stronger and my pace picked up.

The stream of riders continued for the next 15 minutes or so. I knew that CT would be somewhere in the group, and I was looking forward to seeing her, but I could also feel the emotion building in me as I waited for her to arrive. All this running has proven to me that the more you exert your body, the more fragile your emotions become. If you ever want to see emotion from adults who are not accustomed to showing it, hang about at the finish line of a marathon or ironman event and you will see the raw emotion flow.

I heard CT before I saw her, and the emotions rushed to the surface. As she pulled up alongside me, I kept running at first, unable to talk, knowing that the floodgates would open if I looked her in the eye. However, I was overcome by the need to hug the one person who means more to me than anyone else. I stopped, and as we wrapped our arms around each other, the emotions were there for all to see.

The riders went on to Wat Yan Yao and I headed straight for Baan Tharn Namchai. The idea, I learnt later, was for the riders to form an archway for me to run through to welcome me into Baan Tharn Namchai. The problem was that I beat them to the finish line, and so it was me standing in the crowd welcoming them home.

The day was a huge success, but it brought home the enormity of the task that was before me. My whole body was sore, not just my knee. I had blisters on my feet, which was to be expected, and as a result of running in wet shorts I had chafing that had led to bleeding, which I hadn't even been aware of until I stopped running. My energy levels were low, and while I took confidence from the fact I got the 56 kilometres done, I couldn't imagine repeating it the next day. We would return to Baan Tharn Namchai that night for dinner and dancing with the kids, and as I sat and watched the others dance, I couldn't help but wonder how I was going to do this again, plus some, for 26 days straight. It did unnerve me, sitting there with the rawness of the chafing, the blisters on my feet, the pain in my knee and the general fatigue, wondering how on earth I could recover sufficiently overnight to repeat this day after day. However, that was exactly what I had signed up for, and that was a problem for tomorrow.

I continued in the training in the lead-up to my next ultra, which was the 50-kilometre run through the incredibly spectacular and world-famous Blue Mountains National Park that I had run the previous year. The difference between this and the Thailand run was massive. The run was part of a weekend festival of trail running, starting with 10- and 20-kilometre runs on the Friday and 50- and 100-kilometre runs on the Saturday. The Saturday runners left from Scenic World and ran along the rim of a valley, then dropped down to the bottom of the valley before making their way back up. This meant climbing either 2500 or 4500 vertical metres over a period of time that could range from 6 to 30 hours – a stark difference to my flat run in Thailand. The other difference was the temperature: in previous years the Blue Mountains run, which is held in May, had experienced snow, which you don't get in Thailand.

I went into this run in probably my best physical shape ever due to the amount of running I had been doing. However, none of the training helped once the ITB issue reared its head again. I was fine going up and OK on the flat, but as soon as we headed downhill I was in between a walk and a hobble. I had dismissed the pain in my knee during the Buffalo Stampede, and then again after the Thailand run, but given this was now the third time in a row that it had appeared beyond the 35-kilometre mark of a run, I had to get it sorted. It really slowed me up in this run, but I wasn't worried about the time I recorded.

After this run, I engaged Matty Abel as my running coach, and he applied structure and logic to my training, which up until that point I had been making up as I went along. I had talked about doing a 100-kilometre trail run prior to December, but we decided it presented more risk of injury than potential benefit, so I would stick to distances that best resembled what I would be doing in December.

In July, I was back in Thailand leading another corporate bike ride, this time over five days in the Isan region and finishing at Baan Home Hug. I saw this as another opportunity to get some decent time on my feet in the Thai conditions, so after four days and 400 kilometres on the bike, I was up at 3 a.m. to meet the crew in the car park for a 3.30 a.m. start, with Baan Home Hug some 68 kilometres away my destination. Learning from the first Thailand run, I had set up the support vehicle that would see me through the day, and the route was set using Google Maps. I was with two new support crew members who hadn't done this before and wouldn't do it again – it was only ever a one-off event for them.

We left the hotel at 3.30 a.m., and as I headed out, setting off all the local dogs, the first four turns I made that morning were all incorrect. Not a brilliant start, but nothing we couldn't recover from. However, only a couple of kilometres from the finish, we got lost, and I found myself running laps around a lake – additional kilometres that I certainly didn't need at the end of a 68-kilometre day. I came close to losing my shit when I realised what was happening. When we stopped and discussed the error, the response was, "I think it is this way," to which I replied, "I don't want you to guess the route. I want you to be 100% before I start running again". I was given assurances that all was sorted after a ten-minute navigation stop with a lot of zooming in and out on Google Maps. I saw the car head off down a road that my gut was telling me didn't feel right, but I was too fatigued to be deciding the route, and I trusted them to follow the map. The car drove off into the distance, and several hundred metres down the road I saw it stop. Nothing to be alarmed about – I assumed it was marking a turn that I couldn't see given how far in the distance it was. I ran towards the support car, by this stage just wanting the run to be over. I knew the bike riders were waiting to welcome me in at Baan Home Hug, and by my calculations they had been there for a while and were no doubt all ready to return to the hotel and get out of their lycra.

As I got close to the car, I couldn't see a side street, so I wondered what they were waiting for. I ran up to the driver's window, and the passenger leant across and said, "Sorry Peter, this is not the right way. We need to turn around and go back". I could understand that they had made a mistake, even though at the lake I had told them not to move until they were 100% certain of the direction, but what I couldn't understand was why they had stopped so far ahead of me and watched me run all the way up to them. Why not do a U-turn and stop me rather than let me run the wrong way?

I couldn't speak. All I could do was turn around and start running back in the direction I had just come from. Nothing I could say would have been helpful to anyone. I knew they felt shit about it; I knew they were doing their best; I knew they had been on the road since 3.30 a.m. as well and were equally as buggered as I was. But why make me run to them!? My rise in blood pressure was matched by an increase in my running pace, and as we ran through the last small village for the day I was on the heels of the support crew. We made it to the end, and I ran into the warmest of welcomes at Baan Home Hug from the kids and the riders. Within five minutes of arriving, the angst I had felt about the extra kilometres and wrong turns was all gone. All had been forgiven, and I was once again grateful for the support offered by those who were there doing their best in support of the crazy idea that was mine, not theirs.

11

Warm up or wake-up call?

With the last of the scheduled event-style runs over in the lead-up to December, the one thing that was missing from my training was some serious back-to-back running in Thailand. I had put in two decent days on the road of 56 kilometres and 68 kilometres in pretty exhausting conditions, but they had been in isolation, with no running before or after to speak of. Granted, I had ridden over 400 kilometres in the lead-up to both days, but time on the bike doesn't come close to the impact on the body of 60 kilometres running on the road.

The other thing I didn't have was an understanding of the route from Baan Home Hug to the southern side of Bangkok. Our northern bike rides in Thailand follow the Mekong River and finish at Baan Home Hug, and the southern rides start at Phetchaburi, a couple of hours' drive south of Bangkok. I knew that once we got south of Bangkok on the run, I would pick up the route of the ride and it would feel like I was heading towards home. But how was I going to get around Bangkok? It was nigh on impossible to think that we could run through Bangkok with the support vehicles, so we had to head around it. As I wasn't planning on carrying a phone or navigation device on me during the run, I would be totally reliant on the crew to mark the corners so I knew where I had to turn. This would be easy to do on the country roads – the vehicle just pulls up at the corner and waits – but not so easy in busy cities or large towns. I needed to test this out, and I couldn't rely on doing it virtually from the computer. We needed to be on the ground.

I was speaking at a conference in Bangkok in mid-August, so I decided to add extra days to my trip and run five days of back-to-back marathons. Chris would come with me and drive the support vehicle. After the last run I had done in Thailand, we needed to get the navigation sorted and we needed to test it out. I also needed Chris to be my support person, as he was going to be there with me in December.

Each of the big runs I did in 2024 were learning experiences. I learnt that I needed to have the right running kit to deal with the environmental conditions I would experience. I learnt that getting injuries treated early was essential – I was no longer in my 30s, and just hoping the niggles would pass wasn't going to work. I learnt that my mindset would be one of my weak points if we didn't get the route right – changes to the route would occur, and I was prepared for that, but running unnecessary extra kilometres because we didn't do what was required from a navigation point of view didn't serve me or the team well. However, the biggest lesson I learnt in my trial runs would come during this August simulation run, and it was the need to get my nutrition right. I could have multiple changes of clothes as needed, my injuries attended to and a route that was 100% accurate, but none of that would matter if I didn't get my nutrition right.

I met Chris at Bangkok airport on the Monday morning for our domestic flight up to Ubon Ratchathani. The plan was to pick up a hire car, head to the local shops to pick up the supplies needed for the week, and then drive the hour and a half out to Baan Home Hug. After some time with Mae Thiew, I would get on the road and knock out a 20-kilometre run. However, I realised the biggest problem with the plan once I passed through the sliding glass doors into the air-conditioned expanse that is the Big C. For those unfamiliar with a Big C store, think of a cross between a Woolworths or Coles and a Kmart, or a slightly smaller version of a Costco. Standing there with our trolley, staring at the endless rows of products, I realised I had no plan for what supplies to get. I couldn't defer to the shopping list because I didn't have one, which upon reflection might have been a good idea given I was buying supplies to get me through multiple back-to-back marathons and this was the only real opportunity to buy food. It was a bloody disaster, and I was setting myself up for failure.

As we wandered the aisles, I randomly selected drinks, snacks and food that I assumed would serve us well. I felt the pressure of time, as I had probably two and a half hours ahead of me before I could hit the road and it was now approaching lunchtime. We passed through the checkout, and alarm bells should have been ringing, as there was bugger-all in the trolley apart from drinks and snacks. A decent Netflix binge on the lounge could have cleaned up all I had in the trolley in a day, but this was supposed to feed the two of us for a week.

After a quick feed at that health food store called KFC, we got back into the car and out to Baan Home Hug. I hadn't alerted Mae Thiew to our impending arrival because last time we spoke about me running, she wanted to send a car out to support me. As lovely as the gesture was, I didn't need that; Chris and I just needed to sort ourselves out in our own time. The price I paid for not alerting Mae Thiew to my arrival was the disconcertion this caused when the staff saw me. They hadn't planned for my welcome, and they ran around trying to find Mae Thiew, getting us cold water and wanting to feed us. Delightful as the offer was, I just needed to say hello to Mae Thiew and get running. The time continued to tick down. We eventually found Mae Thiew at another property up the road, and then I had to do a tour of the property to see how the pigs had grown and the new duck enclosure that had been built. This was all fantastic, but I needed to get on the road.

It was well past lunchtime when we eventually got underway, but we got the 20 kilometres done as planned. I would have liked to run further, but time was against us. I ran a third of what I would on day one in December, and then I had to drive to the town to find accommodation for the night. I hadn't booked any accommodation as I wasn't sure where we would end up and I didn't want to be stuck to a plan, and I figured surely it wouldn't be a drama to find a hotel with two rooms available. It was dark by the time we got to the town, and I found a good-sized hotel on Google and headed there. I was joking to Chris that all we had to hope for was that there wasn't a Rotary conference in town that had taken all the rooms. Well, there might not have been a Rotary conference but the best they could do was one room with one double bed. A shared room with Chris was less than desirable given his ability to snore with the best of them, but a shared bed was never an option. We found another place with a vacancy, a small hotel on the outskirts of town, but now we had to find a suitable feed for dinner. We were in a town that didn't have even local tourists, let alone those from faraway shores, and as 8 p.m. approached and no likely dinner options appeared, we headed for KFC. I can go a year or more without eating the dirty bird, here I was eating it twice in a day. Our meal plan was unravelling very quickly – or rather, the lack of a meal plan was coming home to roost.

If there is one meal in Thailand that contrasts most with our dietary habits in Australia, it is breakfast. I can never really tell the difference between the breakfast, lunch and dinner offerings at the food station of a hotel in Thailand – they just look the same. And the level of chilli is not dialled down for breakfast – it smacks you in the face first thing in the morning. If you can find fried eggs, they are likely to have been cooked the night before and be sitting just below room temperature, and they are usually not done enough. None of that mattered to us, though, because hotels in Thailand don't typically serve breakfast until at least 7 a.m., and we were up around 5 a.m. and wanted to be on the road running as soon as possible.

Unsurprisingly, the lack of nutritious food quickly impacted me on the road. Not having a good base of food meant that I lost my appetite to eat while running, and this had a compounding effect. The worse I felt in my guts, the less likely I was to eat, which made me feel even worse. I was struggling through a marathon a day, which was only two thirds of what I needed to do come December, and my lack of meal planning was letting me down big time. I found myself vomiting on the side of the road and then having to run another 10 or 20 kilometres to the end of the day's run. It would take me a good couple of hours to recover after the run before I could stomach a decent-sized meal at dinner. But you don't need a nutritionist to tell you one decent meal a day is not sufficient when running a marathon in the heat of Thailand. And it was hot; Chris said it got to 41 degrees in the car while I was out running, so who knows what the actual temperature on the road was when factoring in the radiant heat from the bitumen I was running on.

I learned from this run that I simply couldn't entertain the thought of getting through 60 kilometres a day for 26 days without some major change to how I was managing my nutrition. I had to eat while I was running; there was no alternative. The cumulative impact of not doing so would be dangerous not just to the ultimate goal of finishing the run but also to my health.

The navigation of the route also delivered some lessons. I had never travelled between Baan Home Hug and Bangkok via road; I had only ever flown to Ubon Ratchathani and driven out from there. I was surprised by the size of some of the cities as we approached Bangkok and the major roadways with flyovers that looked like something out of Los Angeles. The number of small waterways was also something I hadn't appreciated – there are thousands of rivers and water catchments that all require a way around or over. The routing I had done for this run via Komoot had me running along some pretty major roads, which was not only a horrible experience but a dangerous one. It was clear I needed to do some work to find alternative options.

While this run had served as a bit of wake-up call, I also took some comfort from knowing that it should be a lot cooler in December than what I had experienced in both April and August, and there would be a team to support and prepare meals and thus address my nutritional needs. I also had another three months of solid training ahead of me that would see a bit of a reduction in the kilometres run on the road and more time in the gym focused on strength training. Now, I could look beyond the failings of the past runs and look forward to applying the lessons from them. I had done back-to-back marathons now, and I had time to correct and adjust as needed. Little did I know about the infection that would risk ending the run before it started.

During my training, from September 2023 right up to the run, I had the opportunity to run in various places under various conditions. I ran in the snow in Japan and in humidity as thick as honey in Singapore, as well as spending hours upon hours running the roads surrounding our farm in everything from the stifling heat of summer to the freezing temperatures of winter. I ran in the morning, I ran during the day and, when it was required, I ran late at night.

Our farm at Turondale sits on the top of a ridge, offering stunning and limitless views with nothing but native bush to be seen. I had been working hard on getting the landscaping done during the day but was committed to the training. So, after a day on the tools, I layered up with jackets, beanie and headlamp and headed out for a night-time run. It was −4 degrees. The next morning, I flew to Thailand to speak at a conference, and when I arrived in Bangkok at 6 p.m. it was still 40 degrees – but I had a run to do. Within 24 hours I had a 44-degree swing between runs. However, I have adopted a saying I heard once: "Whatever the conditions, they're my favourite".

The travel I undertake for work sees me on a plane weekly and overseas every three to four weeks, which certainly made it challenging to maintain a consistent approach to my training, but that is my life, and I feel incredibly fortunate to do what I do. I was also blessed to have a running coach who actually customised and responded to my life, rather than delivering a program based on a template rolled out for all his athletes. Initially, I think Matty was surprised by what I was doing, but as we got closer as athlete and coach, he worked harder to respond to my needs, which

I will always be grateful for and which is testament to why he is so good and in such demand as a coach.

The experience of running in a range of conditions would serve me really well during the run in Thailand. It was going to be hot, it was just a question of how hot. But there was nothing I could do to change that. If I embraced those conditions, I would have positive head chat rather than negative. I never heard the crew complain about the heat – I actually never heard the crew complain about anything, come to think of it – but while we didn't explicitly decide not to speak about the heat, no one ever did.

One of the real lessons to come out of the August run for me was that it is far better to embrace the conditions we find ourselves in when we have no power or influence to change them and invest our energy in how we respond. I couldn't change the weather, but I could manage and control my response to it.

12

Comparison is the thief of joy

Returning home after the August simulation run, everything felt very real. I had gone from counting down to the run in December in years, then in months, and now it could be measured in weeks. The time I was spending with Matty was incredibly helpful, and he had me dialled into a solid program of running and time in the gym. He was adjusting my training on a weekly basis to accommodate the travel I was doing, both internationally and locally, all of which impacted the training.

Many people commented to me both before and after my run that they couldn't comprehend the enormity of running 60 kilometres every day for 26 days, and I understand that. How could you until you have done something remotely similar that gives you a window into that world? I can't understand the work and discipline, let alone the years of practice and training, that is required for a ballerina to stand on pointe. I have no perception of the mastery at play because it is so foreign to me.

To be honest, I didn't truly understand the enormity of the run either. I just hadn't done anything that big before over such a long time, so I couldn't truly appreciate what I was getting myself into. But something would happen in those final months before the run that would provide some harsh perspective.

I was introduced to Matty midway through 2024, when my run plans were well underway. A client of Matty's who came on one of the charity bike rides in Thailand heard about the plans for the run and casually asked me if I had a running coach. "No, mate," I responded, "just kind of making it up as I go". He offered to reach out to Matty, who wasn't accepting new clients at the time as his books were full, but he would introduce me and see if the project was of interest to Matty. A few months after the introduction, an opening appeared, and I became a client of Matty's for the final six months of my training.

As I got closer to Matty, I also got closer to his other athletes, which I found pretty intimidating to say the least. One of these athletes was Nedd Brockmann, who had set his sights on the 1000-mile time record. His plan to achieve this was to run 160 kilometres a day for ten days around Homebush Stadium in Sydney. He had previously run across Australia from Perth to Sydney, capturing the hearts and minds of the Australian public. Matty coached Nedd in his run across Australia and was with him every step of the way at Homebush.

How could you not marvel at what Nedd was doing? Becoming a client of Matty's gave me many things, one of which was a close insight into the enormity of the task Nedd was undertaking. Matty and I would review in significant detail the logistics of Nedd's run, taking lessons from it to assist me in the Run to Remember.

However, having this connection to Nedd's run didn't serve me well. I allowed myself to fall unconsciously into a world of comparison. Nedd was running further than I had planned to in about one third of the time, and would raise several times the money I had in mind. The more closely I followed Nedd's preparation, the more I heard from Matty and the more active the runners' group chat was, the greater the negative impact on my mindset.

I knew logically that I wasn't competing against Nedd in any shape or form. I wasn't copying him – I didn't set out to do the run in Thailand because I was inspired by him. But the closer I got to the run, the more unhelpful questions I asked myself: "Who do I think I am to undertake this run? Is it lame in comparison to what Nedd is doing? Will I just be seen as a wannabe?" I stopped talking about my run, I stopped sharing what I was doing via social media and I retreated into myself. I don't know that I ever got to the point of seriously considering not doing the run because of all this, but I certainly withdrew from promoting it. It was a good thing his run would finish before mine with sufficient time to allow me to shift and refocus.

Drawing comparisons between us was crazy and of no value whatsoever. The beginning and end of our similarities was that we shared Matty as our coach and were in a WhatsApp group chat together. Nedd was 28; I would turn 58 on my run. Nedd was a professional athlete who had run across the country and had the backing of a machine behind him; my full-time gig was Hands Across the Water and speaking at conferences, and I was anything but a professional athlete. He is a good-looking rooster with long blond hair, loved by all; I am a ranga who is loved by a handful of people but known to few. As Matty says, "Comparison is the thief of joy". That doesn't mean we can't learn from others, but comparisons can be unhelpful.

I wondered why Nedd's run had taken a toll on me, why I was even comparing myself to him and what he was doing. My run was never about setting records; it was about acknowledging the 20 years since the tsunami. There was very little that was even similar to what Nedd was doing. And I should have known better.

Ever since I started speaking in 2006 and sharing the stories of the work I had done in Bali and Thailand, audience members would come up to me to tell me how insignificant they felt when comparing their life achievements to mine. My response was always to dismiss that thinking and suggest to them that what we had done was just different – not better or worse, just different. The other times I hear these comparisons is when people compare their challenges to what others have gone through. There is a balance to be found between taking perspective from what others have faced and overcome, and dismissing our own suffering. Indeed our experiences are our own, and we shouldn't dismiss them because someone, somewhere, has experienced something "greater".

Reflecting on my thought process during Nedd's run, it was almost arrogant of me to draw comparisons between us. It was just my proximity to what he was doing that really reeled me in. When I line up for a trail run alongside hundreds of other runners, I have not a care or thought for where I will finish within the group. I consistently finish among the slowest 10% to 20% of runners, and it has never worried me. The trail runs are about my own journey. So, I'm not sure why, for a time there, I allowed the December run to be anything other than what it was meant to be. I would never run at Nedd's pace, I would never raise the money or awareness that he did for his cause, but that didn't make my journey or the dollars I raised any less valuable or worthy.

The saying "Comparison is the thief of joy" is not mine, but I have certainly embraced it. There is immense value in learning from others who have gone before us, but little value in comparing ourselves to them or their achievements.

PART III
WE CAN CHANGE WHAT HAPPENS NEXT

13

The ceremony and the send-off

The original plan was that the main crew of CT, Chris, Wendy and myself would fly into Thailand on 26 November, and Greg, Jules and Claire would follow a day or two later. This would allow CT and Wendy time to plan, procure the necessary supplies and pack the vehicles without time pressure. The timing would also allow me to adjust to the time zone, get a little bit acclimatised and just settle into the feeling of the run that I was about to embark on.

When we travel to and compete in events, whether it's the bike rides, my ultramarathons or CT's ironman and triathlon events, we love to arrive a full day prior to the start of the event when possible so we can immerse ourselves in the atmosphere, check in and register for the event, and basically set ourselves up for an enjoyable event without the anxiety of rushing. There are always pre-event nerves, and they are best settled by removing time pressures and getting everything sorted out before the day of the event. There is nothing worse than getting ready on the morning of an event and realising that a piece of kit or equipment has been left at home or damaged on the plane.

That was our plan. Our flights were booked, and there was something nice about the four of us heading over as a team to share the excitement, the nerves and just the entire experience. However, the plan would change.

I make my living speaking at conferences all over the place, sharing stories and observations around leadership from the work I have done over the last 20 years. I find every invitation a privilege, and it is a humbling experience when an organisation decides that what I have to say is worth listening to. I received an invitation to speak at an event in Brisbane on Thursday 28 November, and given I was about to enter into a period of a couple of months when I wouldn't be drawing an income from the speaking – being in Thailand for the run and then the 20th-anniversary bike ride – I decided to take the speaking event. This meant I would have to fly from Brisbane back to Sydney on the Thursday evening, then on the Friday morning I would fly to Bangkok, stay overnight near the airport and take an early morning flight to Ubon Ratchathani the next morning. I would arrive at Baan Home Hug less than 24 hours prior to the start of the run. Less than ideal, not the original plan, but again, given the lead-up I was just happy to be there.

Because of the leg infection I sustained three weeks out from the start of the run, my training had gone out the window. The wound on my leg refused to close, let alone heal, and after getting confirmation that I could indeed travel and run, I found myself in an inner battle: get out and train, or refrain from running and give myself the best chance at turning up with the wound healed? I really didn't like the thought of arriving in Thailand and running in the conditions there with an open wound; that, to me, was just an invitation for the infection to flare up again. However, the idea of sitting out the next three weeks and just waiting for the run to arrive wasn't appealing either. More than once during those three weeks, I convinced myself that I was indeed good to run, only to get a couple of hundred metres out from home and feel the scab crack open and fluid seep down my leg. My lack of patience was not serving me well. Eventually, I conceded that there probably wasn't a lot to gain from training over those last couple of weeks, and I would be better served by sitting out the remaining time and giving my leg every chance to heal.

This gave my body a chance to rest. I couldn't underestimate the toll I had placed on it with all the training and fighting the infection, which had, obviously, been a serious one. I was also still struggling mentally from the incorrect prescription of the medication and the impact it may have had on me should I have continued with it. I was still taking antibiotics and would continue to do so for the first couple of weeks of the run. While they were doing their job keeping the infection under control, it wasn't necessarily great for my gut health to be on antibiotics for six weeks.

I accepted that I would rebuild the fitness I had lost over the last month during the first week or so of the run, and I would need both patience and acceptance. I needed to respond to the conditions that I found myself in, not the ones that I was hoping for.

I needed to respond to the conditions that I found myself in, not the ones that I was hoping for.

Sitting in the Qantas lounge after breakfast on Friday morning with time until the flight, I was more than a little consumed by thoughts about how the next month would play out. I kept thinking, *This will be the last time I am in this lounge without knowing how the run pans out.* Boarding the plane, I was thinking, *This will be the last time I fly to Thailand without knowing the outcome of the run.* No matter the outcome of the run, this was going to shape me and how I thought of myself more than I cared to realise.

I was flying to Bangkok with Finn, the son of Dale and Katherine Beaumont, who have been supporting Hands since it first began. Each year, Dale leads 50 to 60 of his clients on the Business Blueprint ride in support of Hands, and they are deeply valued supporters of Hands and, more importantly, deeply valued friends. Finn, the eldest of their two boys, has a creative streak that is surely a gift. His ability to capture life through the lens of a camera is beyond his years, and his work looks like that of someone with decades of experience and professional training. Finn was only 16 but a seasoned traveller nonetheless. When I approached Dale and Katherine with the request that they consider trusting us with Finn for a week or so of the run, they warmly agreed. Finn would be with us for the first week or so, and the only regret I have is that he wasn't with us for the entire journey. What a talent, and what a remarkable young man.

As the plane dropped below the clouds and Bangkok revealed itself below, it wasn't lost on me that all the land I could see from 20,000 feet in the air I would cover on foot over the next month. It was such a wide expanse of land. I had spent literally days poring over maps of Thailand on various mapping programs identifying the route, but seeing just a small section of it from the air was more than a little intimidating. I tried to work out how many days it would take me to cover the land that I could see from this height. What would it be like? How would I feel? Would things be going to plan? Just how achievable *was* this run? Again, the realisation came to me that this was the last time I would fly into the country without knowing the outcome. It was almost like there was a sense of innocence leading up to the run; without an outcome it was just an intention. I couldn't fail without starting – but, of course, I couldn't succeed either. I was really clear, though, that action would always surpass intention, that what I was about to do would matter more than any plans, no matter how solid or robust. It was what I did on the road that I would measure myself against, and that I was sure others would measure me and the run against.

We descended into our final approach, and the land below revealed itself with greater clarity. The roads that had looked like an arterial system bringing life to the outer reaches of Bangkok now looked clogged and in urgent need of a bypass. How many of these roads would I run on? Could I avoid the traffic that dominated the landscape? The other thing I noticed was just how much water there is in Bangkok. There are thousands of creeks, canals and small rivers, all feeding into the main rivers that head south towards the Gulf of Thailand. The Chao Phraya River divides Bangkok and is the main drainage basin for the city, and is known as the River of Kings. I would need to cross this river and hundreds of others as I made my way from the north to the south of the country. The sheer volume of water and number of waterways was just not something I had appreciated prior to the run.

Arriving in Bangkok, I met a journalist for an interview for a foreign magazine about the tsunami, Hands and the run, then headed to the hotel for bed, ready for an early start the next morning. The domestic flight from Bangkok to Ubon Ratchathani was another opportunity to explore the land I would be running across from a vantage point like no other. I fly helicopters in Australia, and the view from 500 or 1000 feet just totally changes the way you view the land, as well as your perspective on speed over distance. I knew my speed over distance for the next month was going to be painfully slow.

Stepping out of Ubon Ratchathani Airport, I was greeted by the person I most wanted to see: CT. She had come into Ubon to meet me, which gave us a good 90 minutes together to catch up before we arrived at Baan Home Hug for the ceremonies and festivities that would precede the run. Other than very early in the morning or late at night, the car trip, with Finn dozing in the back seat, was one of the last times we would get to spend alone together for the next month. It was a chance for both of us to check in and see how the other was feeling. I was eager to hear how the planning was going, and CT reassured me that everything was in hand logistically. There was very little to do now and even less that would influence the overall outcome of the run. Within hours, it would just come down to what I was willing to do out on the road, and that would matter more than what I perceived I was capable of doing.

The starting point of the run was always a given. Hands had been supporting Baan Home Hug since I first met Mae Thiew, the director of the home, back in 2010. Due to its location and the children that it cared for, it had faced a unique set of challenges in the years both prior to Hands's support and since. Tucked away in the Isan region of north-east Thailand, it didn't receive too many visitors. It isn't a short drive from the hotels frequented by tourists, and this was both a blessing and a curse: the kids weren't put on show for tourists, but it's hard for people to support what they don't know about or can't see.

The ceremony and the send-off

Upon learning of the Run, Mae Thiew decided that she would ride a bike with me from Baan Home Hug to Bangkok. Then, as the start of the run got closer, she changed her mind: she would ride from Baan Home Hug to the end of the journey. We didn't have a role for her, weren't sure how she would contribute and had no accommodation booked for her, but we would find a way to embrace her presence. We didn't know what her contribution would be, but we did know her presence would be a positive contribution to the run.

Arriving at Baan Home Hug, it was clear that the run was important to Mae Thiew and she had wholeheartedly embraced it. Stepping out of the car and into the sanctuary that is Baan Home Hug, I was greeted by a sea of bright orange. Sitting on specially erected platforms were more than a dozen monks, a number of whom I had met before, all assembled to offer me blessings. And there, right in the thick of them, was Mae Thiew. She retained her expected composure until we made eye contact, and then her face broke into a beaming smile. There was pride in her face, and I took it to be pride in what she had assembled to send me off. She was acknowledging the enormity of what I was about to do, and this was her way of saying "thank you". I know that after decades of feeling disrespected, discriminated against and shunned by members of the community because of the nature of the illnesses the kids had, she was also saying "Thank you for choosing Baan Home Hug": not just for starting the run from there but for choosing to support and be part of her life and the lives of the kids. I couldn't help but think of the journey that we had travelled together almost 15 years since we first met at this very place, where now I was hours away from starting what could potentially be one of the most important things I had ever done, and certainly the biggest. I wondered if she thought back to that first meeting. Had she thought I was just one of those who might never return, or had she seen something on that first day that led her to believe differently?

We would receive blessings from over a dozen Buddhist monks, including the head monk for the region. Many of them had travelled several hundred kilometres to send us on our way with their prayers and blessings. The monks led a ceremony with chanting, and it was a meditative, peaceful experience. It was a deep privilege to be the guest of honour at such a ceremony, and I have to wonder how many other foreigners have had such an honour bestowed upon them. Of course, this was not a recognition of my importance but of the high regard in which Mae Thiew is held throughout Thailand.

Sitting in the garden of Baan Home Hug in the shade of the trees gently swaying in the midday breeze, with the monks on their elevated platform, surrounded by the kids this run would benefit, I found it to be a reassuring time to reflect on how what I was about to do was on every level the right thing. I felt calm, composed and ready. I am not sure I could have wished for much more at that point in time.

The calmness wasn't just created by the monks and their chanting; it was a state within the team, which was so reassuring and reaffirmed we were ready. There was no rushing around with last-minute things to do or buy or people to see. CT had created this calmness through preparation and commitment. I thought back to the last time I was at Baan Home Hug with Chris for the simulation run and just how different it was this time. We were prepared and ready. I felt an increasing closeness and connection to CT, and this would only intensify over the 26 days on the road. This run would deliver so many gifts, and that was one.

My night in Yasothon prior to the start of the run was a low-key event. CT had ensured dinner would be just for the team and close to the hotel. I was clear I wanted an early night, but it is not uncommon for agendas to mean little at Baan Home Hug. I ended up getting to bed at 10 p.m., which, given the four-hour time difference, was 2 a.m. according to my body. Going to bed that night was a strange feeling. I had planned this run, I had thought about it every day, and every night my last thought before going to sleep had been to wonder what it would look like. Two years of planning, dreaming and training had come down to this last night. I was nervous, I was excited, I was grateful to be there, and to be honest, I was ready to get it underway.

We had a 4.30 a.m. alarm set, which would be the case for the next 24 days. We gathered downstairs and, in what would become a significant moment for the team, we formed a huddle and I thanked them all for what we were about to do. My call to them was, "Together we can". It wasn't something that I had thought about or planned, and not sure where it even came from, but it felt right.

A number of the monks had returned to Baan Home Hug to wish us well; a final blessing, a sprinkle of holy water and we were ready to go. I ensured I caught as much of the water that was being showered on us by the head monk as I could, as I figured I needed every little advantage I could get – real, perceived, divine or otherwise, I would take it.

As we filed out past the monks, CT was beside me, and holding hands with her I could feel and see the emotion in her. Here we were; after two years, it was time to run. I am not sure either of us appreciated the magnitude of what we were about to do, but we felt the emotion of the moment. As we took those first tentative steps, I found Greg in the crowd and, arms around each other, we wished each other well for the journey ahead. We were accompanied by 30 or so of the kids from Baan Home Hug, who would run with us for some portion of the day. For some it was a flat-out sprint for 60 metres before they reached their limits, bent over gasping for breath; others hung on for several kilometres. CT was with me for the first kilometre as we left the home surrounded by kids, cars and a whole heap of fanfare.

It was finally here. I was finally off and running. After two years of planning, after a crazy three weeks leading into the run when it could have all fallen apart, we now had feet on the ground and were inching our way south towards Baan Tharn Namchai 1411 kilometres away.

The first day on the road felt like a bit of circus, to be honest. While it was a beautiful gesture, I was concerned about the kids running with us and the impact it would have on them. Were they getting the electrolytes they needed? Were they pushing too hard to try to keep up? A bit disconcerting was the fact that we had not one but two local ambulances following us for the entire day. Had they taken a look at me and decided they would be needed? None of our team had asked them to join us – on the contrary, CT specifically requested they not. They were with us for one day and then disappeared, never to be seen again. I'm not sure if they got bored very quickly or if our unwillingness to pay their expenses had more to do with their departure.

From the second day, we would have only the team that would be with us until the finish line, and we could start to settle into the run. However, I quickly realised that the impact of missing the last three weeks of training would bite me, and it bit hard on day two.

Above: Morning of day 1, with Mae Thiew on my left as we prepare to leave Home Hug. Below: Receiving the final blessing from the monks.

Above: Greg and I prior to the start. Below left: With the Mothership in the background. Below right: The hot and dusty road.

Above: Time on the road. Below: running on day 11 through one of the busier towns with CT, Garry Browne and Mae Thiew.

Above: A typical water stop with ice vest to bring body temperature down.
Below: Mae Thiew in deep reflection in between our run legs.

Top: Makeshift shade water stop. Below left: Beachfront water stop. Below top right: My Together We Can drink bottle. Below bottom right: Day 14, a hug for energy.

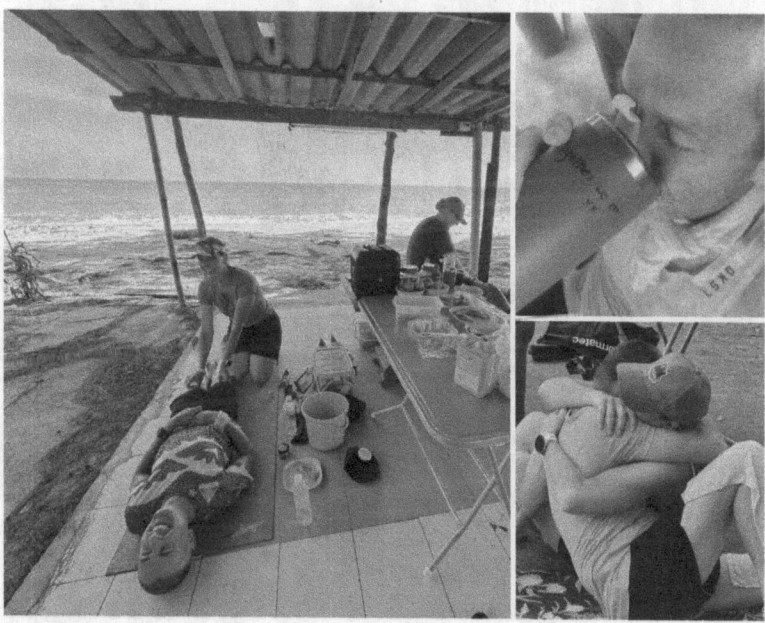

Above: The team celebrating the 500km mark. Below left: Smiles from the ice bath. Below right: My feet were in constant need of attention.

14
Finding our feet

I woke on the morning of day two in uncharted territory. I had run 60 kilometres the day before (or 59.9 to be exact), and now I had to rise and repeat the effort. With the blisters, the chafing and the stiffness from the previous day to accompany me, day two would be the longest on tour and one of the hardest. We would start in the darkness, which we would repeat every day up until day 24, but we also ended the day running in the dark. That just shouldn't have happened, and it was the result of my slow pace over the entire day and spending longer at the water stops than I should have.

The second, third and fourth day of running were the slowest and, therefore, the longest days on the road, not in distance but in time on our feet. The longer days obviously meant more time exposed to the elements and less recovery time, which impacted not just me but the entire team. In planning the run I had looked at the worst-case scenario in terms of time on the road and determined that if for some reason I had to walk an entire day,

I would do that at a pace of 12 minutes per kilometre, and with an average of 60 kilometres per day that would mean a 12-hour day on the road. This was certainly less than ideal and hopefully would only be needed in the case of injury, but it did give me confidence that if I needed to, I could walk an entire day and still get the job done. The problem with that plan was that it didn't include water breaks or time on the road when I wasn't moving, such as morning tea and lunch.

Upon reflection, it seems like a pretty obvious oversight. How did I miss this? Well, in each of the simulation runs I had done in Thailand, I hadn't stopped for a long break such as lunch or morning tea; I had only taken the regular drink stops. I hadn't changed clothing or shoes, and there certainly hadn't been any mid-run massages. Also, during the simulation run in August with Chris, I'd only run 40 kilometres a day.

The first couple of days on the road really did reveal a couple of concerns. The first was I certainly wasn't where I needed to be from a fitness perspective – I felt as though I was well underdone. The second was that arriving in Thailand the day before the start of the run wasn't ideal, and a few extra days to acclimatise to the heat and humidity would have served me well. My physical state over those first few days, which shifted between various states of distress, had an impact on the team that I wasn't aware of at the time. All they could see was my performance on the road and my distress at the water stops, and several of them were concerned as to whether I was up to the challenge or if I had bitten off more than I could chew. What they didn't have insight into, though, was my mindset and belief.

Another problem I suffered during the first few days of the run was chafing, which I found really strange because I was running in the same shorts I had run in through all my long training runs and I had never suffered from chafing, apart from the run into Baan Tharn Namchai after the ride the previous April. I guess I hadn't run for 60 kilometres in wet shorts before, day after day, so something was bound to give. After applying enough lubricant in all the right places during the run, and then paw paw cream in recovery overnight, I still couldn't get on top of the chafing, and it was certainly more than an annoyance. Step forward Greg and Jules with their advice: cut out the inners of the shorts and hang free as a bird. I protested, saying I had the shorts specifically because of the inners, but I decided I would sacrifice one pair of shorts and give their advice a go. Lo and behold, the inners of the shorts, which were designed to prevent chafing, were causing the chafing, and their removal gave instant relief. The extra and uninhibited air flow up in the nether region was a great relief. My lack of physical endowment down in that region didn't cause any problems with bouncing or discomfort for onlookers; in my case, it was more a bob than a bounce. Problem solved and onwards I ran.

During that first week, we learnt a lot about what the experience would be like and the lessons the road had in store for us all. We settled into our rhythm, and I started to feel stronger on the road. As obvious as my lack of form was in the first couple of days, so was the rebuild – not just to the team, who were commenting on how I was looking stronger each day, but mates at home following along and analysing my Strava data could also see the increased pace of the run. Importantly, though, I felt my strength return, and with that came increased pace and significantly increased enjoyment running on the road.

The definitive sign that I was back in good shape came on day six.

It was after lunch and we were heading towards one of the last few water stops for the day. I had been walking for a bit. It was hot, and we were exposed to the heat of the afternoon sun with no cloud or shade cover, no buildings around to offer shade and no tree over waist height that could offer some relief. It was certainly a grind, and there wasn't a lot of fun to be had. I was counting down to the water stop, and I could feel a sense of frustration building inside me as each bend in the road that Greg and I turned revealed a long straight ahead with no Ford Ranger waiting for me. I wanted and needed to take on fluid, but more than that, I just wanted relief from what I was doing. The water stop would give me a legitimate and justifiable excuse to stop, sit down, put a sponge with cold water on my head, don the ice vest and regather my energy to go again.

As we continued our march along the road, CT was riding along with us on her bike, and no doubt she could sense my darkening mood and knew well enough that the best thing she could say to me was…well, nothing at all. I didn't need encouragement, motivation or a reminder of this being my choice. I just needed to suffer in silence.

We then heard over CT's radio that our road support crew was struggling to find a suitable place for a water stop, so they were pushing on a bit further. No doubt that made complete sense to them, and it was only a couple of kilometres, but here's the thing: a couple more kilometres in the cabin of an air-conditioned car causes no duress or angst, but for me, at that time of day, when I was counting down the distance to the next stop, having changes made on the road messed with my head. Of course, I knew it wasn't adding to the overall distance of the day, but I became so focused on small, incremental stages that changes to those stages seemed monumental at the time. To make it worse, because I was hearing the chat from the radio about the team not being able to find a suitable spot to pull off to the side of the road, every spot on the side of the road I ran past looked to me like a perfect spot to stop. *What's wrong with this spot?* I'd say in my head. *They could stop here. Or here. Or here.* I am grateful that the disdain I was feeling for the crew at this time remained inside my head. Of course, they were looking for the best spot *for me*, and while it didn't feel like it at the time, they as always had my best interests at heart. My feet were hurting, my blisters were rubbing, and I could feel the heat radiating up from the bitumen road. And as I thought of all of these things, I became aggravated, and the pain and noise just got louder and more intense. I could feel myself spiralling pretty quickly, and I wasn't in a great space.

Without her knowing it, CT's presence on the bike that day kept me moving forward. She and Greg chatted as we made progress along the road, and if they were doing it easy then obviously I needed to rethink my attitude, or at least keep it internal. Not for the first or last time, I reminded myself that it was my choice to be on the road and it was a privilege to have this opportunity.

We turned another bend in the road and, to my delight, there was the crew, parked in a small clearing that had shade – something none of the other "perfectly suitable" spots I had seen had, and to be honest I think they found the only tree above waist height for kilometres around. My ill feeling towards the crew and the world at large dissipated, but no doubt I hadn't masked my mood as well as I had hoped, and I am sure they could all see where I was and just did the best thing, which was to ignore me.

We had ten more kilometres to run that day, and given the mood I had carried into the water stop I just wanted to finish the job for the day and immerse myself in the recovery stage. I knew there was an ice bath waiting for me, and the longer I took to get there, the longer I would have to put up with the pain. So, I took on fluid and then announced to Greg and the team that I was heading back out onto the road to continue walking. Greg had no issues or concerns with this, expecting he would reel me in pretty quickly. To be honest, he was probably happy to put a bit of distance between us so he didn't have to deal with my less-than-pleasant mood.

I headed straight back out onto the road. With five kilometres of straight road ahead, there were no decisions to be made other than to cover that as quickly as possible. I started to shuffle, which turned into a jog, which for the first time since we left Baan Home Hug turned into a decent running pace. I was on my own, Greg was yet to catch up, the support vehicle hadn't passed me and I was running five-minute-something pace, which was the fastest pace I had put down the entire week. I felt strong and I felt fast. With 50 kilometres in my legs for the day, six days of running and an accumulated distance of around 350 kilometres, I was feeling the best I had since the start of the run. This was what I had been waiting for. This was what I knew I had in me. This was the joy of running I had been holding out for – not to limp into the finish line like a beaten dog but to run in strong, my head held high, looking and feeling as though I could keep going. I was back, baby, and it felt amazing.

I celebrated as each kilometre ticked over with no sight of the support vehicle. It felt like a challenge to get as far down the road as I could before the support vehicle caught up to me. I knew I hadn't taken a wrong turn as there were none to take; I was just finally putting down a decent pace. When it did catch up, I received surprise and encouragement from Chris and Jules, who must have thought they had somehow passed me along the way. On the evidence of the first six days, they were justifiably surprised to see me running as strongly as I was. In what would become a weird pattern of the run, the fastest ten kilometres of the day would be the final ten. During those ten kilometres, I would run at the pace at which I would do a five-kilometre run at home and not what you would expect from the final stages of a 60-kilometre day.

When Chris and Jules passed me, I could feel their joy as they acknowledged my pace, and I felt myself lift another notch. My mood was so infectious to the entire team. On previous days, when I limped into a water stop or the end point of the day with my head down, the mood was like a wake, with no one too sure how they should act. It reminded me of that saying, "Leaders bring the weather," meaning that how I was turning up was setting the tone for the rest of the group. It's one thing to be aware of this, but it's another thing to rise above the absolute emptiness that I felt on some days. Now, though, they could celebrate in my energy.

My pace actually created a problem for the car crew. As we entered the final kilometres and the town where the finish point was located, Greg and I were separated on the road by some distance for the first time. How could the car crew mark the corner I needed to turn at and then get to the next one, while also ensuring Greg knew where to run? This was made more difficult by the fact that the GPS and mapping software sometimes needed to be right on top of a corner before it was clear which road to take, particularly in the villages and towns where there seemed to be crossroads going in all directions. However, right there, right then, I didn't care. That was their problem to sort out; I was running fast and loving life. I truly felt unstoppable, and it was a feeling I wanted to enjoy as long as I could. As the tough times on the road had passed that day, I knew the feeling I had right then would pass as well, so I was determined to enjoy it while it lasted.

The feeling of running so strongly for the final ten kilometres of that day was really important to me. It confirmed that the work I had done in the lead-up, the hours and hours of training I had put in and following the plan laid down by Matty, had given me the strength to complete this run. Above all of that, though, I think the greatest takeaway was that this run wasn't going to be a grind for the entire 1400 kilometres – there would be joy to be found in the running, and I should embrace that. It also confirmed that yesterday couldn't define tomorrow. A tough leg, stage or day on the road didn't mean that what lay before me had to be the same. I had to be present, be patient and follow the process, and the reward would come on the back of the struggle and sacrifice.

There is a Buddhist belief that everything is impermanent. What I would go through each day on the road was very much in a state of impermanence. The pain, the joy and indeed the experience of running on those roads in Thailand with this amazing crew would come to an end. I needed to appreciate and show gratitude for all that I was experiencing.

15

All in a day's work

Seldom did my 4.30 a.m. alarm wake me. My nights were filled with periods of rest and sleep rather than continuous sleep woken by the alarm. I had a mini celebration each time I woke and looked at the clock knowing I still had an hour or more before the alarm would sound to signal the beginning of another day. Hours before, when I went to bed, I would lay awake hoping not to fall asleep, because I knew that once I woke the pain of the next day would be upon me.

A good night's sleep meant being in bed by 9.30 p.m. and waking to go to the toilet before midnight, rejoicing that there were still four and a half hours before the alarm. I found that I was drinking at least a litre of water each night, and so there were always going to be multiple trips to the toilet. The challenge was navigating my way to the bathroom in the dark in a new hotel every night. Each night, before bed, I would ensure there was a clear runway between my side of the bed and the bathroom, removing all possible toe-stubbing obstacles.

A restless night's sleep was always preceded by pain in my feet as the sheet settled onto them. It became the ritual that each night, once I laid my head on the pillow, CT would take a needle to my blisters and drain the fluid from them. I was glad to leave this ritual behind near the back end of the run, by which time my feet had formed hard calluses.

When the alarm sounded, CT would rise and start packing up the room, removing the clothesline strung across the room on which the running kit from the previous day was drying. She would tear off two strips of tape and apply one to each of my nipples to prevent chafing. Then, she would move to the bottom of the bed and carefully and lovingly take to my blisters for the second time in seven hours, draining the fluid that had built up over night. She would then tape my feet as well as she could. It was my first step onto the tiled floor each morning that really brought me awake. It always hurt; the surprise was just how much and where it would hurt the most.

After a morning weigh-in to check how much weight I had put back on from the previous afternoon, I had a quick breakfast and a mandatory coffee, put on my hi-vis vest and headlamp, and away we went.

CT had committed to support the run and participate in her own way. On day one of the run she ran one kilometre, and each day she would increase her running load by one kilometre, culminating in a 26km run on the final day. As we headed out each day, I looked forward to the extra time running together as her distances increased. She had personally set her goal, and I was really hoping that the logistics of managing the entire event wouldn't prevent her from running each day. By the end of the run, CT would cover 351 kilometres on the road with us, which was huge, and I enjoyed every one of those kilometres we shared.

Sometimes we started the day at the hotel, and sometimes we had to take a short drive to the finish point from the previous day. Due to the remote locations we were running in, it just wasn't possible to finish each day at a hotel and maintain the 60-kilometre daily average I had planned on. When we had to drive, it was normally somewhere between 15 and 30 kilometres to pick up the mark from the previous day. Chris would take great pride and purpose in spray-painting "R2R" onto the road to signify tomorrow's start point.

The first ten kilometres of each day were normally run in the dark and slipped by fairly quickly. If we were running in the north through the villages, the sound of our feet hitting the pavement and the sight of our bobbing headlamps brought the local dogs out to say hello in their own special way. Greg was less comfortable with the dogs than me and was keen to be in front. "I only have to be able to outrun you," he would remind me when the dogs were about.

No matter where we found ourselves – running through rice fields or small villages, in the light or heavy industrial areas of outer Bangkok, or down the coast of the Gulf of Thailand – each morning we were greeted with a sunrise that was a gift to start the day. As our headlamps became less effective and were replaced by the light of the day, looking out to the east was an opportunity to welcome in the day and the sun that would soon greet us. In the early morning the sun was a beacon of light, but it wouldn't be long before it turned from friend to foe.

If the first ten kilometres were on the highways and busy expressways, it was always pleasing to get it done. It was bit like broccoli: get it off your plate first so it is done and you can enjoy the rest. The traffic and trucks were respectful for the entire 1400 kilometres, and I simply can't imagine that happening in any other country. To travel the entire distance without any abuse, horns blasted or suggestions that I should get off the road was outstanding. In saying that, hugging the verge was never enjoyable, and I always breathed lighter when we were off those roads.

The model I put in place right from the beginning was that we would run five kilometres at a time and then meet the support vehicle. Then, we would take on food, water and electrolytes, apply suncream and receive a briefing on anything we needed to know for the next five kilometres. Sometimes the stools would be out, and sometimes we simply handed over empty water bottles and took on new ones without stopping. I was pretty adamant that I wanted to maintain the five-kilometre water stops so that I never got myself into a state of dehydration or distress due to the heat. Each day I ran, my thought process was that I needed to manage the run today to put myself in the best position for tomorrow. There would be plenty of occasions when I would absolutely empty the tank; I didn't need to add to that by missing fuel or hydration stops.

The first 20 kilometres passed by relatively easily, and the more time that CT was running with us, the more enjoyable those first 20 kilometres felt. If our days were broken up into milestones, the first significant one came around the 20-kilometre mark, as it was here that we would run into the grounds of a local temple to be met by the crew and the Mothership – our roving kitchen, office space and storage area – for morning tea.

One of the things CT implemented that set us up really well was "Mother's Famous Bento Box". Before we set off each morning, Wendy would load this big, flat fishing-tackle box with all sorts of goodies, including cheese and Vegemite sandwiches, peanut butter and honey sandwiches, watermelon, jelly beans, salted chips, snakes, nuts, pikelets with jam and cream (or scones on alternate days) and, the absolute highlight that appeared at the end of the day, frozen jelly! Something I found running 60 kilometres a day back to back in heat and humidity is that my tolerances around food changed day by day and even hour by hour. We could plan to have food available that was high in sodium and calories, the two things I needed the most, but I could turn up to a water stop and find that what was tasty and appealing an hour ago now turned my stomach. But I had to eat – I knew it was hugely important, even just to graze all day. The key was having enough options that at least something would appeal, and there was always something in the bento box that was easy to digest and added to the calories I was trying to replace. Within the first week or so on tour, the Mothership became somewhat temperamental and having the power to cook was no longer a certainty, which presented Wendy with additional challenges. Not that I ever noticed – I was always fed and never left a major stop hungry.

Morning tea was also when I would normally see medic Claire for the first time each day. Claire's role was pretty straightforward: assess my immediate needs or any new injuries. Then we would go through the transition process. After taking on food and fluids, I would go through a complete kit change, including shoes, socks and shorts. (I would already be on my third or fourth shirt of the day.) Claire would assess my pre-existing injuries, which at the beginning of the tour consisted of the infection on my leg, but others would come throughout the run. Claire would massage my legs, which was always a welcome relief, and then send me on my way. The process through lunch was exactly the same, just a little bit longer.

After 30 or 40 minutes, morning tea would be done and it was back out onto the road, and quite predictably, the rise in temperature was immediate. The two hardest and slowest kilometres each day, without fail, were the first kilometre on the road after each of morning tea and lunch. This wasn't so much about the tiredness or the pain in the legs – that would come later in the tour – but those first tentative steps back onto the blisters. They would scream at you to stop, but they would give up the fight and submit once they knew they weren't going to win. I swear, for the first couple of hundred metres each day that the blisters were present, it felt like I was walking on broken glass. But it was just pain, and it would pass.

In the first few days of the run, progress between morning tea and lunch was slow and involved a lot more walking than I would have liked. Arriving in Thailand with only one training run in the three weeks prior always meant I was going to be underdone. I had said to Matty that I suspected the first week would involve rebuilding after the training that I had missed. It might not have taken a full week to regain my strength, but it was a lot slower for those first few days than I planned.

Lunch, which was around the 40-kilometre mark, was always a significant milestone in the day, as it meant we had run a marathon and only had half a marathon to go for the day. It was more often than not in the grounds of a temple, the parking area of a service station or just on the side of the road – seldom did the location matter to me, but I always looked forward to the break it offered. The lunch break was slightly longer than morning tea and gave us a good break off the road and out of the hottest part of the day. Wendy would provide a high-calorie lunch for the runners and ensure the crew were fed, and I would do another complete kit change, now rotating back through some of the shirts from the morning and into my fourth pair of shoes for the day. The highlight of lunch, without question, was the imported lemonade

Zooper Doopers that came out from the Mothership when it was time to return to the road. The ice, the sugar, the familiar taste – never has something so small made such a difference.

Leaving lunch, CT would often join Greg and I on the bike for the first ten kilometres before heading to the hotel to prepare for our arrival. I always thought of the final 20 kilometres as two legs of ten and the first ten was always the hottest part of the day's run. Get through that and we were down to single-digit kilometres and close to home.

Some things we do in life are meant to be hard, and the joy and reward comes from that. I think it was the internal celebration and acknowledgement of the fact that I was approaching the finish line of another day that propelled me forward. Running those final kilometres, there was a mind shift. It wasn't about counting down the kilometres; it was about gratitude for the experience I was having. I was so grateful for the people around me and the significance of what we were doing; the once-in-a-lifetime opportunity wasn't lost on me. It was during those final kilometres that I internally celebrated the day on the road. To find growth, we have to leave comfort behind, and the events of each day – the struggle, the grind, the pain – all contributed to my personal growth. What a privilege it was to have this experience.

If the final kilometres of each day on the road were a celebration, then finishing and being greeted by the team was the encore. The hotel finishes were the best. A few of the team would walk out to meet us and direct us to the final turn. That we had reached our final destination would be signalled by the sight of the Mothership and the sound of Andra Day's "Rise Up". They timed it perfectly every day, and it was such a fitting song to finish to; it will be forever embedded within the very fabric of my soul, and as I write this months on from the end of the run, it still triggers the emotion of each day on the road and the joy of the finish.

Within five minutes of finishing each day, and with the team assembled, we would have our daily huddle. This usually consisted of me thanking the team for their efforts and acknowledging the contribution that everyone was making towards the goal of reaching our final destination. We carried this 1 by 1.5-metre board around with us that displayed 26 days each in its own box, and I would conclude the huddle by inviting one of the team to come up and cross off the day we had just completed, add in the kilometres run and calculate the cumulative total. It was a celebration of everyone's efforts, and it became a hugely symbolic act for each day.

How we finished and celebrated the events of each day was one of the things that made the run the incredible experience it was. Even on those days when I finished in distress, my discomfort quickly passed when I was surrounded by my people. Watching the team enjoy their post-run Leo beers was something I delighted in – not as much as they did, though, I am sure. Each day, one of the team would hand Squid an ice-cold longneck, and each day he pretended to be surprised by the gift. Even up until the end of the tour, he still feigned surprise, and the whole charade added to the joy of each day.

My immediate post-run recovery process consisted of an ice bath, shower and 45 minutes in the Normatec compression boots. I don't know the benefits of the process I went through and how much it aided in the recovery, but I do know that when I didn't have time for the recovery process on day 13, the following day was a shocker.

When I was shivering in the ice bath, Claire the medic, in one of those voices that could be used for a meditation on Spotify, would talk me through the day and a meditation. Just listening to her voice brought calmness and light to the end of each day. More than once we would conclude the meditation and she would invite me to get out of the ice bath, but I would remain, immersed, calm and at peace. I looked forward to these ice baths. They provided obvious relief from the high temperatures we were running in, but I think they also served as a subconscious signal to me that physically and mentally, the day's work was done. Nothing hard needed to be done now until the following day.

Each day of the run was remarkably similar to the day previous, yet also so incredibly different. The model changed very little until the final three days. We woke at 4.30 a.m. We had breakfast and ran. Morning tea at 20 kilometres, lunch was at 40 kilometres, and the finish was somewhere between 55 and 65 kilometres. Yet, each day delivered its own experiences and made the run the incredible, life-changing experience it was.

16

Injury hits the run

The morning of day nine on the run would be a huge turning point for Greg.

By this stage, I was well into the run and had found the form I had been missing due to the lack of training over those last three weeks of November. We were running strongly and had reduced our daily time per kilometre by two minutes, which was huge. We had shortened some of the breaks, and we were now finishing each day two or more hours earlier than at the start of the run, which was hugely significant when it came to recovery time.

We were running with a bit of pace down the side of a bridge when Greg immediately pulled up sore, and in his head knew that something wasn't right. He continued running, but now with a limp, which certainly wasn't a good sign with 17 days to go. Greg started to run more slowly and we decided that I would continue at my pace, and he would get some help from the team in the support vehicle and reassess. I ran on to the morning tea stop, and I was ready to head back out again by the time Greg arrived about half an hour later. This wasn't a scenario that any of us had predicted. Greg and I discussed the possibility of him dropping back with a support vehicle while I went ahead, but it quickly became clear that we were not set up to support two runners on the road who were drifting further and further apart from one another.

It certainly didn't look good, and I considered the implications. Greg said he would walk the rest of the day if necessary to get it done, but with 40 kilometres to go, that made for a long day, a night-time finish and splitting the crew. I headed out with Chris, who was now alone in the lead vehicle as Jules stayed with Greg while he received treatment from the team. It wasn't all that long, though, before the second vehicle passed me. Seeing the forlorn figure of Greg in the passenger's seat caught me by surprise. He looked childlike and tiny, and in that moment had a look of defeat on his face. He reached out the window, we shook hands and he offered some encouraging words, and then the vehicle headed off into the distance. A wave of emotion washed over me. I was gutted for Greg. He and Jules had committed so much to be on the run and to support my efforts to get to the finish, and of all the scenarios that could have played out, I couldn't believe this was where we had ended up. With Greg off the road, in a strange way I almost felt a deeper sense of responsibility and a newfound determination to perform well, for Greg as much as for me. The impact was that my pace picked up, and it would end up being one of my fastest days on the road.

Only a few days prior, I had been running with Greg, CT and Alison Flemming (a Hands supporter who had joined us for three days), and Mae Thiew had been on the bike along with one of our long-term riders and supporters, Paul Lambert, who had joined us for a day riding. It was a little posse of six. Now, it was just me running and Mae Thiew in her position a few metres back.

I felt for what Greg was going through. I knew that the injury would have shaken Greg and Jules, because if anyone would have been expected to succumb to the rigours of the road, it was me. I was very much aware of what completing the run meant to me and how devastated I would be to have an injury stop that. I'd had a scare leading into the run, which had shown me what pulling out might have looked like, but now that I was on the road I just didn't see that happening to me.

Greg had sustained a soft tissue injury, and as he consulted with his physio back in Australia to try and identify the extent of the injury and pathway forward, all I could do was continue to run and make forward progress.

Greg's injury would see him off the road as a runner for a week. During this time, he showed more grace and courage than any time he was on the road. It was a massive thing for him and Jules to be sitting in the vehicle watching me run. They had both taken leave from their jobs and paid their own way to be in Thailand for the month, and that wasn't to sit in a car for a week and watch me run. But whatever conversations and challenges were going on behind the door of the hotel room, they didn't allow any negativity or emotion to creep into the run. Though their support had to take a different form than they expected, their approach was still to support me and the mission of getting to the end. "Together we can" just looked a bit different now than when we had set off on 1 December.

Early in his week off the road, when it became clear that Greg would need decent time away from running, I ensured that Greg knew there was no obligation to remain. Given that we still had more than two weeks to run, we discussed him and Jules leaving the tour and heading to a resort somewhere, and rejoining when the time was right. Greg's response was, "If we head to a resort, all we will do is sit and look at each other and cry". Thankfully for me, they remained on the tour. Greg continued to be a source of wisdom and encouragement and just found other ways to bring huge value to what we were doing. Selfishly, I then got to enjoy all of the support that Jules had to offer. She possesses such wisdom when it comes to endurance events, and I was blessed to have both of them on the tour, even if Greg was not on the road beside me.

Greg's return to the road on day 15 went without incident, and we would run the final 11 days together. We started the tour together and, importantly, we finished the tour together on the road. The way the middle part of the run played out, from my perspective, took nothing away from the tour. I suspect that deep down, Greg has unfinished business on the roads of Thailand, but in my mind the contribution he made to me during the run, particularly in that first week, set me up for success, and without his presence and wisdom, who knows what the outcome would have been.

Behind every step: a crew's-eye view

Jules Wallace, Runner Support

It's strange how time moves on a road trip: days blur into nights, kilometres blend into memories. Everything starts to feel surreal.

Fourteen hundred kilometres of planning and uncertainty. Twenty-six days of shared effort. Twenty hotels that became fleeting homes. Eleven people tied together on one journey. Three vehicles carrying our collective purpose, and only one ending.

The days started out as unknowns. There had been meticulous preparation, of course – charts, maps and spreadsheets filled with questionnaires, calculations and contingencies. But Thailand has its own rhythm, its own way of unravelling the most careful plans. I had arrived with my mind deliberately unlatched, ready to receive whatever came at me, yet I still found myself at times ambushed by unexpected emotions and obstacles that materialised like a sudden rain shower on a sunny day. *Stay calm, adapt, it'll be OK* were words I whispered over and over in my mind before departing that first day. I think I knew these words would probably become a sort of mantra along the way, but what I couldn't have known was how often I would need to silently repeat them, like prayers, over the 26 days to come.

In those early mornings, as we travelled ahead in the Ranger, I would look in the side mirror and watch Pete and Greg's silhouettes grow smaller, tiny blurs bobbing against the rising sun. As they disappeared from view, my mind would shift to the rhythmic sounds of the day – the tyres on the road, steady footsteps on gravel, the wind passing by my window – creating the heartbeat of the vast expanse of the kilometres ahead.

For 26 days, we existed in a time bubble, a world entirely our own where nothing outside our mission really mattered. We were suspended from regular life, our only purpose to move forward, kilometre by kilometre.

Each day's route and each five-kilometre stretch of road carried its own challenges: there were unexpected detours, sometimes no road at all, relentless blistering heat, pain and aching exhaustion. There were also beautiful rewards: breathtaking sunrises over misty rice fields, hundreds of noisy ducks being shepherded by villagers, moments of shared laughter with the crew and the boys, quiet reflections as waterways carpeted with lilies appeared through morning fog like a dream sequence. I intentionally lingered in these moments, savouring their beauty, their uniqueness, wanting the weight of the memories to last.

Thailand unfolded before us like a living tapestry. We passed through villages where children would run alongside Pete and Greg for a few hundred metres, their laughter and chatter echoing long after they'd turned back. Elderly women in colourful mismatched garb would pause their work in the fields and villages to wave, their curious weathered faces breaking into broad smiles that required no translation.

As Greg's dedicated crew member, my days blurred into a constant cycle of preparation and recovery. Every five kilometres, we'd spring into action – fresh water bottles ready, electrolyte tablets dissolved, dry shirts and sunscreen waiting. In the punishing Thai humidity, clothes would be soaked through in minutes – Pete was the champion in the sweat department – as the midday sun turned rural roads into shimmering mirages stretching endlessly before us.

Crewing requires its own kind of endurance, but it was the emotional terrain that always proved the most unpredictable for me. Cheering from the back of the roadside ute as another milestone was conquered; finding words of encouragement as the emotional and physical lows demanded attention – it was a lucky dip of needs every five kilometres, a new gamble of emotions every day, and the entire month was a whirlwind of work that required everything to be thrown at it.

One of the things I cherish most about crewing, and especially for Run to Remember, is the freedom to give myself completely to others. There was no agenda other than knowing the reward was bigger than anything I would immediately see. Knowing why we were there – for the kids – was all the reason I needed to rise each morning. There were times when ego surfaced (for all involved), when personal discomforts or differences threatened to overshadow purpose, but in those moments the finish line and the kids were all I needed to bring myself back in check and recentre. We were all there for the same purpose.

It's not always about keeping someone running; it's also about keeping the spirit of the journey alive, especially a journey with such a purpose as Run to Remember.

There were moments when the road seemed endless, the sun torturing and the air stifling. Pete and Greg would arrive at a stop, their faces masks of exhaustion. They would wince as they lowered themselves onto their stools in the "borrowed" shade with aching legs, new blisters maybe forming on already tender feet, overheated skin, bodies depleted. Yet somehow, after wet towels on heads, iced water, snacks and the cherished cold facecloth to dry off a little, they would stand again. "Ready?" And back into the sun they would go.

Then came the ninth day. Greg had been flying, his spirits high and everything in tune, his stride a metronome for kilometres conquered – until, at the 500-kilometre mark, with quiet cruelty, tendonitis claimed his knee, a reminder of the many kilometres it had already endured and the vulnerabilities of ultrarunners. This invisible saboteur brought Greg's journey to an abrupt halt.

We were both utterly gutted. The injury stole not just kilometres but an identity of sorts for us both; our choreographed and existing roles were suddenly dissolved. In those first hours, we drifted like boats untethered from their moorings. Greg carried the weight of what felt like failure. Over the next few days, I watched him wrestle with the ghost of expectation while he diligently exercised, rehabbing his knee.

What kept us going, what I kept returning to, was who we were doing this for: the radiant faces we had met at the beginning, who had sung for us, danced with us and shared meals around their tables with us, children who had lost everything in the 2004 tsunami but had gained family, hope and care through Hands Across the Water. And it was for Pete: it was for him to succeed and for us all to succeed with him, to finish what we had started.

We were 11 individuals who arrived as semi-strangers, yet we departed as something far more significant. For 26 days, we moved as a single organism across 1400 kilometres, each person an essential component of this living, breathing expedition. Our purpose was singular and clear: to help Pete complete his monumental run.

The beauty lay in how our distinctly defined roles interlocked to form a seamless operation. Bew charted our course with meticulous precision through unfamiliar terrain, making critical route decisions that could mean the difference between smooth progress and unexpected setbacks. Squid maintained the Mothership, adapting to changing road conditions while keeping us on track at all times. Greg remained in constant motion, attending to the running experience and providing the immediate support that kept Pete's legs moving kilometre after kilometre. Am served as our cultural bridge, translating not just language but customs and contexts, ensuring the Mothership moved with ease through each community we encountered and gathered the necessary supplies. In the Mothership, our rolling, sweltering sanctuary, Wendy created nourishment that was both fuel and comfort, that restored body and spirit on gruelling days. Our two media specialists, Rod and Finn, captured moments both triumphant and tender, preserving the journey's essence while also sharing our story with the wider world following along. And overseeing it all, CT coordinated the moving parts with quiet efficiency while tackling the heat and road each morning with the boys for her own challenge and fundraising efforts.

"Together we can" became more than a motto – it became our daily reality. We learned each other's rhythms, anticipated needs and developed the shorthand language of people who have weathered challenges together. Strangers became teammates, teammates became friends and, ultimately, we became something like a family, bound not by blood but by the shared experience of helping one person achieve something extraordinary.

As we packed up for the last time on that final morning, exchanging hugs that were heavier with meaning than words can express, the reality of what we had achieved hit hard. Crossing the finish line felt like the culmination of so much more than kilometres; it was a celebration of teamwork, determination and the strength of human spirit. As a team, we'd travelled far together, and as a team we'd all grown closer. The finish line was more than a destination – it was a team built, memories forged, hearts touched, awareness raised and hope inspired.

The children of Hands Across the Water – from Baan Tharn Namchai, from Baan Home Hug – are the inspiration for these thoughts. They see only what's in front of them, and they smile and laugh and are humble and grateful, giving and gracious. They are vessels of love and light, given hope through the work of this charity and everyone who supports it.

The Run to Remember opened my eyes to just how much we are built from our imperfections, how we are sketched as humans from the sum of our interactions, observations and reactions with people, animals and our surroundings. We are all just vessels in this borrowed life, gathering and shedding. We are fragile and strong, vulnerable and brave. Our reactions to such rich and cherished experiences as the Run to Remember only shape us further and, if we're willing, they'll leave imprints deep within our souls.

It was named the "Run to Remember" and, for me, that's exactly what it will always be.

17

I can, I can

When Mae Thiew committed to the run, we were all uncertain about the role that she would perform. Having worked with Mae Thiew for 15 years, I knew it was always important to keep your plans somewhat fluid, as she is known to deviate from the plans that have been made and agreed upon. Those changes don't come with forewarning and need to be embraced as the path of least resistance.

While neither we nor she knew what role she would perform, her commitment was to ride her bike with me. Initially, I was hesitant at the thought of not just Mae Thiew but anyone riding with me. My concern was that if they rode by my side or in front of me, they would inevitably ride at a faster pace than I wanted or was able to run. I knew my limitations and that I had to run at my pace, not anyone else's. I also know that riding a bike at a really, really slow pace is hard. It is draining and frustrating.

After spending the first couple of days riding ahead of us, which was of no value to anyone, Mae Thiew found herself behind me, and that was where she would stay for the best part of 1350 kilometres. She held her position consistently around five metres behind me, until there were dogs. Then, like a member of the close protection detail tasked with protecting a highly valued asset – think royalty, presidents, prime ministers or the pope – she would spring from the shadows to be front and centre, protecting her asset at all costs. She had this innate ability to calm charging dogs who appeared set on taking a lump of flesh from Greg's or my calves. Mostly it was with a few words to the dogs, speaking calmly and helping the dogs realise they were embarrassing themselves and should return home; with other dogs that were more intent and committed, she would physically position her bike between them and us.

When Mae Thiew wasn't warding off dogs, she would ride behind me in silence. Her orange robes offered a warning to the motorists approaching from the rear, not just through their brightness but because of what they represent in Thailand and the inherent respect offered to Buddhist monks by the population. In the larger cities, and particularly during the days spent skirting the western side of Bangkok, I spent plenty of time running on major roads on my own with Mae Thiew behind me.

When Greg or I would stop for a call of nature by the side of the road, we would alert Mae Thiew with the call "hong nam khrap" ("bathroom") so there was no chance she would be exposed to us, well, exposing ourselves, and she would ride on and wait for us to catch up.

There was a day when she drifted way off the back. It was after lunch; I was running on my own and CT was riding beside me. I was running at a decent pace and was neither up for nor capable of holding a conversation. Besides, what could we possibly have had to talk about? CT had a speaker in her riding vest and asked for any song requests, and the song that I knew would pump me up was none other than Eminem's "Lose Yourself". It's not just the beat of the song – which, by the way, I challenge you to listen to while running or riding and not see an increase in effort – but some of the lyrics that speak to me: "you better never let it go … you only get one shot … opportunity comes once in a lifetime". Now, if you're not familiar with the song, perhaps don't play it for the first time with the kiddies in the car – there are references in that song to those who fornicate with mothers, which might have been offensive to our Buddhist monk, but I like to believe she drifted off the back as she wanted time on her own rather than as a reflection of my song choice.

There are a number of moments I experienced with Mae Thiew on the run that will remain with me. Her level of service to my needs above and beyond any of her own was such an incredible and humbling experience that it will take me time to truly grasp the honour she bestowed upon me. I can imagine the only thing more uncomfortable than running 1400 kilometres in that heat was riding it at the pace I was running while dressed in multiple layers of fabric covering your entire body. When I ride my bike in Thailand on our charity rides, the hottest part of the day is when you stop riding. No matter how hot it is, when you ride at pace you generate a breeze that cools you even on the hottest of days. Riding at the pace I was running at offered no breeze, but she did so without complaint and without deviating from the mission she had set herself.

The way she independently pursued her role of service without deviation was admirable and at times amusing. As we travelled around the outskirts of Bangkok, we were crossing major highways and the flyovers were just too dangerous to run or cycle across, which meant loading her bike into the rear of Chris's car as we negotiated them. Now, the bike that she was riding was one of our tour ebikes, and they are fairly weighty given the battery pack and awkward to lift into the rear of the ute. But if I went near the bike to help her, she would yell at me, "I can, I can," and quite literally push me out of the way. At the end of each day, if we needed a car transfer to the hotel, we would again need to load her bike into the ute, and she would rise from her usual placid, peaceful, meditative state to yell at me, "I can, I can," often climbing up into the back of the ute herself to stand on the top of the eskies and drag her bike up. Adding to the spectacle was the fact that this Buddhist monk, dressed in her bright orange robes, was wearing a cycling helmet and snow goggles; where on earth she found the goggles in Thailand I have no idea, but to her credit they were effective. After several days of being yelled at by the monk, I decided to stop getting yelled at and just hope that others would be there to assist her if needed.

Another moment that will remain with me occurred on day ten. It had been a long, hard day. It was one of the days running down the western side of Bangkok, when we encountered the busiest roads, which was my least favourite section of the route. The speed of the traffic passing us, their proximity and their toxic fumes made the running less than enjoyable. We were in the final ten kilometres of the day and, for reasons I am not sure of now, there were only three of us out on the road: I was running, Mae Thiew was on the bike behind me where she always was, and Chris was in the car on his own. Jules had returned to the hotel with the other support vehicle, I think probably because it was a straight run to the finish line along the highway, so there was no real navigation to be done, and her returning early freed up space in the vehicle for Mae Thiew and I to travel to the hotel for the finish.

I was running hard, keen to get the day done. It was a grind – it was hot, and there was nothing really enjoyable about it. The afternoon had been punctuated by several river- and multi-lane-highway crossings, all of which were anything but straightforward and broke our rhythm and momentum. Several of the highways we crossed had flyovers that we were able to negotiate because there was a wide enough gap between the traffic and the wall of the flyover. This wasn't ideal and these were not pedestrian thoroughfares, but it felt safe enough. Where the gap wasn't wide enough, Chris would either drive slowly behind us to prevent cars approaching us at speed, or we would jump into the vehicle for 100 metres or so to pass the most dangerous section before returning to the road to run once again.

As I ran towards the next flyover, I saw that to get to it we would have to cross two lanes of traffic diverting off the road leading to the flyover. Also, I couldn't see from my approach how long the flyover was or where it came down; the only way to find out would be to head up onto it, at which point it would be difficult to back out. Chris wasn't at the base of the flyover, so I assumed there must be a safe and viable option for Mae Thiew and I to cross it, but the closer I got, the more concerned I became. I couldn't see a lane for me to run in, and the traffic was just moving too fast; the speed limit was 100 kilometres per hour, but as is custom in Thailand, it was not being adhered to. My gut was telling me not to take the chance – there was just too much risk involved.

We stopped at the side of the road, and I told Mae Thiew to wait while I assessed our options. I crossed the two lanes of the slipway and got to the concrete barriers that formed the left side of the flyover. There was absolutely no way we could take it – there was no lane gap for us, and the flyover rose for probably 75 to

100 metres before the crest and I had no idea what was beyond that. If we took the risk, we could find ourselves in a dangerous position with no way back. I assumed there must be an alternate route under the flyover somehow, so we continued in the direction of travel but underneath the flyover. However, about 100 metres on, we came to a river of significance, hence the big flyover. I didn't know what to do. We had no line of communication with Chris, and having been separated from the support vehicle for some time, I knew he would be wondering what had happened. I learned later that he was dealing with his own dilemma: he was indeed concerned about us, but where he was waiting for us was a major road of four lanes in each direction, so turning around was not an option, and he expected we would cross the bridge at any time and wanted to make sure we could see his vehicle when we did. So, Mae Thiew and I were stuck on one side of the river while Chris was stuck somewhere else along the road.

I went back to the road to see if maybe I hadn't considered the options with a sound mind, but it really was as bad as I thought: there was no way I was crossing that flyover. So, I went back to the river, and under the bridge I found a set of concrete stairs that led to the top of the flyover. It rose about five stories from the riverbank, but still it seemed like a better option than crossing the flyover. I left Mae Thiew at the bottom with her bike and climbed the stairs, and to my relief found that the stairs led to a raised concrete walkway that ran parallel to the traffic. We had found our way over the bridge.

I descended the stairs and told Mae Thiew that we had to climb up and carry her bike to the top. There was no "I can, I can" this time around, no yelling or pushing me out of the way. There was no way we were getting that bike up five flights of stairs without a great combined effort. I said to her, "Together we can," and once again that catchcry rang so true. At that time of day, after 55 kilometres on the road, neither of us was going to be able to climb those stairs carrying the bike alone, but together we could. We climbed the stairs one flight at a time, and that bike, with its big-arse battery, seemed to get heavier with each flight. As we got to the top of the stairs, I felt physically sick and in desperate need of water. Mae Thiew shared her water bottle with me, and the warm water almost induced me to vomit – and there is never a good time to vomit on the feet of a monk.

We now had safe passage across the bridge, and as I ran high above the water and to the left of the trucks passing at high speed, I felt a strange sense of delight in the decision that I had made to climb the stairs rather than risk it all and run up the bridge. It had taken us a lot more time and effort than expected, but it was the right decision. We crossed the high side of the bridge and came to the end of the walkway, which meant taking five more flights of stairs back down. By now there was no argument between us: Mae Thiew took the front wheel and handlebars, I took the rear wheel, and down we went. The trip up and over the bridge, carrying the bike on those flights of stairs until I had vomit in the back of my throat, was an experience that we shared in isolation from the rest of the team; I won't forget it, and I recall it with great fondness and gratitude.

We hit the road and were back on track. As I ran, I could see what I thought was our orange Ford Ranger support vehicle parked on the side of the highway. Nothing strange about that, but there looked to be someone walking towards us and away from the vehicle. It was Chris, and as we met, his opening question was, "Where have you been?" When I explained what had happened and that we couldn't cross the bridge, he was mortified that he had put us in that position. He assured me that he had believed there was room for us to run up the side of the bridge safely. When I explained that there was pedestrian access only once you reached the top, he was beside himself with regret. It was interesting that during the entire process of getting across the bridge, I felt no anger or negative emotion; I wasn't pissed off at Chris or the team. I think I was just grateful that we had found our way across and shared an experience together.

Mae Thiew's commitment to be on the run was of huge significance. Each morning, as I stepped out of the Mothership following breakfast, ready to take on the day, we would exchange brief pleasantries. I would say, "How are you, Mae Thiew?", and her response was as predictable as the sun rising: "I am strong". It was such a trademark response from her. I normally had to ask her the same question three times before I got any other answer. Then, she would say, "I'm OK, how are you? I worry about you". Knowing she was with me on the road, even though we travelled in silence, brought me great comfort, and she will never understand the deep appreciation I have for her and the commitment she made during that month of December.

18

The hardest day

I ran solo for the next week (aside from CT running her one extra kilometre each day), with Mae Thiew, my guardian angel, always a few metres behind. Running alone didn't concern me, as seldom in training had I run with a companion. And it wasn't as though I had been a real conversationalist when Greg had been on the road. It had become a bit of a joke that I didn't really speak to anyone from 4.30 a.m. until we finished the run for the day, so Greg was probably happy to be in the vehicle with people who could hold a conversation.

The morning of 14 December, I woke up in a really shitty mood for the first time on tour. The day before had been my birthday, and we had held a fundraising event in the town of Hua Hin with local expats. The timing of the dinner meant that it was a pretty quick turnaround from when we arrived at the hotel to when we had to be back in the foyer and on our way to the event. Through the support from one of our sponsors, we were booked into the Anantara Hotel, which is a stunning property and way above the standard of the rest of the run. To try to make the most of the resort facilities on offer – a swim in the pool at minimum, and perhaps a massage – we agreed that I would push the pace during the day and reduce the length of the water and rest stops to get to the hotel earlier. We did get to the hotel with a bit more time than usual, but for some reason that didn't translate into a massage, a swim or even my normal post-run recovery. There was no ice bath and no 45-minute session in the compression boots. The time just evaporated as we met with sponsors at the hotel and got ready for an earlier dinner than usual, and we even found ourselves having to rush to get there on time. It was the first time during the run that our post-run process went out the window, and it is probably no coincidence that the next day, things turned ugly.

The evening, which I attended with CT, Chris and Wendy, began with pre-dinner drinks on the lawn of a beautiful beachside hotel, which would normally be delightful. However, this involved talking, mingling and networking while standing. Standing. I could see chairs, and I so wanted to go and sit down, but no – stand and mingle was my task. This was made more uncomfortable by the fact that I was wearing R.M.Williams boots, which are my go-to for such an event, but normally my feet aren't covered in blisters and dressings. I thought about going to dinner in my Hokas, but CT was never letting me out of the hotel in running shoes, unless I was going to run to dinner. And just to top it off, I had to tie a dressing-gown cord around my jeans to keep them up, as I had by this time lost sufficient weight that they would otherwise have dropped down to make me look like a wannabe 1980s gangster.

It was difficult to make a quick exit given the event was being held to raise funds for the run, so when we left at 10 p.m. it was well past time for me to be in bed. I was more than a little bit jealous of the rest of the crew, who'd had room service and a night in.

Waking up at 4.30 a.m. for what was now the 14th day in a row, we went through the normal routine, none of which was fun by this stage. As I dressed and prepared to head to the Mothership for breakfast, I realised that my watch hadn't charged overnight and was sitting on 0% battery, meaning I had no way of tracking the run distance for the day – not that big a deal upon reflection, but it was enough to send me into a mini meltdown at 4.50 a.m. Part of my daily routine was knowing how far I had run, how far I had left to go for the day and how far the next water stop was; I didn't want to be guessing that stuff, and I didn't want to change the routine. CT headed to reception, and I sat in the room to charge my watch. Of course, due to the early start we couldn't enjoy the exquisite buffet breakfast that was on offer, and because of the state I was in I hadn't listened clearly when CT left the room to take the luggage to reception: I thought she was dropping off our bags and returning to the hotel room with breakfast, but she had said she would meet me at reception and we would have breakfast at the Mothership. I sat on the bed, watching my watch charge and waiting for breakfast, and CT was waiting in reception for me to arrive, both of us wondering what the other was doing. I eventually headed to reception to check what was going on and found Chris, CT and Mae Thiew waiting for me to hit the road. I grabbed whatever breakfast I could carry, and we left.

There was a bit of urgency as CT and I headed out on the road: the local run club was joining us at 6 a.m. at a designated point on the route, and that meant we had to get our skates on. Again, this urgency was not part of the morning routine, and this added to my deteriorating mood. To make up the time and cover the distance necessary to meet the run club, we ran through our normal water stops, eventually catching the runners at the 12-kilometre mark. I didn't want to be caught up in the five-minute-kilometre pace they ran at. They would run whatever distance they had in mind and then return home for showers, all before 8 a.m.; my day was going to be long, and when I eventually finished running for the day I would need to make the four-hour return trip to Bangkok to be ready for the fun run the next morning.

As it turned out, the runners were entirely respectful of what I had done in my 13 days on the road and were happy to run next to me and behind me, and at my pace. It was nice to have the support of the dozen runners, most of whom were running in our Run to Remember singlets. They would run a few kilometres with me before pulling up for photos and well wishes. I appreciated their contribution to the awareness we were striving for, but I also appreciated the opportunity to settle back into my rhythm after a hectic, almost chaotic start to the day. We had broken with routine, and it was time to return to what had served me so well over the previous 13 days.

As it was the 14th day of the run, CT's running finished at kilometre 14. After that, she went back into the Mothership to take care of marketing and run logistics, and I was on my own.

I have suffered from shin splints once before, but that was at least 20 years ago. Also known as medial tibial stress syndrome (MTSS), they are a common overuse injury causing pain along the shinbone (tibia). I remember how quickly they came on. I was travelling for work at the time and had gone for an afternoon run. Feeling the pain in my leg, I had turned around and headed back to the hotel, where I took cans of soft drink out of the minibar and held them against my shin to offer relief. I certainly didn't head out for a run later that evening, or the next day, or, I suspect, the week after.

It was around the 28-kilometre mark that I felt discomfort in my left shin as I ran down a small incline heading to the next water stop two kilometres away. My immediate thought was, *Hello, where did you come from?* I made it to the water stop and told Jules of the pain. I took some pain medication in the form of tablets and rubbed some Voltaren gel into the leg, and then headed back out. As soon as I left the water stop, the pain was immediate and intense. It felt like someone was driving a screwdriver into my shinbone each time my foot hit the pavement.

I continued to run, albeit quite slowly now. Walking didn't really relieve me of the pain – it just meant I was a whole lot slower, and that meant I was going to be out on the road and on my feet for longer. As I ran, the pain increased. I ran with a steady stream of tears running down my face and snot running out of my nose. I had gotten myself in a right old state, but I continued to run.

Until I couldn't. For the first time in 14 days of running, I stopped. I leant against a light post on the side of the road and wondered how I could finish the day.

Mae Thiew, who had been witness to this, immediately stopped her bike and started pouring cold water onto my head. She called the support team on the phone and told them I had stopped and they needed to move the lunch stop to where I was as I couldn't continue. Hearing Mae Thiew on the phone was enough to push me forward, to take the next step, and to follow that with another. I would later learn that the team had told Mae Thiew they wouldn't move the lunch stop and I had to get to them. It was exactly the call I would have wanted them to make. This was evidence of the importance of having those communication protocols in place prior to the run. No doubt CT, as my wife, hearing for the first time in 14 days Mae Thiew call to advise that I was in pain and needed the crew, would have wanted to come to me. However, that wasn't what we had agreed during planning. The role of the team was not to abandon plans because I was in pain or to change things because I was doing it tough – it was to give me the best chance of making it through each day and, ultimately, to the end of the run. I needed to find a way to get to the crew. This was my choice, and these hard times were always going to be part of the journey. This was a defining moment of the run, and I would be defined by what I would do over the next couple of hours.

The lead support vehicle with Chris and Jules turned around and drove back several kilometres to meet me. They gave me more pain medication and took up a position driving behind me to offer anything they could. Chris's message to me was clear: "We are here behind you, mate, and you just stop whenever you need to". Jules would tell me later that she could see from the passenger's seat how the injury was impacting the muscles in my leg and changing my running form.

I somehow got to lunch and just lay on the concrete ground. The relief, while not complete, was certainly welcome.

This lunch stop was pretty impactful for the entire team. They certainly hadn't seen me in such a state of distress; I had been in pain previously, but nothing like this. CT consulted with Matty, and everything the support team could do, they did. Laying on the concrete, I regained composure, and with pressure off my leg I could take in food and rest.

This was, without question, the lowest point of the run. I was in more pain than I had ever experienced in my life, and while the pain was intense, it was the act of continuing to run that created the most discomfort. Despite this, though, never did I consider withdrawing from the run. It never even occurred to me that we should call it a day and return tomorrow. My only thought was that I needed to get back up and start running. I knew it would hurt, but that was something I just needed to embrace.

The lunch stop had no timeframe attached to it; I could stay for as long as I needed to. I had 18 kilometres to go in the day, and they could wait. The only pressing issue was that as soon as I finished running, whenever that might be, CT and I needed to get into the car and drive back to Bangkok. Several hundred runners would be turning up to participate in our fundraising fun run, along with sponsors and their teams, the Governor of Bangkok and the Australian Ambassador to Thailand. Not attending wasn't an option.

So, while the team gave me all the time I needed to try and get back on the road, I also knew that the longer I stayed, the later we would get to Bangkok and the later we would be in bed. We still had a 4.30 a.m. alarm to meet.

I'm not sure where the motivation came from during that lunch stop, the willpower to rise up and start changing clothes and getting ready to head back out. I don't know what conversations the team had, whether they feared the rest of the day or even the whole run was in jeopardy. As you'd expect, they kept all of that from me. I know now that it pained CT to see me in so much pain. How could it not have, seeing your person, the one you love, in pain and then going back for more?

The act of pulling on my shoes and socks was the trigger that I was committed to going. In the lead-up to the run, I found excuses not to go for a run probably more often than I should have, but never did I put my shoes on and then not go. That was always the action that there was no coming back from. So, as I sat there slowly tying my laces, in my mind at least, I was committed.

When I stood, that screwdriver returned, driving into my shin. Bew held me upright as I struggled to put weight on my leg. At this point, all that mattered was I needed to move forward. As I took the first couple of steps, I knew I had to run – walking at that pace just wouldn't get it done. Starting was the most painful part, but at least it gave me momentum.

With 18 kilometres to run for the day, I would have normally had three water stops to go, but once I started running I just didn't want to experience the pain of stopping and starting again. Actually, I was afraid that if I stopped, I wouldn't be able to start again. Chris and Jules had resumed their position behind me rather than driving on to the next five-kilometre mark, and the agreement was that I would just stop when I wanted to and that would be the next water stop, irrespective of the kilometre marker or the number of times I needed to stop.

There was no doubt that the "why" of the run was important to me, but among a number of lessons I took from those 18 kilometres on the road was the importance of "how". The "why" just seemed too big and too far out of reach at this time, so focusing on the "how" was what got me through and would, of course, ultimately get me to my "why".

I had a soft half-litre flask in my hand and would drink from that between water stops. When I emptied it, I looked around, and Mae Thiew rode up and took it from me, returned to the car, exchanged it for a full one and returned. It meant I didn't have to break stride, let alone stop. It was almost like the Tour de France, when the riders simply raise their arm to call their team car forward and it arrives to meet whatever need they have. I just kept running, and each time I emptied the flask, I held it out to the side and Mae Thiew got me a full one. Not a word was spoken other than when I said "khop khun mak khrap" (thank you very much) each time she returned.

I passed what should have been my first water stop after lunch at the 13-kilometre mark and found strength in the fact that I hadn't stopped. I ran through the next at the 8-kilometre mark, and rather than feel fatigued or burdened by the pain in my leg, I was feeling stronger. At that point I was committed to running without stopping until I reached the hotel. It was such an important turnaround for me and the team to have limped into lunch in such a state of distress and to now have the end of the day in sight. I wasn't just limping, either – the closer I got, the stronger I got. I was sending a clear message, most importantly to myself, that there would indeed be incredibly tough times, but they would pass. As long as I stayed on the road and continued moving forward, I was giving myself a chance to finish not only the toughest day I would face but, importantly, the whole run.

Running into the small villages dotted along the coast of the Gulf of Thailand, the first sign that you are getting close is the houses that appear on the outskirts. There is one on its lonesome to start with, and then another, then they are side by side, and then you start to pass the restaurants and hotels. This was a very familiar road to me from the rides, but I wasn't sure which hotel this particular leg finished at. All I knew was that my watch was telling me I was inside the last couple of kilometres, and then it was down to the final kilometre. In six and a half minutes, the day would be over. I ran with such conviction, so bloody proud of my efforts since lunch. For the first time, I had run with music, listening to a playlist I had built for exactly this moment containing the likes of the Foo Fighters, Silverchair, Wolfmother and Eminem, and it had done what it was supposed to do.

As I ran the last kilometre to the hotel, I was loving the feelings I was experiencing. I loved where the pain of the run had taken me and that I had risen above it all. I had responded to the conditions I had found myself in, not the ones I was hoping for. Greg had come out of the hotel and met me a couple of hundred metres out from the finish in what would be his first time back running since the injury. "Keep your head up, mate," he was saying to me, but at that point I didn't need the encouragement – the euphoria that this run offered had been delivered.

I turned into the hotel and could see the crew, who came to meet me one by one. It was one of the most emotional finishes of any of the 26 days on the road. I had run 18 kilometres without a shirt change and I couldn't have been wetter if I had just risen from a swimming pool, but that didn't matter to any of them. There weren't just a few tears – there were genuine sobs. Each crew member had ridden the highs and lows of the tour up to this point and had been with me every step of the way.

The embrace from Chris that day was something special, and I am so grateful it was captured on video.

"That was toughest thing I have ever fucking seen," he told me as he slapped me on the back. "If you do nothing else this run, that was worth every fucking minute. Well done. Well done."

Chris's approval matters to me a lot, and I know that day, on the back of the efforts he had witnessed on the road, I had it. He had driven every one of those last 18 kilometres with me and witnessed each step I took. I had felt his and Jules's presence and the proximity of the car, and knowing they were literally behind me spurred me on. Who knows how the day would have ended if I had been out there on my own, but I wasn't. This was another day when the team got me home; together, we got the job done.

That day could have turned out a number of different ways. I could have surrendered to the pain at lunch or against that light post, promising myself that I would return and pick it up the next day. If I had done that, I would have gone to bed that night defeated. I would have had questions around my ability to finish, and I would have been 18 to 20 kilometres behind where I needed to be.

I knew when I finished that day that it was something special, and when I look back on it, I consider it a clear defining moment of the run. I can't think of anything in my life that was harder on a physical level. I think finishing that day and rising above the adversity was a clear sign of the importance of the run to me and how deeply committed I was to it.

I had originally planned to overshoot the hotel by five kilometres, so I ended up five kilometres short of the planned distance for the day, but given the state I was in at lunch it definitely could have been a lot worse. I could easily pick that up the next day once we returned from Bangkok. It was now time for a shower and to get into the car for the four-hour car trip back to Bangkok to attend the fun run the following morning.

The car trip turned out to be a godsend. I was able to lie flat the middle seats of the loaned Ford Explorer so I could sit in the rear and have my legs elevated and fully extended for the entire journey. As well as allowing me to be out of the heat and to recover, the trip also gave CT and I the chance to catch up, and it allowed me to catch up on some of the messages of support that had been coming in. Despite the significant discomfort I had been in, it was a great finish to a really hard day. It gave me confidence that I could overcome sustained pain and continue to run, and it gave me the self-belief that if I faced further difficulties, I could overcome them as well.

Behind every step: a crew's-eye view

Chris Thomas, Captain on the Road

I was approached in early 2024 and asked if I would be interested in supporting Peter on the Run to Remember. In coming to my decision, I felt there were a lot of factors I had to consider: Would I be of use to Peter and the endeavour, or would I simply be a "hanger on"? Would I have the stamina to perform when no one knew what was going to be thrown at us? The questions in my head were numerous, but looking back I can say with certainty the decision I made to participate is up there with the best I have made in my 70 years.

What evolved over December 2024 was nothing short of incredible. The team contained a mix of personalities, nationalities and ages, and some were complete strangers. The group grew from humble beginnings and a lot of trepidation to believing "together we can" and finally "together we did". At what point we started to believe is hard to pinpoint, but needless to say, we all took strength and belief from each other, and it wasn't long before we were as one in our determination to see it through no matter what.

The month was not without its difficulties, but we overcame them all – and some. I need to make special mention of our Thailand crew – Am, Squid and Bew – who had to put up with my ranting and raving when we came across road closures, dead ends, floods, King's celebrations… you name it. We always came through with a plan that would have the least impact on the runners, which at the end of the day is why we were all there.

To Jules, my trusty offsider in the Ranger, what can I say other than that I was blessed to have you by my side. Again, we had bumps along the way, but our reasons for being there carried us through. Greg is one lucky guy having you to support him.

Reflecting now, after four months, I personally feel very privileged that I was asked to be part of such a momentous feat of endurance and determination. We faced physical challenges, exhaustion, tough weather conditions and long hours on the road, but we came through with flying colours and always had each other's backs.

The memories made in December 2024 will live with me forever. I will never be able to thank everybody involved enough for providing me with this invaluable experience that took me from the lowest of the lows to the highest of highs. It reminds me of the 1996 movie *A Time to Kill* – we certainly killed it. Together we did!

19

Kilometres mattered

When I think about the most important things the crew did for me on the road, it is a long list, and everyone contributed in such meaningful ways that allowed me to focus solely on running. The success of the run can ultimately be attributed to all the work they did to get the small things right. This is what made for a safe and successful tour that will go down as the best thing I have ever done, full stop. To have a crew of eleven people on the road for 26 days, working from 4.30 a.m. until as late as 10 p.m. at night without a day off, all the while maintaining a team-first and goal-focused approach, is a worthy case study in teamwork and leadership.

In preparing for the run, I shared with Chris that one of the things that would matter most to me on the run would be knowing how far I had to go – how far to the next water stop, how far to the main break and how far until the end of the day. The actual distances didn't worry me – whatever I needed to do, whatever distance I needed to cover, I would do that – but what fired me up was getting the distances wrong. One of the clear lessons from the run I did the previous July, when we got the navigation wrong and it added extra distance to the beginning and end of the day, was, "If we are unsure of which direction to take, we will stop and wait". I didn't want the team guessing the route under pressure from me to keep moving. I was clear that my preference was to stop and wait, giving the team time to find the solution. I wasn't racing to beat someone else's time or trying to set any records; we had the luxury of time, and I wanted the team to take their time if they needed to make adjustments to the route. When changes were needed due to dangerous flyover crossings or closed roads, I simply removed myself from the conversation until Chris needed a decision from me or wanted to update me on the changes. Running back over roads you have already run is demoralising and was the last thing I wanted to do.

The other thing I tied myself up in knots about was the distance I had to run until I would next see Chris's orange Ford Ranger parked off the side of the road. Again, it wasn't the distance remaining that was important – I would run what I needed to – but the accuracy of the distance compared with what I was told.

On day 16 of the run, we found ourselves off course and walking between the tracks of a train line for some six kilometres without water. This wasn't the fault of the team or a breakdown in our process; it was a case (and not the first instance) of roads shown on our navigation app simply not appearing in real life. We couldn't run alongside the tracks because there was too much vegetation. The alternative was to backtrack a fair way, which is never a good option, so we chose the railway route with eyes wide open, understanding the risk that the exit point we identified on the map might also not exist. While we were on the tracks, CT was pushing her bike and trying to find songs for Greg and

I that would lighten the mood. We couldn't run: the concrete slabs between the tracks were too close to one another, and the presence of ballast rock tempted fate in the form of a twisted ankle if we tried to run and got it wrong. Those six kilometres on the railway line were probably the slowest of the entire tour, but we just needed to accept our fate and get it done.

We continued to make forward progress, and each awkward step brought us closer to firmer ground and surer footing. We found a well-defined exit road that led out to the main highway the support crew was on, and CT gave our location to the crew. While we couldn't see the support vehicle, we could see traffic moving at high speed in both directions on the highway. The road was straight as an arrow and probably two kilometres in length. I hoped to see the support vehicle approaching at high speed with the food and water I was desperately keen to take on, but as we continued to run, no support vehicle appeared.

About halfway down the road, I finally saw the orange Ford Ranger turn onto our road from the highway, but then it stopped more than a kilometre away, waiting for us. It didn't make sense, and I became frustrated. When we finally reached the car, we discovered that the road we were running on was in a national park and the staff at the checkpoint wouldn't allow the vehicle down the road.

It was great to see the crew, to take on water again and to know that the end of the day was in sight. It had been a hard day, and I was looking forward to the ice bath. Because we had been off route for the last eight kilometres, with six of it on the train line, what we had covered no longer correlated with what remained, and so I no longer knew how far it was to the hotel. I asked Jules, who was riding shotgun in the car with Chris. "Eight k" was her response. That meant five kilometres to the final water stop and then a three-kilometre cool-down to the hotel.

The new route had Greg and I running along a wide and safe verge of a pretty busy highway. We had been on a lot worse, but it's never pleasing running with cars and trucks passing you at 100 kilometres an hour a couple of metres away. I decided it was time to get this done. We headed out at a steady pace that progressively increased as we approached the finish, figuring we didn't need to finish with anything left in the tank, and we ran straight through the final water stop. As I handed Chris my empty flask in exchange for a fresh one, I said, "So, three k to go, mate!", expecting him to give me a thumbs up and reassurance, but his response caught me off-guard: "No, you have seven k to the hotel".

An extra four on top of 60 was no big deal, but when I was dialled into three left, three turning into seven was not great news. I needed accuracy to measure my output. I left the water stop with all the momentum from the last five gone and suffered for the remaining seven. Instead of the finish being somewhere between 16 and 18 minutes away, it ballooned out to 49 minutes.

We ended up running 64.4 kilometres that day, the most of any day on the tour. Once again, the fastest ten kilometres of the day would be the last, and on this day we ran sub-six-minute kilometres, which at the back end of a 64-kilometre day was good going. That adding kilometres to the day happened only a couple of times over 26 days was testament to the care that Chris and the crew took in getting this right.

20

Passing milestones

I was pretty fortunate to connect with Domonique Doyle, a sports psychologist, a few months prior to the run, and one of the things we spoke about was the importance of celebrating milestones. We didn't consciously identify and label milestones, but there were some obvious ones, including the halfway mark, the 1000-kilometre mark and, of course, the final run into Baan Tharn Namchai.

Our board that had each of the days of the run for us to cross off once completed was a bit of an afterthought of mine and one of the few things, apart from identifying the route and running it, that I actually contributed to the tour. However, I think all of us who were on the tour would agree on the value the board provided and the joy that came from celebrating the team as they stepped forward and crossed off another day.

It wasn't until we were all gathered around the board on the first night and looked at just how many days there were to cross off that I think we appreciated just how big this thing was.

Sitting on the stool at the end of the first day, exhausted, chafed and blistered, I don't think I was alone in my deep realisation of what lay before us. But the board served as recognition of each significant milestone, because that's what each day was: a significant milestone. Running 60 kilometres is an ultramarathon, which is huge and should be celebrated, but when you put 24 of them back to back, it is easy to lose sight of just how big each one is. Every day deserved its own celebration.

After we crossed off the first day, Jules said, "Imagine how good it will be to cross off a row". The top row of the board contained seven days, so the first week became a milestone to be celebrated. By day two, we were into triple-figure kilometres covered, so the next milestone became the 400-kilometre mark, which would mean we were less than 1000 kilometres from the finish. Once we passed that on day seven, the target became reaching 700 kilometres, which would signal halfway in distance, while day 13 was halfway in terms of time on the road.

Not only were there milestones in terms of kilometres but also in terms of the country that we moved through. For the first nine or ten days, our direction was generally west as we headed from Yasothon in the east to the western side of Bangkok. We then turned left and started heading south, and even that subtle change in direction felt like a significant sign that we were making good progress.

Day 11 was run on the outskirts of Bangkok, through industrial areas, which came with traffic and trucks on the road. However, this day was memorable for two reasons that weren't about where we ran. The first memorable thing about the day was that CT and I were joined on the road by Garry Browne AM, a wonderful supporter of Hands, who had flown into Thailand to run with me for a day, and for the pleasure – or displeasure – he raised $100,000. It is humbling to know someone would go to those lengths to support our endeavours. The second memorable aspect of the day was the finish, running with Garry a short distance away from the shores of the Gulf of Thailand. I could see the salt water, and God knows I could taste it. It was such a delight; it signalled to me that I was on familiar territory. I would soon be running on the roads of our 800-kilometre southern bike ride. We had turned for home.

Covering somewhere between 50 and 60 kilometres each day meant that every second day we were covering more than 100 kilometres, and so it felt like we were stripping the kilometres off the total at a serious pace. The end was fast approaching.

While I never considered not finishing, I guess if I think about when I truly believed I would finish, there are two distinct moments that come to mind. The first was passing the 1000-kilometre mark, and the second, which signalled the success of the run before actually finishing it, was arriving at the Cliff & River Jungle Resort in Khao Lak.

We reached the 1000-kilometre mark as I ran into lunch on day 18 of the run. It was the last of the milestones that I was measuring in kilometres. The team were very much aware of the milestone and were out to celebrate, and the biggest cheer came from CT.

Dinner that night was at a beachside restaurant a short walk from the hotel. I felt jubilant and light. Passing 1000 kilometres was an undeniable mental victory not just for me but for the whole team. Our hard work, the struggles, the sacrifices – it was all paying off. We had passed 1000 kilometres!

I remember when I went to bed that night, as CT and I lay in the darkness, I said to her, "Lover, we just passed 1000 kilometres. That's big". She responded, "It's more than big, it's huge". Having such a huge number of kilometres behind me and a rapidly decreasing number of kilometres to go, any doubt or uncertainty that I would reach the finish line was gone. There was just over a week left, and I could almost see the finish line. That there were still 400 kilometres to run at this point is a clear indication of the scale of the run; running 400 kilometres over a week is no insignificant feat, yet here I was already tasting the sweetness of victory.

21

The final nights

Every year (with the exception of COVID-19 years) since we started the bike rides in 2009, be it the eight-day 800-kilometre ride in January or one of our many five-day 500-kilometre corporate rides, the last night on tour was always spent at the Cliff & River Jungle Resort. It is a stunning hotel set at the base of the towering, majestic limestone cliffs that make this part of Thailand, which has become known within our riding group as *"Avatar* country", so remarkable. The accommodation is nothing like what we experience elsewhere on the rides. It has the traditional thatched roofs and a pool, and sits on the side of a mountain above a fast-flowing river, on the other side of which are towering limestone cliff walls. The views are unique and challenge for the best in all of Thailand.

In planning the run, at one point I considered CT and I staying in the Mothership each night to give us the consistency that changing hotels every night would not. We thought it would offer sanctuary and consistent sleep, and remove the need to check in and out of hotels for the entire tour. It sounded good in practice, but it was never going to work. The noise of the generator (when it worked) that supplied power to run the air conditioner (when it worked) was enough to put that theory to bed. Besides, the Mothership was just full of shit. It was so full of gear that we needed and had accumulated over the tour that I couldn't have lain down in one of the six beds if I had wanted to.

Building the route was a process of identifying the daily route and then trying to find accommodation nearby. So many of the hotels we stayed at along the way were new to me and selected because of their proximity to the end of the day's run. There was nothing fancy about them, but there was nothing wrong with them either. Some were quite plain and vanilla and I forgot them within hours of leaving, some were quirky, and some offered amazing views of the surrounding countryside. The minimum requirement in the brief was that we needed enough air-conditioned rooms for the entire crew; a hot shower was desirable but not essential. However, as I planned the back end of the route, I knew I wanted to stay at the Cliff & River Jungle Resort for a few nights. We would finish the 23 December run about 52 kilometres from the resort and drive for 40 minutes to stay there that night, then return the next morning and keep running from where we left off, and stay at the resort the next night as well. All going to plan, we would spend a truly unique Christmas Day there and celebrate as a team and family.

It was always my intent to run on Boxing Day and arrive at Baan Tharn Namchai that day, but I wanted to keep it a short day so that if anything derailed the run and injury forced me off the road for a day or so, I could make it up at the finish. However, other than the hiccup on 14 December and the dropping of five kilometres, which we picked up the following day, the run had gone entirely according to plan. There was no need for a spare day, which meant we could spread Christmas Day's kilometres over the last two days. It was almost a wind down, with 48 kilometres to run on 24 December, 25 kilometres on the 25th and 26 kilometres on the 26th and final day of the run.

On the evening of 23 December, as the car turned left off the road into the driveway of the hotel, it truly felt like we were home. The run was as good as done, and nothing short of breaking my leg would stop me from finishing now. I have this feeling every time I pull into this hotel, be it at the end of our January ride or a corporate ride – the final day from the hotel to Baan Tharn Namchai is 56 kilometres, which is a couple of hours' riding or a regular day of running. The end was in sight.

I received so many messages before and during the run. Each night, I would read them, and many moved me to tears. Some of those messages were encouraging in their intent but slightly condescending in language, saying things like, "It doesn't matter if you don't make it, you've done so much already," and, "Don't push too hard and hurt yourself," which I read as, "Baines, you have fuck-all chance of running 1400 kilometres; stop now, old man, before you kill yourself". I accept that they meant well, but that was exactly the type of language I had told the crew was not helpful. I didn't need subliminal messages telling me to stop.

As I got closer, I also noted the silence from some people who I would have expected to have the time and interest to share their thoughts, either publicly or privately via a simple text message. I have no doubt the lack of response from some people was because my success was not their desired outcome; there was a small number of people who I know would have rejoiced in my failure to complete the run. That me running 1400 kilometres and raising hundreds of thousands of dollars for charity was offensive to them is just what it is and is more about them than a sign that what I was doing was wrong. Not everyone will cheer you on or want you to succeed, and that just comes with putting yourself out there and doing big personal things. Nothing, though, would take away from the euphoria I felt stepping out of the car on the last of the 50-plus-kilometre days. Here I was, 99 kilometres from the finish of a 1400-kilometre journey. At the age of 58, I was about to do something that many had thought might be just a stretch too far.

We parked by the rooms at the bottom of the resort, and I entered through a garden walkway that surrounds the pool at the bottom of the cliff. I was in such a buoyant mood. It honestly felt like I was done. The crew was there, waiting. CT had set up chairs for Greg and I, and our daily theme song, "Rise Up" by Andra Day, was playing. It is such a powerful song. More than once during the run, when I was in a state of distress, I would give CT a hug and whisper in her ear, "I've just got to rise up". That was all I needed to do: in spite of the ache, just rise up again. But that day, as I walked through the archway, the ache was gone. The strapping was still on my knee, I still had ice bags attached to my leg, but the pain was gone in that moment.

I greeted CT with a long hug. We both knew we had done it. After all the work, the training, the sacrifice, the struggle and the financial expense, we were so close to home. This was our finish. The rest was our lap of honour, our victory lap, the last day of the Tour de France when the winners ride with champagne flutes. At any other time, running 99 kilometres would seem like a massive undertaking, but it's funny what perspective does for you. The next day, I would run a 48-kilometre ultramarathon, and I was viewing that as a half day.

CT ushered me over to the two chairs that were set up for Greg and me by the pool, next to our board where we would cross off another day. As I walked around the pool, it just looked too good, so I dived into the pool fully clothed, with running shoes and ice bags still attached to my leg. Why not? I allowed myself to stay underwater rather than immediately surfacing, and in that short moment I felt two things: weightlessness and silence. Nothing hurt. Gliding through that water for a few seconds, it felt much longer. It felt cleansing and purifying.

As I resurfaced, I looked back towards the crew and saw CT standing there with a smile on her face and a look of, "Well, that wasn't the plan!" Then, I saw my kids Jack and Kelsey bolting across the grass towards the pool, removing layers of clothing as they got closer before they both dived into the water as well to greet me. I'd known they were coming to Thailand for the last three days of the run, I knew they would be at the hotel that night, but I didn't know they were already there. It was an incredible moment to hug them both in the pool. It was captured on video and will remain with me as one of the absolute highlights of my life. I was overflowing with gratitude to have the kids there as we approached the end of the run.

What I didn't know was how concerned the kids had been for my physical health and safety in undertaking the run. Jack, in particular, had faced a few demons worrying about me finishing, me coming home – nothing was for certain. That concern and worry was washed away by the water in the pool that day, just like the sweat and road grime.

The kids' mum, Nic, had committed to coming to the run from the moment CT and I first invited her. To have her run to the finish with two of our kids and the rest of the crew was hugely meaningful to me and all of us there.

The touring party had grown; the morning of Christmas Eve, which also happens to be Jack's birthday, I headed out with CT, Greg, Jack, Kels, Nic, Jack's partner Jordan and Kels's partner Josh to tick off another day. Both Jack and Kels had been training for the run ever since we invited them more than 12 months previously. They had both been running the same model as CT, which was a huge effort for Jack especially, who was working in civil construction each day and then running half-marathons at night. The day would see yet another milestone: they would both run the full 48 kilometres and thus complete their first marathon and ultramarathon. To run with the kids for the entire day without needing to change my pace was a testament to the work they had both put in to be part of the run. This wasn't some token gesture on their behalf; they stepped off a plane, drove to the hotel and, starting the next morning, ran 99 kilometres in three days, including an ultramarathon. Afterwards, Kels told me that running the entire day was never part of her plan; she hadn't put that pressure on herself. She was just going to run until she felt she could run no more. However, they didn't understand the power of "together we can". They experienced what I had been experiencing for the past 23 days: how the support of those around you lifts you to achieve what might otherwise not be possible.

Those last three days running towards Baan Tharn Namchai with CT, Kels and Jack are one of the fondest and most treasured memories of my life. The fact that the three of them had chosen to be there, had chosen to train and were running side by side with me... I can't articulate the love and deep gratitude I hold for each of them.

Behind every step: a crew's-eye view
Kelsey Baines, Peter's daughter

When Dad told me he was going to do the run, I must admit that the distance he was going to run didn't register, and neither did the amount of time it would take. I didn't have a concept of just how far, how big or how epic it was, and to be honest I still struggle to comprehend it. All I heard were big numbers, and I thought, "Yep, here he goes again, another crazy thing, and he'll probably get it done".

I believed Dad would get it done not because he had run anything like that in the past but because I knew how mentally strong he is.

Mum was the first person I spoke to who really seemed to have a decent grasp of just how far the run was going to be. She made me realise that finishing was no certainty and even coming out of it OK was no guarantee, regardless of how mentally tough Dad was.

When Dad and CT invited all us kids and our partners to join them at the end of the run, it was an absolute "yes" from me straightaway. I never had to give it a second thought; there was no way I was going to miss it. I knew this was going to be special and perhaps never to be repeated. I had ridden many times on the charity bike rides in Thailand with Dad. I did the very first ride in 2009 with Jack and Lachie when I was 14. I have ridden plenty of times since, and I know from personal experience how hot it can be. I know how busy the roads are and how fast people drive there at times. I also know how special the end is when people are there to welcome in the riders.

The opportunity to be there at the end of the run had a number of layers for me. Of course, I just had to be there to watch

Dad cross the finish line, but the opportunity for me to run with him and CT as well was really special. The final layer was that Josh, my partner, would get to visit Hands and see why it has had such a big impact on my life and means so much.

I think it was pretty much straight after the idea of the run and the opportunity for us to be there was presented to us that Jack and I started talking about running some portion of it with Dad. Jack's birthday is 24 December, and we both thought it would be pretty cool to run some part of that day – and, of course, to run on the last day would be awesome too. Neither of us had a plan for how far we could run with Dad, but we both recognised it as something we wanted to do and that we would need to train for. My goal was to run a full day if I could make that work.

I was travelling around Australia with Josh for the entire 12 months prior to the run, and I could see via Strava the runs Dad was doing in preparation. Dad travels so much for work, but he maintained the training. I would wake up in some remote campsite in Far North Queensland and see that he was running in Thailand or Japan, or around the farm. He was so dedicated, and his dedication motivated me to run during my trip. The more he ran, the more I wanted to be out running. So, I adopted the same model as CT, running one kilometre one day, two kilometres the next, and then building on that. At first it was cute, but very quickly it got intense. Soon I was running back-to-back half-marathons. This gave me some appreciation of what they were doing over there, but I wasn't doing it in the heat of Thailand. It wasn't until I actually got over there that what Dad and CT were doing really blew my mind.

During my time travelling, the run gave me something to aim for, it gave me some structure and purpose to my days, but it also gave me incredible experiences that I wouldn't have had otherwise. I found myself running on the most remote roads, along deserted beaches, even being chased by emus. I grew mentally and physically from the training – and this was all the result of Dad's run. There were so many benefits that came from it, and so many people benefited in different ways. Mum even took up running, which I didn't expect. I fell in love with running, and without the Run to Remember that just wouldn't have happened.

When the run finally got underway and Dad was on the road, I was watching it all via social media. At first, I was excited to see what was happening, and I was constantly checking social media for updates, but as I started to see how hard it was and how raw the videos were, I couldn't watch them anymore. It was too distressing to see Dad in so much pain. I would get Josh to watch them and then update me on what I needed to know. Having ridden those roads myself in the heat just made me worry even more. I worried a lot about how Dad would adequately fuel his body, as I have seen him not get this right at different times and it hits hard. The thing that brought me the most comfort was seeing how CT was supporting Dad. I just adore her, and it wouldn't have been possible without her.

As the run continued, it started to sink in that there were no certainties, and I got more worried about what this could mean. I could actually see how Dad's mental strength could work against him. I could see the moment on the run when, for all types of logical reasons, he should stop, but that mental toughness or stubbornness would push him forward to a place he might not come back from, and that scared me. Could he do long-term damage, or even worse, by pushing too far and too hard?

I also worried about the impact it would have on him mentally if he didn't finish. I had more confidence in his ability to cope with the pressures and pain of the run than not finishing.

My mind was at peace once Dad had finished the run and he was safe. I was so proud of him. What a relief that his vision had come to life, and it couldn't have gone better. I am so proud of his decision to push the barrier and to continue to care for the kids, 20 years on from first arriving at that temple. And I still don't know how he did that run; I don't know how that was physically possible.

Selfishly, I want to go back and do it again. Not only am I so incredibly proud, but I also feel so grateful. Hands has been a big part of my life, and the run was an opportunity to remember the "why" behind it all. I feel incredibly grateful to have a parent like Dad who is so inspiring to be around. Learning through experiences is what Dad has taught me, and I can't wait to pass that on to my kids.

There is no doubt in my mind that I'm in the best space in my life, and a huge part of why is because of the run – not just the three days and 100 kilometres that I spent running with Dad but the entire 12-month campaign that got me there. What a gift.

22

Mae Thiew bids farewell

Mae Thiew would depart from the run just prior to the end of day 24. As her announcement to join the run had come as a surprise and without discussion, so too did her departure. We were informed on the morning of day 24 that once we reached the hotel, she would leave the tour and return to Baan Home Hug. Of course, we wanted her at the end of this remarkable journey, especially given she was the one person with whom I had spent the entire 1350 kilometres on the road so far, but I have come to accept that once she has made a decision, she knows her reasons for it and I have to accept it. It is not my job or position to question or even understand her decision.

Saying goodbye to her was an incredibly emotional experience. It was at one of the last stops for the day, and I was lying on the ground, going through the final stages of preparation and recovery prior to heading back out on the road, when I sat up to see her sitting at my feet. She looked different. The tinted snow goggles that she wore as sunglasses out on the bike were gone. She had changed out of her cycling robes (those are not two words you use together too often) and was wearing fresh robes for the occasion, devoid of road dirt, dust and sweat. She looked almost more spiritual, if that is possible. She had a presence that was different to the last 23 and a half days.

She spoke about her time with me on the road. She spoke about the love that exists between us both and the shared commitment that we have to support the children. She told me it was time for her to go, and I was overcome with emotion and unable to speak. I tried to thank her for all she had done, not just over the last 24 days but since I had first met her in 2010, but words failed me and were replaced with sobs. She hugged CT, then Wendy, Jules and Claire, and they were special hugs. The last was for Am, and she too was shedding plenty of tears. As a female monk, one of the rules she abides by prohibits any physical touch between her and a male, so my hug was delivered vicariously through CT. It had been a massive journey for all of us, no matter how you measured it, and it was indeed a sad moment to bid her farewell.

Why did she leave with two days and 51 kilometres to go until the run was over? Why did she leave home for 24 days and travel so far but leave in sight of the finish? I think there are a couple of reasons. The first was very practical: she had a decent understanding of the festivities that the final day would bring, and as a monk I believe that she saw it as conflicting with her teachings to be part of that.

That leads into the second reason. By day 24, we were finished with running through villages. I was on the road with Kels, Jack, CT and Greg, and I feel as though Mae Thiew believed her job was done. I believe that her commitment to me and to herself was to do all she could to deliver me to the finish line, and now that we were in sight of it, her job was done. She didn't need to go any further; she had done what she had set out to do.

If that is the case – and I truly believe it is – it speaks to what is important to her. I can't imagine committing to a journey of running 1400 kilometres and then stepping off the road within sight of the finish, saying, "I have done what I needed to do. I don't need the celebration of crossing the finish line". I think her state of mind speaks to the vast gap between her awareness and mine. Perhaps it also is evidence of her values as a Buddhist monk and those of us in Western society who chase celebration, adulation and applause for our accomplishments. Imagine the contentment and peace, the higher state of enlightenment that must exist in her soul for her to complete her task and simply walk away. How sad and shallow is our society, built around creating artificial lifestyles to seek the approval of people we will never meet through likes on social platforms.

I think about the run daily, and I often think of Mae Thiew. I think of her riding behind me like a guardian angel, warning approaching motorists of our presence. I think of her timely response to the dogs, and how I went home with my skin intact as a direct result of her ability to keep them away from us. I smile fondly at her relentless desire to be independent, and the rise in her voice as she scolded me when I tried to help her. Chris never got used to it, but no one controls Mae Thiew. I think about when we were stuck on the highway and needed to carry the bike up and down the stairs together – together we could, and together we did. And I think about the closing 18 kilometres of day 14, when she kept me fuelled so that I didn't have to stop running.

What a deep privilege it is to have her in my life and to have shared that time together on the road.

I asked Mae Thiew when the last time was that she had spent a month away from her kids and Baan Home Hug. Her response revealed the depth of her commitment to me and the Run to Remember: "Have not".

Behind every step: a crew's-eye view

Rod Reid, Film Crew

We all have a story. We're all carrying something – joy, pain, trauma. Some chapters are loud and messy; others are quiet and filled with questions.

A couple of years ago, I hit pause on mine. I took a year off. I needed room to breathe, to reflect, to reset. I didn't know exactly what I was looking for, but I knew I had to step away from the noise for a while to find it.

That journey took me to Japan, and at the very start of that trip, I ran into Pete and CT. That's Pete for you – he just seems to appear when needed, even when it's not planned. It had been years since I'd seen him and CT. Sure, we'd texted and spoken here and there over the years, but there's something different about being in the presence of those you care about and respect.

Fast-forward a few years, and I needed a recharge. Planning to go back to Japan to hit the slopes, I checked in with Pete and asked if he was going to be in Japan with CT after Christmas. And with that classic Pete mix of calm and quiet intensity, he said something like, "Nah, mate, I'm running 1400 kilometres to raise money for the kids and to reflect on 20 years…"

And before he finished, I just blurted out, "Can I come? Can I help?" I didn't know what the role would be. I didn't care. I just knew I wanted to be part of it.

Pete, being Pete, found a way to bring me in. No fluff, just trust. That's the kind of leader he is. That's the kind of heart he has.

It wasn't the first time Pete had impacted my life without knowing it. Years ago, we'd crossed paths when I was leading a team that was, honestly, struggling. It had good people but no alignment, no clarity. I left the role and looked to the next. He offered a little support, a program, which helped me get to the next role. Pete sparked something in me back then. I didn't fully get it at the time, but looking back I see how he was already planting the seeds of lessons I'd carry with me. Listen properly. Lead with purpose. Turn up when it matters.

Since then, I've tried to pay it forward – sometimes directly, often in my own way, when no one notices. And that's the thing about Pete: he doesn't ask for credit, he asks you to reflect. He asks you to be real. He asks you to show up in the quiet moments and do the right thing, even when nobody's watching.

And that's what I saw from Pete during the run. What matters is what people do when no one's watching, when there are no accolades or Instagram moments. Even when he could barely walk, talk, or comprehend what was happening, he made time to appreciate those around him: to thank people, to acknowledge every tiny act that helped move the mission forward. That's the essence of "together we can", and it's why people follow him, not just with their feet but with their hearts.

Over the course of that journey, I was lucky enough to be surrounded by so many who gave their all. Runners, crew, volunteers, supporters – each one touched my heart in some way. But two people, two lights, live rent-free in my heart now. If I were to leave this world tomorrow, just having had the chance to meet them would be enough to feel like I'd lived a life worth living.

Their names are Am and Mae Thiew.

Raised at Baan Home Hug, Am grew up with the love and support of the Hands community after experiencing unimaginable loss at a young age. What struck me wasn't just her story but her presence. Am is one of the most resilient, grounded and joyful humans I've ever met. She is calm, centred and generous. When you meet Am, you don't see her past; you feel her strength, her grace and her ability to make you feel seen. She carries her story like a lantern, lighting the way for others. She reminded me that we don't need to be defined by our beginnings; we can choose how we show up for others.

But if Am is a lantern, Mae Thiew is the fire that lit it in the first place. She is love in motion. Her story, her decision to open her home and heart to children who had nowhere else to go, has touched more lives than anyone can count. Her selflessness, her humour, her unwavering compassion are impossible to put into words. But I'll try.

Mae Thiew's presence commands respect. I'm loud, I'm silly, and I was hoping that my energy would be a small contribution that might lift the crew, pep up the runners, lighten the load a little; what I wasn't expecting was how quickly she could meet that energy and calm it. She didn't dim it – she grounded it. We had some special moments. She flew a drone. She passed on some wisdom. She met my silliness with an entirely new level of her own.

When we arrived in a new village and the locals saw Mae Thiew, something shifted. They recognised what she represented, and all barriers dissolved. Nothing needed to be said. Mae Thiew's calming presence, her discipline, even the way animals responded to her, all told you this was someone special. Dogs calmed. Farmers opened up. You could feel that she was special.

When you're around Mae Thiew, you feel peace. You feel warmth. You feel what it's like to be wrapped in a type of love that asks for nothing in return. Her legacy isn't awards or achievements – it's the hundreds of children she's given a future to and the ripple effect of every person she's inspired to lead with heart. To sit in their presence, to laugh with them, to hear their stories – it changed me. It softened parts of me that had grown hard. It filled gaps I hadn't realised were still open. And it reminded me of one simple truth: we are all part of each other's stories.

Having always been a supporter and in awe of Pete, I've stayed close to the cause, but I knew this run was different. It was not just an epic feat of human endurance to raise awareness; this was a once-in-a-lifetime movement. People who barely knew Pete showed up to support. And by the time we reached the final stretch, half the town did too.

As we approached the finish, the tension built. It was overwhelming. We were coming to the end. I set up for a final tracking shot. The bridge. The temple. No second take.

Now, a bit of context: growing up, and even into my adult life, my experiences with police were rarely positive. If the cops were around, I was probably the reason why. So, when a police bike pulled up, I saw trouble. There were rules being bent, laws possibly being broken. I saw the potential for everything to be derailed in the final stretch. I thought, *No way. Not now. We can't come undone here. We've come too far.*

I slipped into hustle mode. Talk him down. Smooth it over. Distract. Whatever it takes to keep the mission and the convoy moving, take one for the team.

I was mid-sentence, offering him a piece of merch to soften the interaction, trying to distract him and stop him in any way, when he calmly said (in better English than mine in that moment), "Yes, we know Khun Peter. Follow me. I am here to help you".

That moment floored me. This wasn't a bust. This person already understood what we were doing, why we were here, and had shown up early to make sure we got there safely. He was the advanced rider, sent ahead to clear the traffic and guide us in. All my assumptions, all my habits from a different life, fell away in a second. I'd been so ready to go to war, and instead I was met with kindness, understanding and support. It was a moment I'll never forget.

I've taken the time to try and express all this not just because it shaped me but because if you're reading this, you're part of it too. You're already in the ripple. That's how we're connected. That's how "Together we can" becomes "Together we will".

23

Finished with the marathons

Completing my 24th day of running also signalled the last day that we would pass the marathon mark on the road, for the next two days were 25 kilometres and 26 kilometres. The run couldn't have gone better no matter which way you look at it. The success of the campaign also meant that CT would run with me for both days from start to finish, completing her solo effort of 351 kilometres.

The 4.30 a.m. alarm was gone; we were waking at a civilised time of 6 a.m. and enjoying breakfast at the hotel. There was no pack-down of the hotel and no sleep-deprived breakfast in the Mothership – she had served her purpose, but no more was she required. We were like civilised holidaymakers just heading out on Christmas Day for a 25-kilometre run. We would be back for a Christmas lunch that would seem like a gourmet dinner after what our lunches had been for the past 24 days.

Our posse had grown significantly. We had welcomed in Greg and Jules's three kids and son-in-law, and they also joined us on the road to run with their dad and celebrate all that he had achieved, not just on this epic run but in life. The significance of having our adult kids want to join us and run in Thailand is so incredibly special and something I will cherish for the rest of my life. We were banking memories that can never be taken away from us, no matter what happens. Hannah, Greg and Jules's daughter, had previously ridden a couple of times with Hands, including with Kels; now, here they were, so many years later, on the road together running in support of their dads.

Christmas Day also saw Game, the director of Baan Tharn Namchai, and a host of the older kids join us on the road. The journey had certainly come full circle. I had started this run 25 days prior, leaving Baan Home Hug surrounded by the love of the kids we have been supporting since 2010; now, within reach of the finish line, I was joined on the road by the kids from Baan Tharn Namchai as we made our way to their home. It wasn't lost on me that running beside me, in front of me and behind me were the kids, now young adults, who benefited from the support that Hands has been able to offer them for the past 20 years. There were also staff members from Baan Tharn Namchai running with me who were once children of our home, having lost parents and family capable of supporting them, who had now graduated university and were the leaders and carers of kids like they had been.

The thought also wasn't lost on me as I ran with the future leaders of Baan Tharn Namchai that perhaps I was also running with the future leaders of Hands: my kids. The impact of the tsunami on their lives had been equally as profound as on mine, though they were swept up in it without choice, unlike I was in choosing to deploy and to continually return.

CT loves Christmas, so it was no surprise to anyone who knows her that we would all be running dressed in our Grinch pyjamas for the first leg. I can't imagine what the locals must have thought seeing a group of foreigners running down the road in pyjamas. That leg delivered us "the hill", which is known by all the southern Hands bike riders, and for first-time riders it is dreaded if not feared. Leaving the hotel, it is an 11-kilometre ride (or run, depending on your choice) to the base of the hill, and then a four-kilometre rise of varying gradients. It always appears worse than it actually is, hence my instruction to first-time riders: "Don't ride the hill before you get there". Many a rider has tied themselves up in knots worrying about the hill only to summit it and question why they had worried so much.

That day was not the first time I had run the hill. In April 2024, as part of my training, I was on a corporate bike ride and got up at 3.30 a.m. to run the last day of the ride – 60 kilometres to Baan Tharn Namchai – with CT and Game. We ran the hill in darkness, and by time we reached the top, the first signs of daybreak were appearing, revealing a low-level cloud base that surrounded us. It was certainly a solemn morning with just the three of us. We were among the clouds.

This time, as I approached the hill on foot for the second time, I would run it with my kids and the majority of the crew that had been on the road with me since 1 December. Mother had decided that she would walk the hill, along with CT, Jords, Nic, Jules and many others. I started up the hill with Jack and Kels by my side, which was fitting, as the very first time I climbed the hill back in 2009 on our inaugural bike ride, they were there summiting the hill for the first time as well. Unlike my first time running up the hill, the sun was out and already raising the temperature.

As I started up the hill, I was quickly passed by a number of the older kids from Baan Tharn Namchai, who challenged me to keep up with them. Of course, I took the bait and set off after them. I caught them, and they allowed me to move to the front. As the gradient started to bite, the chat and laughter of the kids quickly died down, as did the number of slapping feet around me, but a couple of them held on. Upwards we pushed. As the humidity climbed like the road, the pace stayed constant. We were settling in for a run all the way to top. *How did I let myself get into this situation,* I thought, *to be goaded by teenage kids, and why do I feel like I can't let them win?* I am sure they were thinking, *Surely we can outrun the old man. He has to be tired – he has run 1350 kilometres.* But I was enjoying the burn in my legs. It wasn't pain in my shin or my knee I could feel – this was muscle burn from hard work, and it felt good. The hills had been few and far between over the course of my journey, and I hadn't anticipated running this one in a foot race with two kids from Baan Tharn Namchai, but this burn was a sign of the work I had put in over the last 25 days on the road and 18 months training. The steeper the incline, the more I leaned into the run; aerobically, I was in my comfort zone.

We pushed on until we reached the top, and I turned to congratulate the two boys who had stuck with me, Boss and Ton Nam, only to find Jack joining us. He had seen me take off with the older kids towards the bottom and had set about chasing us. It felt really good arriving at the top of the hill, working hard all the way and not faltering. I could tell we all had gas left in the tank – not much, but enough. It was such a contrast to when

I had arrived at water stops early in the tour just feeling defeated. What an outstanding way to finish this incredible experience.

What goes up must come down, and on the other side of the hill was a seven-kilometre descent, which is the absolute highlight of any bike ride for me. I often say I ride 780 kilometres on our eight-day bike ride just to ride the seven kilometres down that hill. Running down the hill certainly took longer than riding down it, and it was a good workout for the quads. Greg had set off early to head down the hill as he was super conscious of not aggravating his soft tissue injury; his nemesis was the downhill, and this would be a long way. He was happy to walk down rather than risk injury.

CT and I have ridden down that hill dozens of times over the years. Kels and Jack have also ridden it numerous times, and here we were running it on the penultimate day of this 1400-kilometre journey. The four of us ran together, accompanied by a number of the kids from Baan Tharn Namchai. This was a Christmas Day like no other and unlikely to be ever repeated. All I could think was how lucky I was to be doing this surrounded by those I love the most.

We pulled up on the side of the road at the end of the day with exactly 26 kilometres remaining to be run. For the last time, Chris sprayed "R2R" on the road, signifying the end of day 25 and the start point for the last day. The crew was all reunited and with the vehicles, ready to return to the hotel, but as we looked back up, there was a steady stream of kids and staff from Baan Tharn Namchai making their way down the hill to the end of their day on the road. With the exception of Boss and Ton Nam, I think they were more than happy to leave the running to us. Waiting and cheering the last of them in, I am sure their running that day had given them a deeper appreciation of the epic nature of what we were doing.

We piled into the support vehicle and headed back to the hotel for a Christmas lunch that was somewhat different, you could say, to years gone by. My family has a few traditions for Christmas lunch, and one of them is the inclusion of a very nice New Zealand sauvignon blanc called Cloudy Bay. It's not on the wine list at the Cliff & River Jungle Resort, I can assure you of that, but Jack and Jords arrived with two bottles that were appropriately chilled and very much enjoyed by a surprised team for Christmas lunch.

Heading to bed that night was a strange feeling. Packing up for the last day on the road, it was hard to believe it was coming to an end. The end was so close now. One more sleep, one more day of 26 kilometres, and it would be over.

Behind every step: a crew's-eye view
Jack Baines, Peter's son

The Run to Remember was a massive undertaking, and right from when Dad told me that he was going to do it I did think, *Dad's lost the plot*, but I knew he was serious and I had full confidence in his ability. Dad wouldn't have shared the idea if he hadn't given it a lot of thought. I could tell that this was something that meant a lot to him, and when that's the case, Dad just makes it happen.

I think part of the confidence that I had in Dad – which wasn't shared by everyone, I have to admit – was that I knew he would prepare for the run and I knew he would turn up ready and in the best shape to take it on. It was a massive undertaking, the scale of which wasn't lost on me, but I never doubted him.

Over the year or so in the lead-up to the run, I shared what Dad was planning to do with mates and other people, and some doubted his ability to get the job done because of how big it was, but also because the heat of Thailand was always going to be a major factor. I first rode in Thailand in 2009 on the inaugural ride and have ridden on ten additional occasions, so I certainly know how hot it gets, but I think because Dad has spent so much time in Thailand on the rides and in the training he did, he appreciated what he was in for, and the team, under the leadership of CT, was ready to respond to the conditions they would face.

In the lead-up to the run, I watched as Dad got his body and (I assume) his head ready for the challenge of 26 days on the road. He travels so much for work, and I don't know what country he is in half the time. I will see him on the weekend, and then two days later he will pop up on Strava running in Bangkok, Singapore or Japan. I really took a lot of inspiration from his commitment to the training, even while he was travelling so much. We talked about the program that Matty had designed for him, and I know Dad felt like he was letting Matty down if he missed a training session.

The invitation to all of us kids to join Dad and CT on the run was incredible, and right from the first time it was mentioned I knew I would be there and was excited to be part of it. Speaking with Kels, we both just felt so grateful to be invited across and have the opportunity to be part of something so big. I knew it was going to be massive, but I have to admit I didn't realise the impact it would have. I have been fortunate to be part of so many experiences in Thailand with the bike rides, the Renovation Taskforce projects and now the run. It was another incredible shared experience to be part of.

I started running months out from the run because I knew that if I was going to be there on the road, there was no way I wanted to be watching Dad run from inside a car. I knew this was too special an opportunity not to be beside him on the road. The model that CT was doing, with one kilometre the first day and then building on that with one additional kilometre each day, seemed like a great idea and a great way to be part of it. It started off easy enough, but as I got towards the back end of December I was working each day and then running a half-marathon, and that brought home the enormity of what they were doing on the roads of Thailand.

As the days got longer and harder in Thailand, it became harder to watch. It was pretty tough to watch Dad in pain, but I was so proud of him that he just kept pushing through. I know there was nothing I could do, but seeing him in those really tough times just made me want to be there even more.

When we landed and drove up to meet Dad and CT, everything felt familiar, and I knew it was 100% the right place to be. I'll never forget when I first saw Dad in the pool at the end of day 23, when we surprised him. To have the opportunity to spend a couple of days running with Dad and CT was so special.

The thing about the time on the road is that it wasn't just those running who benefited. I saw the impact it had on my fiancée Jordan, on Mum, who ran with us, and everyone who was there in some way – this would impact and change their lives. It certainly changed my life in the most positive way.

The run into Wat Yan Yao and the emotion around that place is hard to describe. It means so much to Dad and the entire Hands community. I had ridden in there plenty of times, and here I was, one of five who would have the opportunity to run through the gates on the 20th anniversary of what started this incredible journey. When I reflect, I have such gratitude for the experience.

The only regret that I have from the entire thing is that I didn't spend more time on the road running with Dad, but work commitments prevented that. I am grateful for the three days on the road and the 100 kilometres we got to share out of the 1400 kilometres.

My time in Thailand has given me a lot of perspective. It has shown me how hard life can be and, thanks to Hands, how good it can be. It has had such a positive impact on my life, creating so many amazing experiences, and if I can take the baton from Dad and do the run at the next anniversary then I will do it.

24

The final day

The ultimate milestone was upon us: Boxing Day 2024, 20 years to the day since the earthquake off the coast of Indonesia triggered the Indian Ocean tsunami.

Sleep hadn't been coming easily to me as I got towards the back end of the tour, and I had been taking sleeping tablets to ensure I had at least six hours' sleep a night. I was feeling strong in my body, with the exception of the shin splint, which Jules and Claire now felt was likely a stress fracture, and an irritated ITB to go with it. I had lost over seven kilograms during the run and would weigh in on the final morning at 68 kilograms, a weight I haven't been since I was a teenager. My body was fatigued and I needed to sleep. However, going to bed on Christmas night, which was probably when I needed the sleeping tablets the most due to the emotion of the day ahead, I couldn't take any, as I had a 3 a.m. wake-up call to appear on Channel 7's *Sunrise* breakfast TV show to talk about the day ahead and the run to date. As the leading commercial television breakfast program in Australia, it was not an invitation I could forgo.

Knowing I had to get up at 3 a.m. meant that the time between laying my head on the pillow and the alarm was pretty restless. When I returned to the room after the TV interview, returning to bed was not an option due to other media commitments I had before setting off for the day. Because of the four-hour time difference between Australia and Thailand, catching even the end of the breakfast media meant calls before 5 a.m. for me, but was important to do these media calls as they would help raise awareness of the run and our efforts on the ground.

The feeling on the morning of 26 December was mixed. I was excited to run with our crew, and I was really happy that Greg had recovered enough to complete the run and run with his kids. I was also feeling an incredible depth of gratitude that I would run with CT, Kels and Jack on this final leg. CT had been able to juggle so many commitments over the past month and yet retain her model of running one more kilometre than the day before. She would run with me all the way that day, as would Kels and Jack. We had also arranged for the entire crew who had been with me on the road since 1 December (minus Mae Thiew) to participate in the final stages of the run rather than be supporters or observers; everyone would be on the road for the last couple of kilometres into Baan Tharn Namchai.

However, despite my excitement, there was a part of me – a big part of me, to be honest – that didn't want this bubble to burst. I didn't want this epic and incredible experience to end. Within hours, two years of planning, hundreds of kilometres run in training, and the sacrifice and struggles would be over, and I knew that I would miss it all. I knew there would be a massive comedown from this high that I had been on.

The final day

Our bags were packed for the last time on the road. Today was it. There was no need for end-of-day washing tonight, and no need for recovery and ice baths. We had 26 kilometres to go – less than 2% of the run. As is customary on our rides when we leave the Cliff & River Jungle Resort on the final morning, we gathered at the top of the property with the backdrop of the sheer cliff face behind us, an expanded but equally connected group. There was the Baines and Thomas family, there was the Wallace clan, and there were those who had joined us for the 26 days prior that belonged to both, not by birth or name but by shared experience. As the clouds danced in the valley surrounding us, we huddled together, welcoming and anticipating the finish but in some weird way wanting to prolong it as well. It didn't feel quite complete to do these final days without Mae Thiew, but I took comfort in knowing that she was now back with the children at Baan Home Hug who gave her life meaning and purpose.

There was a 20-minute drive from the Cliff & River Jungle Resort to the mark on the road that signalled the start of the last day. The kids and staff from Baan Tharn Namchai had intended to join us for the second time in two days, but they realised that running back-to-back days is difficult when you haven't trained, so they decided to rest their weary legs and see us at the end. Although we could almost hear the celebration drums beating from Baan Tharn Namchai, we still had 26 kilometres to run, which in isolation is not a walk in the park – in fact, for the parkrunners out there who do a five-kilometre loop each Saturday morning, it is five loops around the park.

We ran as a team of five – Greg, CT, Jack, Kels and myself – all dressed in our Run to Remember singlets and all running in complete unison. We ran at a fairly decent pace, driven by our desire to meet the time commitments first at Wat Yan Yao and then at Baan Tharn Namchai. We had been advised that there were a couple of hundred people gathered at Wat Yan Yao who were there to run the final four kilometres with us to Baan Tharn Namchai. The other driver of our pace was the energy in the group. Jules had strapped my knee again that morning as best she could for what would be the last time, and as I ran I could feel the pressure and pain, but I just willed it to hold out for the final 20-odd kilometres. I didn't want to limp or hobble to the finish line; I wanted to run the last day as it deserved to be run.

The team ran through the backstreets of Old Town in Takua Pa, a town I knew well, having first come there in the days after the Boxing Day tsunami that brought such loss to the people who called this area home and those who had been visiting from afar. I felt composed. Each of the water stops on the last day was a fairly quick in and out, taking on fluids, filling our water bottles and heading straight back out onto the road. There was no fatigue. There was nothing holding us back. We were now inside the final ten kilometres of what had been an incredible experience. I was running with those who meant the most to me in my life, and I could have kept running all day.

We ran past the football stadium that I had attended in January 2005 among thousands of people, all dressed in white, who had come to mourn and pay their respects for those lost. We had sat for hours in the sun as the silent Australian representatives at the event. As the sun sank, taking with it the bite of the heat, thousands of monks dressed in various shades of orange robes took their place in the stands. Once seated, they began chanting in unison, thousands of them. As the chanting came to an end, those seated on the field of the stadium formed small groups and lit floating lanterns that filled with hot air and rose under their own power into the sky. The vision of thousands of lanterns rising into

The final day

the dark night sky is forever etched in my memory. I can close my eyes and see those lanterns with such clarity, as if it was yesterday. It truly was an experience that I will never forget. Running past the stadium, I shared with the others the significance of the stadium and just how spectacular the event had been.

Running over the iron bridge that leads into the town, designed for pedestrians but used by motorcyclists, was like a movie playing at full speed backwards in my mind. I was trying to process all that had happened over the last 20 years; it was like a series of flash cards going off in my head. The sound of our feet thundered to announce our approach, and the motorcycle riders heading in the opposite direction stopped and waited for us to pass. The sun had real bite, and I could feel its intensity on my exposed skin. As usual, I was drenched from perspiration, but I felt invincible as we were now down to single-digit kilometres remaining.

The 20 years since I first landed in Thailand felt like the blink of an eye, but so much had changed. So many people had been impacted, both positively and negatively. I would like to think that on balance, there has been a far greater positive impact than negative. Kels and Jack were ten and eight years old respectively when I first deployed, and here they were, running 100 kilometres with me over the final three days of the run. Together with CT and Greg, we were closing on the finish line.

We turned left onto Phet Kasem Road, the main road leading through town, and ran the 300 metres to the Takua Pa River and Wat Yan Yao immediately beyond. A number of police on motorbikes were there to close down the road and escort us for the final stretch into the temple. While the temple was not the official end of the run, it certainly was the place that best represented so much loss and heartbreak and therefore held so much meaning for so many people.

The emotions were rising in all of us. We had made it. After 1389 kilometres, the equivalent of 33 marathons, over 26 days in the heat and humidity of Thailand, we were about to finish this run. I had felt in control of my emotions all day, which had surprised me, but no more. Fifty metres before the gates of the temple, I broke, and the tears flowed. To arrive at the temple with CT, Kels, Jack, Greg and the entire support team is something I will be forever grateful for. We had all ridden into the temple together on various charity bike rides since 2009, but none of those experiences came close to what we were feeling that day. It was one of the greatest moments of my life.

We ran into the temple to be greeted by hundreds of well-wishers, including friends, supporters of Hands, former colleagues from the tsunami response 20 years prior and members of the local Thai community. The Thais love a souvenir running shirt, and I would say 90% of those gathered in the grounds of the temple were dressed in a run shirt. The immediate hugs were between those of us who had left Baan Home Hug on 1 December and, over the past 26 days, made our way to where we now stood, and they were hugs to cherish, the type you don't want to end, the type that say, "Together we did". Those gathered at the temple respected the space and time needed for those hugs.

The circle of hugs then expanded to the wider team, and then pandemonium broke out. All of the Thais who were there wanted a selfie with each of us. I'm not sure they could tell who was who, but it didn't matter – they wanted that photo and weren't afraid to manhandle you into position to get their best angle. The time at the temple allowed us to rejoice in the achievement of this truly remarkable feat. I know that I didn't appreciate the significance or scale of this endeavour leading into it, and it would take some time for me to reconcile what we had achieved together as a team.

The final day

After a moment of celebration, those of us who had been running since 1 December changed from our Run to Remember blue singlets into our yellow running shirts from when we left Baan Home Hug on day one so that we would stand out from all the shirts worn by supporters, sponsors and their teams, and no one would get lost. CT and I had agreed that we would cover the four remaining kilometres from the temple to Baan Tharn Namchai as a team. Arrangements had been made for the transfer of the vehicles, meaning that Chris, Squid and Bew would be on the road with us too.

The idea had been to walk the final four kilometres together, given that a few of our crew weren't necessarily in the condition to run four kilometres, but many of those in the crowd had turned out for a run. As we left the temple, the crew was at the front of the pack, but it was a bit like holding back the rising tide – those who had come to run wanted to run. I had spent most of the last 1389 kilometres running with no more than one or two other people, and several hundred kilometres on my own, so it was almost intimidating to have what became a bit of push and shove from the Thai runners who were jostling to get next to me to take a selfie. I quickly lost sight of all but CT, Kels and Jack. Greg was with Jules, and the remaining crew were somewhere in the middle of the crowd, quickly drifting backwards. Squid hadn't been briefed on the day's end and was running in a pair of jeans and thongs, and it might have been the first time in a decade or so that he'd had cause to run more than 50 metres, so he was quickly at the back of the pack.

I started to feel a little uncomfortable about all the jostling and pushing that was going on as people just wanted to run shoulder to shoulder with me, and I could see that someone was going to fall over. The only way I could see to take back control was to increase the pace. The idea of the crew covering those last four kilometres together was now long gone, and I needed another plan. CT said that she was going to drop back with her mum and dad; Chris was 70 and only a year removed from a double knee replacement, and wasn't necessarily up for the four-kilometre run either. As CT drifted back, I picked up the pace, and the jostling stopped; those who could hold the pace were runners and showed respect for space and what we were doing.

We didn't really have a plan for the end of the run, but I knew that what was unfolding was not it. As we rounded the lake that sits behind Baan Tharn Namchai, I could see another large group of people off to the side of the road waiting to welcome us home, and about 100 metres beyond that group I could see the rooftop of Baan Tharn Namchai. I hatched a cunning plan right there. As we got to the new group of people, I stopped in the middle of the road, turned to face those running beside me and stretched my arms out, stopping the entire group. It was just like back in my early police days of crowd control. I wouldn't let anyone pass, and quickly the Thais caught on and assisted. Then, I spotted one of the yellow shirts from our team in the crowd and called them forward. First came Jack and Kels, then Greg and Jules. Am, Bew and Claire arrived, along with Squid and Mother, and CT and Chris. We had everyone; the team was back together, all dressed in our yellow shirts. I asked everyone to hold hands and form a line across the road. Then, as a team, we walked the last 100 metres together. No sponsors or supporters were in front of us – they understood what was happening and followed us into Baan Tharn Namchai. We turned the last corner together and 25 metres in front of us saw an archway of inflated balloons, scores of people lining the side of the road, all of the kids from Baan Tharn Namchai dressed in their Run to Remember shirts, and

The final day

the finishing tape held out across the archway. We would finish this run as we started: together.

As the team passed under the archway of balloons and broke the finishers tape, we raised our arms in ecstasy and in celebration of what we had achieved together. There was an explosion of confetti, which filled the air and then rained down upon us. There was noise, there was cheering, yet there was this space that was just for us. We came together for what would be our last group huddle. It was filled with emotion, tears and the pure joy of what we had all achieved. When we started on 1 December, the call was, "Together we can"; now, 26 days later, it was, "Together we did". We did it: 1400 kilometres in 26 days.

An enormous amount of planning had gone into the run. The quite literally thousands of turns we had taken, the kilometres run, the temples visited had all been planned. Very little was unpredicted or unplanned on the run. However, I had put zero consideration or effort into what the finish would look like. Even the location of the finish was up in the air: would we finish at Baan Tharn Namchai or continue down south to the actual tsunami memorial? I wasn't attached to either and was open to whichever felt right on the day. However, given the timing and the events of the day, Baan Tharn Namchai was absolutely the right place to finish. As I write this months after the completion of the run, when I consider crossing the finish line, I can't think of a better way to celebrate the finish than how we did it, crossing together as one team. For something that I had given zero planning or consideration to, it couldn't have been more perfect.

Many had doubted my ability to get this done. Prior to the start, some had said in a polite way, "That's optimistic". My mate Dr Sean Richardson, who works with elite athletes, had said, "That would put you in the elite category of ultra endurance athletes". Even within the crew there were doubters. But from the moment I started, I never considered anything but finishing, and I know in my heart of hearts that CT shared that belief. Even in the darkest of times during the run, I know she believed, and I felt it. I will never be able to effectively articulate what this run meant to me, nor will I be able to convey the love that I feel for CT and the support she shows me.

After lunch at Baan Tharn Namchai, our team drove to the hotel where we would spend our final few days in Thailand. CT and I entered our hotel room, and there was silence. It would take some time to come down from the emotion and energy of the day, and it would take months to process. The hotel staff at the Avani+ had put together a congratulations sign on the bed that read "1400km in 26 days", and they had some nice photos of the run that they had framed for us. It was really touching. There was an ice bucket filled with beers as a gift, and CT and I enjoyed our first beer together since I had given up alcohol in February. To be honest, it wasn't all that special, and I hadn't missed it. But if the beer was a bit anticlimactic, the water pressure in the shower was not. Not since the halfway point in Hua Hin had we enjoyed a shower like this.

Sitting in the air-conditioned room, just the two of us, there was nothing left to do. The running had been done. There was no need to wash clothes and prepare for another day on the road. I didn't feel the need to go through my recovery process. We just sat and shared a quiet moment of reflection.

Behind every step: a crew's-eye view

Greg Wallace, runner

The finish was gradual and progressive. Peter's and my last day running together was a kind of finish. Pete's family joining, then my family joining, then Mae Thiew departing were all small finishes; then, some of the kids from Baan Tharn Namchai joined, past and present, and with Christmas thrown in it felt like each of the last five to six days of the run was a mini-finish in its own right. Even the final day had three finishes: our last water stop on the edge of Takua Pa, our last time together as an R2R team before the temple finish, then the cacophony, love, celebration and welcome of the temple finish before a procession stage with a sea of people – and a police escort the last handful of kilometres to Baan Tharn Namchai. Those last few days also featured roads I had ridden and run before, and there was something "full circle" about that for me personally.

A progressive finish allowed me to enjoy a steady emotional release rather than a massive finish-line eruption. It was a gradual unburdening. Simply put, it felt great.

Our team worked well together, falling into roles as the run developed. Yes, we had challenges from time to time and occasional hiccups, but nothing insurmountable. It's always how you adapt that makes the difference.

Considering our team of 11, with a mix of cultures and experiences, lived together for 26 days in a bubble (a very long bubble), in a different hotel for all but the last few nights, in vehicles all day together, we all coped and worked off each other surprisingly well. All in all, the team delivered, and that's what made R2R possible: good times with good people doing good.

I felt so good throughout, with the exception of injuring my leg (an overused tendon – who'd have thought?) and then reinjuring it on day 23. Fresh food, days of outdoors, a relaxed and wonderful environment and being in my happy place all contributed to an incredible feeling of wellbeing and health. Day after day, road after road, village after village, hotel after hotel, being away brought a real sense of freedom and adventure. I crave those feelings, and the run rekindled how much I crave them.

Together, we helped Peter. Together, we achieved something special. Together, we did some good. Would I do it again? In a heartbeat.

Jules with our Thai team and the Run to Remember board, crossing off the days.

Above: Surprise birthday cake on the road with our Thailand team.
Below left: Mae Thiew and Am. Below right: Smiles with CT as we realise we might just have pulled it off.

Running on the 24th of December with Jack and Kels. It was Jack's birthday and both the kids would run 48km with me that day.

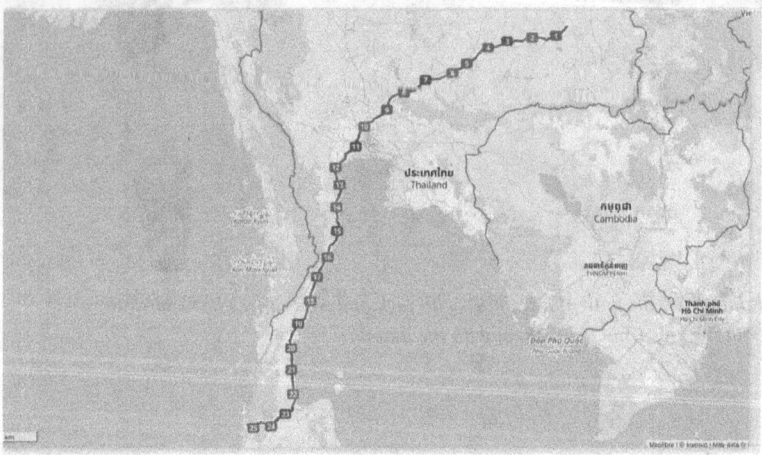

Above: Final day – 15km until the run is over. Below: Looks like a long way on the map.

Above: Mae Thiew, a constant shadow and guardian angel. Below: With CT, Kels and Jack, 2km to Baan Tharn Namchai.

Above: The end! and the celebrations begin. Below: At Baan Tharn Namchai, the whole crew and Kels and Jack.

25

The darkness of succeeding

The international deployments I was fortunate to experience during my time in the police – Bali after the bombings and Thailand after the tsunami – were followed by the return to normal life and the struggle to find purpose and meaning. Bali was less of a personal challenge, as the deployment was much shorter, and I returned to lead the state forensic response to a deadly bushfire season, one crisis replaced with another. Thailand, well, that was different.

As I have said many times, nothing in my life remained the same after my time there – everything that was important and that mattered changed. I returned home after the final tour to the reality of my new life, and I would have happily returned to Thailand to escape it. What followed was a dark and somewhat destructive period personally, the legacy and regret of which I carry today.

How, after leading an international team into the world's largest response to loss of life from a natural disaster, do you find meaning and purpose? Where does it come from? I went into a dark place, and it impacted all levels of my life. I don't suggest it was post-traumatic stress disorder, as I have seen many mates from my forensic days suffer from that, and that was far more acute than what I was experiencing. I think the best way to describe it is as the worst case of post-holiday blues you can imagine, and then multiply that by the power of ten – not quite clinically diagnosable, but we're getting close.

It wouldn't be the last time I would experience the depths of post-holiday blues. I found early on when returning from the annual bike rides in Thailand for Hands that I was experiencing the same type of feelings. Admittedly, and thankfully, not to the same extent as after working in Thailand, but I was certainly questioning my purpose and meaning in the weeks after the rides. Part of the self-prescribed solution was to prepare and launch the next annual ride so the countdown was on once again and the focus could shift, and I could kick the can of misery down the road. Even the high from delivering a kickarse keynote presentation and receiving a standing ovation can be replaced by an almost instant low. Perhaps it says something about my big ego and low self-esteem.

Knowing the run would be big and suspecting there was a good chance of the dark cloud of misery returning after the run was over, I did what I could to prepare for and manage it. I spent many hours on Zoom with sports psychologist Domonique Doyle talking through all aspects of the run. It was with her that I formulated the communication protocols for the run so the team was clear who among them would have the tough conversations with me should I find myself in difficulty and we needed to suspend or, worst-case scenario, abandon the run. We talked about the post-run experience, and her work with elite athletes positioned her well to forecast what I might experience when it all came to an end – she had seen it in other athletes when the bell rings and it's time to call it quits.

Of course, many of the clients Dom has worked with dedicated their lives to their sport; I had dedicated two years out of 58, which was not really in the same ballpark. We both thought that because I had experienced these blues before, because I was dialled into it, that there was a real chance I might, if not avoid it, then perhaps mitigate the impact.

Oh, how wrong I was.

The second morning after the run, I returned from breakfast and sat on the bed in my hotel room, and thought, "Well, what the fuck was that all about?" I didn't feel any sense of elation, pride or even achievement. I didn't feel much at all. Here I was, within 40 hours of completing what was, without question, the biggest physical endeavour of my life, and I felt pretty numb to it. My phone was flooded with beautiful messages of congratulations, and I read them and believed the sentiments they conveyed, but I didn't feel them inside. Deep within my soul – a place that is not open to see, a place that no one can judge because they only know what I tell them about it – there were no positive feelings about what I had done. As my mood parked itself in a dark corner with no signs of coming out, I kept saying to CT, "Can you imagine how dark I would be if I *hadn't* finished the run!" That thought actually scares me.

The surprise was not that I had some "down times"; the surprise was how swiftly the darkness descended. I really didn't give myself a chance to enjoy the moment. What we had achieved was massive. I still struggle to comprehend that we actually pulled it off, and I regret now that I didn't give myself the chance to enjoy the afterglow.

Our return flight from Thailand back to Sydney was on 30 December. I'd wanted to have a couple of days to rest, enjoy a massage and just wind down a little bit. Part of me had also wanted to have a few days up my sleeve in case things went really pear-shaped and I couldn't finish on 26 December, so I could still get the run done before departing Thailand. I hadn't shared that with anyone as I didn't want it to be something that we could default to; it had to be a last-resort option. We also didn't want to hang around too long in Thailand as we had to return on 15 January, just over two weeks after finishing the run, to lead an 800-kilometre, eight-day charity bike ride. It was a sellout ride, and we would both be back riding.

Returning home from the run, we landed in Sydney and the team of people who had supported each other for a month was no more. The bubble had burst, we were back, and like it or not we were about to re-engage with lives that didn't involve running 60 kilometres a day. CT headed north to our home in Terrigal on the Central Coast, and I drove directly to our farm in the Capertee Valley to relieve our dogsitters, who had been looking after Burton and Frankie for a month. After a warm welcome from the dogs, I spent an afternoon on the lounge, binging Netflix and drifting in and out of sleep. I spent the next ten days working to restore Wildnest, our glamping business, to something we could be proud of, which meant time on the tractor slashing paddocks, hours on the ride-on mower and hours with the chainsaw restocking wood for the guests' fire pits.

The messages that came to my phone in the weeks that followed typically followed the same thread: "How is the recovery going? How's the body? Any sign of coming off the runners high yet?" Well, the physical recovery was almost immediate. When I stopped running for a couple of days, the shin pain calmed down, my knee stopped yelling at me and went back to doing what it is supposed to do, and the desire to run returned pretty quickly. Physically, I was fine. When I saw people who had followed the journey, their initial comment was always, "You look so well". I wasn't sure what they expected. Perhaps they were expecting a replica of Forrest Gump when he stops running and has a beard down to his chest. I felt good and was physically in the best shape of my life. But emotionally, the struggle was real. I was extremely fragile. If I saw a puppy with sad eyes, I would start crying. If I had any type of meaningful conversation, if any kind words came my way, I broke. I had a bit over a week after the run without exercise and on the 7th of January Kels and I headed out for a run and it was a weird feeling taking those first steps. It was almost as though I had forgotten how to run, but it came back, slowly. I spoke with Matty after the run and his advice to me was to take it really slow, that my body and mind might take six months to recover and I should run for pleasure now rather than because I had to. Rather than heading out because I "should", run when I felt like it and enjoy it. I had achieved what I set out to do and now it was time to rest and recover.

The weeks between the run finishing and returning to Thailand for the next bike ride were strange, and not just for me: I know that CT and the other members of the crew struggled with what it all meant. CT and I were very much in a quiet, reflective state, and time at the farm served us really well. We could sit in silence and stare out at the cattle moving through the paddock without needing to fill that time with words. We both retreated inwards as we tried to comprehend what we had achieved. Without question, we were grieving what we had lost. As the time since the end of the run increased, so too did our awareness of how unique the experience had been. We missed the routine, the rhythm of each day, the pain and the struggle, and the reward that came when I stopped for the day. Our days weren't finishing with Andra Day and her incredible voice inviting us to "Rise Up". CT wasn't sharing a Leo beer with her dad and the crew and she wasn't sticking needles in my feet, and we missed every goddamn part of it.

December had been about giving on every level, not just physically but emotionally. I felt as though I recovered well from the physical output, but emotionally, mentally, that was different.

I think we also recognised that the two weeks we had at home was only an intermission. Returning to Thailand for the ride, we needed to be present; we needed to be the face of Hands Across the Water and celebrate the 20 years of Hands's presence in Thailand. When planning the run some two years prior, I had reached out to Dr Sean Richardson to ask when I should place the ride in relation to the run, and his response was that I should create as much time as possible between the two events so I could recover from the run and prepare for the ride. As it turned out, the three weeks between the final day of the run and the first day of the 800-kilometre bike ride was the perfect amount of time. It was long enough to return to Australia and have some quiet, reflective time, but wasn't so long that I felt idle. Upon reflection, I really feel like the ride offered the circuit-breaker I needed to shift out of the dark place I had ventured into after the run.

26

Reflections from the bike

We were back at Sydney International Airport on 15 January, just over two weeks since we had returned from the Run to Remember. I sat in the airport lounge and reflected on how I'd felt last time I was there at the end of November, heading over for the run with Finn. My thoughts then were around the potential success or failure of the run. One of the two was guaranteed. What I came to learn was that fear sits with us before we start, but once we are on our way, we become consumed by the doing, and the fear drifts away. Now, six weeks later, I could sit in the lounge and smile internally knowing that failure had not visited the run; indeed, it had been an outstanding success. Now, I could return to the exact same roads I had run and reflect on the experience we had shared and the remarkable gift the run had been.

The January 2025 Ride to Provide from Bangkok to Khao Lak would be my 40th Hands ride in Thailand, but I hadn't given it much thought due to all the attention I was giving to the run. For the couple of years that I was planning the run, my road bike sat sadly in the garage like a forgotten child. I would see it each time I went to the car, but I pretended it was just a collection of carbon fibre, alloy and rubber rather than something that had feelings, and it was feeling neglected, I could tell. There was a period when I was riding upwards of 10,000 kilometres a year at home, and it is fair to say that I loved my bike and my time on it. I used to shun all other forms of transport when I could and elect to ride my bike to meetings, hunting out showers, attending the meeting and then riding home the long way just to get extra time on my bike. It was something that CT and I mutually enjoyed, and each weekend we would ride and then stop for coffee and a bacon and egg roll somewhere on the Northern Beaches.

Our first Hands ride was in 2009, with 17 riders, and every year until COVID-19 we enjoyed year-on-year growth. We started with one ride in January each year, which became a staple of our income, and grew to multiple rides a year as businesses saw the benefits of spending quality time with their teams or clients and enlisted us to deliver a ride just for them. I made a habit of joining as many of the corporate rides as my diary allowed.

In the early years, I would train in the lead-up to a Hands ride, because riding 800 kilometres was just such a massive endeavour. Then, when our January rides started to sell out due to demand, we offered a northern ride at the beginning of the month and a southern ride at the end of the month, separated by two days off the bike as we relocated the team and bikes. Riding for 1600 kilometres over 16 days just seemed so big. Until it wasn't.

When my focus shifted to the run, I only spent time on the bike during the corporate rides in Thailand. I could turn up and, apart from a bit of discomfort from not having sat on a bike seat for several months, my riding legs would return and I could keep pace with the front riders. Knowing that I didn't need to train to complete a 800-kilometre ride meant I didn't spend time on the bike in between tours, devoting that time to running instead. I also felt that running offered a better return on investment of time: a two-hour ride was the minimum I would head out for and meant somewhere between 50 and 60 kilometres covered, which to be honest didn't require a huge investment of energy, but two hours running was a half-marathon.

The ride group departed Bangkok on the morning of 17 January and headed to Phetchaburi, where we would saddle up and start the journey south. For probably 85% of the ride, we would be following the exact route I had taken on the run a few weeks prior. It was going to be a "lap of honour" of sorts.

We set off on the first morning and straight away picked up the route that I had just run. As we rode past temples and service stations, CT and I recognised points where we had stopped on the run, some good and some not so good. "That was a tough stop at that temple," CT commented as we slid past another one.

The reflections from the bike seat were, in the main, super positive. How could they not be? We were passing key places from the run at 25 kilometres an hour and covering double the distance in a day than what I had done on the run, with plenty of time at the end of each day for a swim in the pool and relaxation.

The first day was a bit of an introductory ride covering only 60 kilometres. The second morning, we left the town of Hua Hin, and everyone was in great spirits. We very quickly picked up the route of day 14 of the run, when things had gone pear-shaped. I shared stories and chatted about the run with the riders around me. Then, at a point on the road where I had found myself in distress during the run, I felt the need to ride on my own. I allowed the riders I was with to drift ahead as I slowed to create some personal space. I could feel with great clarity the emotion and the pain of day 14 as I turned the corner onto the road that ran parallel to the beach. I rode without the pain and concern I had felt that day, knowing now how it had turned out, but it was quite an emotional experience to be back so soon after the run riding that stretch of road that had posed the greatest threat to its completion.

Riding along the beachfront, I was surprised by how far I had run that day in such distress. There were no tears and snot running down my face as there had been that day, but it was an emotional ride nonetheless as the kilometres slipped by. I rode at quite a gentle pace, and I could see a gathering of riders ahead who had arrived at the water stop before me. The water stop was an idyllic beach with the gentle waves crashing on the sand only metres from the road's edge. It was picked for a concrete parking area that allowed the vehicles to park off the road, not that there was much traffic to be concerned about. It was the exact place that the run support team had picked for the water stop on day 14.

Of course, no one on the ride knew the significance of this place or the leg leading up to it. The support team for the ride had picked the spot for no other reason than it was an appropriate place to stop, the same as the run team. Arriving at the spot, CT quickly sought me out to give me a hug and check how I felt about returning. I was happy to be there in very different circumstances, but I also wanted to leave. The energy of that water stop didn't feel good, and I needed to get on my bike, both metaphorically and literally.

My body held up really well throughout the ride, and the time on the bike was the therapy I needed to lift my languishing mental state after the fatigue of the previous month and the obvious comedown from the run. I certainly looked at the route through a new lens, and I am not sure that will change with time. Riding for four days, enjoying a rest day and then riding for a further four days felt somewhat luxurious compared to the run, but it was important I didn't transfer that thought process onto the riders – for them, eight days of cycling was significant. Before the end of March, I would return and ride those roads twice more on corporate rides, and the run was ever-present to me.

27

The three outcomes revisited

As I mentioned in chapter 9, there were three clear objectives for the run:

1. to raise awareness of Hands in Thailand
2. to raise $1 million
3. to undertake something epic on a personal level in acknowledgement of the 20 years since the tsunami.

1. Raising awareness

The fun run in Bangkok attracted a great turnout. Having the Governor in attendance and committing to return the following year ensured that local media were also in attendance. The event gave us the opportunity to present to the runners the brand of Hands, which no doubt they were seeing for the first time, and it also gave us an opportunity to showcase our Thailand-based sponsors, some of which took up the opportunity and maximised it.

The idea had been that I would run the nine-kilometre loop with the runners. However, given the calamity of day 14 on the road, I made the very easy decision that the best thing for me to do on the morning of day 15 was to rest my leg and cheer in the runners as they crossed the line. I found this a whole lot more enjoyable anyway, and I was even questioning my decision to run the 1400 kilometres at all. Why didn't I get someone else to run it, and I could meet them at the end and hold the finishers tape? That was looking a whole lot easier than the situation I had found myself in!

If we were to be marked on the amount of awareness created by the run overall, would I consider it a success? I am not sure. Whether we moved the needle in terms of the level of brand recognition of Hands in Thailand, I just don't know. During the 2025 Australia Day celebrations in Thailand, I was identified as one of the top five most influential Australians in Thailand, but how that translates, I'm not too sure either.

2. Fundraising

CT was the custodian of our marketing and communications on the ground during the run, on top of all the other roles she had to keep us heading towards the finish line, and she did an amazing job. As part of that, she continued to put forward the case for our fundraising drive, and people responded. We had both small and large donations, but every donation was appreciated, regardless of its size. The majority of the donations came from Australia, and many from long-time supporters of Hands.

We had set up a trigger through the Hands website, which was the portal for the donations coming in, so that I would receive an email alert every time someone donated to the run. My commitment prior to the run was to personally write to every donor thanking them for their donation. I had been doing something similar for all donations above a certain limit that came into Hands for the bike rides, and I often heard how people appreciated and were surprised to hear from me. Some people wrote back to me directly and others wrote to who they were supporting to let them know how touching and rare it was to hear from me as the founder thanking them for their donation. I kept on top of this commitment in the lead-up to the run. No matter the size of the donation, I sent the donor a personal email that I typed myself, unique to them, and sent it off. It wasn't done by a remote team or AI, and it didn't come from a template. I could have put a few of those systems in place, but it was important to me to connect with the donors and personally thank them. However, once I started the run I realised I just couldn't commit to that, and rather than sending emails I needed to focus on the recovery process.

That didn't mean the commitment was gone, though – it was just delayed. Within three days of finishing the run, I had personally written to everyone who had donated in the ten days prior to the run, and within a week of finishing the run I had personally written to every single person who had made a donation during the run. Whether they acknowledged the email or not was irrelevant; I took pride in writing to everyone with a personal email. They had donated to the cause, and the emails felt like the least I could do in return.

Heading over to Thailand with $300,000 banked, I didn't know where the fundraising would go from there. CT worked as hard as she could to keep the donations rolling in, and there were some activities on the ground in Bangkok that would continue to bring funds in, such as the fun run. We missed opportunities in Australia, where Hands is registered as a foundation, to build momentum through events at home, and this was particularly disappointing given the presence and resources we had and the opportunity that existed. However, while there were disappointments, there was also plenty to celebrate. Our small team of three in the Philippines – Airene, Adrian and Andrea – held their own fun run, met the out-of-pocket costs themselves and raised funds in support of the big run. Their belief, commitment and enthusiasm mean even more than the money they raised.

As the run progressed, we expected to see a rise in donations, and that was certainly the case. Passing $400,000 and then $500,000 were certainly milestones to celebrate. It did become clear, though, that without a massive surge in donations we were going to fall short of our target of $1 million. We ended up raising just north of $670,000 from the run. If we had stuck with the original target of $500,000, we would have been celebrating the overachievement, but here we were somewhat disappointed we didn't hit our goal. Were we happy with raising $670,000, though? Absolutely. If it was a failure then, as my mate Hilly described it, it was a "pretty spectacular failure".

In the months after the run, I spent time reflecting on the fundraising. I am not sure what we could or should have done differently to reach the goal. I could have worked harder on fundraising, I could have invested more time and sent more proposals, but I had to find a balance as to where I committed my time during the year. In the lead-up to the run, it was easy to kick the can a bit further down the road and convince myself that things would change significantly once the run was underway, and that was true to a degree.

It's fair to say I was disappointed with the response from some of the largest Australian companies operating in Thailand, who shunned the initiative, dismissing it out of hand. These companies draw a significant profit from their operations in Thailand, benefiting from the low wages they pay there in comparison to Australia, yet they ignored the opportunity to give back to those very communities from which their workforce may have originated or where they may have family connections.

I was hoping for an increase in donations from within Thailand after the Bangkok fun run, but that never eventuated. If I had to identify a reason for us falling short here, it would be that my personal profile was not big enough or of enough interest to those not already connected to Hands.

Something I have been working towards ever since 2011, with the establishment of our first social enterprise, is the generation of commercial income into the foundation. I have always seen it as an opportunity to increase funding for the charity and reduce reliance on donations as the sole source of income, which ties a charity's success to the will and discretion of its donors. We have long moved away from this model with the charity bike rides and the commercial activities we run. Of course, the benefits of these activities extend well beyond the increased funds: they bring people closer to the charity as well as meeting a need that exists within them. For example, many participants in our bike rides come back time after time because of the shared experience and the value they personally take from the ride. If they weren't enjoying the tour, if it wasn't food for their soul, they wouldn't ride, and we wouldn't receive the charity funds they raise.

A big step towards increased funding and opportunities for our kids – and, indeed, the broader community – are two projects I am looking to fund from the Run to Remember. The first is a hospitality training centre, which will operate from a building Hands funded the construction of back in 2011. It was established at the time as a community centre and has operated as a childcare centre for those in the local community. With 15 individual accommodation rooms at the centre, our plan is to turn it into an operating hotel servicing the lower end of the market. However, it will be much more than a hotel. In collaboration with a hotel partner, we will operate the centre as a training venue for students looking to enter this sector. It won't be just for the kids from our homes; it will be open to the broader community. I see it as an option for the students who have no desire or will to attend university. It won't operate to provide training for the sake of a qualification; it will only provide training in those areas where the industry has identified a resource gap. Right now, that is across the board.

We see the hospitality training centre as a direct pathway to employment that students might not otherwise receive in a more formal or traditional training program. It will meet the needs identified by the local industry in closing the gaps in training and staff while better utilising a resource we have and generating income. There are, of course, many hospitality training centres already in existence in Thailand; the difference here is that the profits from the centre will flow back into the foundation, and it will have a very low barrier to entry for the students. It will allow them to quickly move into paid employment rather than having to complete a four-year university degree. (That can come later, should they choose.)

The second project that will benefit from the funds generated through the Run will be an agricultural learning centre. The governor of the local province first approached Hands to see if we would be interested in utilising land 15 minutes out of Khao Lak to further our work. The concept is not too dissimilar to that of the hospitality training centre: we will conduct operations that meet the needs of the local community while at the same time providing training and employment for those interested in agriculture as a vocation. We are working in collaboration with a global company to build infrastructure that will meet the needs of the community and maximise the unique opportunity before us.

Both of these projects reflect our commitment to provide a life of choice and brighter futures not just for our kids, but the broader community in which we are located.

So, were our fundraising efforts a success? Not reaching the target left me feeling somewhat disappointed, but as Hilly said, raising $670,000 was "a pretty spectacular failure". The other thing I take comfort from is that only a few weeks after the conclusion of the run, we were back in Thailand for our annual charity bike ride, which raised in excess of $500,000. Perhaps on this occasion I was marking myself too hard.

3. My personal challenge

Of the three reasons for taking on the run, I think it's fair to say that it was the personal challenge that drove me to the finish line. To take on something as big as running 33 marathons in 26 days through Thailand, I needed a strong team and a very clear reason for starting, and that had to be rock solid to see me through the difficult times both in the lead-up and during the run.

It's without question that I didn't realise the enormity of the run until I was on the ground, and even after I completed it, the scale of it took time to process. Setting the start and finish points for the run had been straightforward, and the distance was just what it was. If the distance had been more or less, that's what I would have run – the length of the run and the time to complete it weren't particularly important to me as long as it was completed within that 26-day window I had given myself. I never went into the run with an eye on setting any type of records, it was just a matter of getting from Baan Home Hug to Baan Tharn Namchai – no other start and end points made sense.

In the lead-up to the run, in that time between lights out and drifting off to sleep, I thought about the run. I could visualise the days of running, and particularly the southern half of the run because I had ridden it so many times. Since 2009, I had been riding the route from Bangkok to Khao Lak, down the Gulf of Thailand, across the mountains that led to the Andaman Sea, so it was easy to visualise running the roads as I closed my eyes. I visualised the finish each night – not the celebration at the end but how I would feel getting it done.

Of course, I also spent time considering how it could come apart, how I would respond to not finishing, but that didn't occupy too much of my headspace. In the three weeks prior to the run, the feeling that everything was unravelling due to my leg infection kept me awake. The fact I couldn't run during this time was certainly less than ideal, but I quickly got to a place of deep gratitude that I could in fact fly to Thailand and start the run, because that was certainly not a given for a while there. I knew the lead-in wasn't great, but I would sort it out once I was there.

The lack of a good lead-in was evident by the end of day one and reinforced by the extra time it took to complete day two. I was a lot slower than I had planned and did a lot more walking than I had hoped. But I was OK with that; after all, it was a 26-day event and I had time to warm into it. There was no prize for finishing early, I wasn't chasing a record, and it was never about setting an FKT (fastest known time) for the run.

The second day on the road was tough. In some of our final chats before the run, Matty had shared with me that people who start these ultra endurance events and pull out often do so within the first couple of days.

"The first three days will be tough, mate," he said. "Get through those and things will get easier."

But even in those tough first days of the run, I never thought about anything other than finishing the run. It never entered my mind that I was going to be one of the runners who pulled out within the first three days. I just didn't think of it at all. It didn't take a concerted effort to suppress the negative thoughts, because there just weren't any. I did feel better, though, once I had made it through those first three days to know that I hadn't been one of those runners. I just couldn't do that to the team, to the brand of Hands or to myself.

I expected that I would walk out of the hotel on day four and things would be easier, because that was what Matty had said. Well, it didn't get immediately easier, but it certainly didn't get harder.

As the days slipped by, I would, of course, face really hard times on the road, but I knew they would pass, as did the good times. The hard times were all part of the journey, and in some strange way, I had been looking forward to them.

Even on day 14, when I ran through the most pain I have ever experienced while running, still the thought of withdrawing wasn't something I needed to address. I was deep in thought about how I would get through the day, but that was all I needed to overcome.

The first time the conversation about not completing the run came up was on Christmas Day, as the family sat around the table enjoying a unique Christmas lunch. Chris said to me, "Can I ask you, at what point did you truly believe you would make the finish line?"

I didn't need a lot of time to think about the answer: "Chris, from day one when we set off, I never thought about anything other than finishing".

I have reflected on this a lot since finishing. It wasn't arrogance, and as someone who lacks a lot of self-confidence, I found this mindset so left of field from how I would normally go into something like this. I have gone into plenty of ultramarathons wondering if I would finish and dreading a DNF (did not finish) against my name, but here I was signed up for 26 days of running back-to-back ultras and somehow I had the self-belief I would get it done. I've wondered where the confidence came from, because we don't normally have confidence in our ability to do something until we've done it, and until then questions remain. I think I just wouldn't allow myself to consider not finishing. If the run was something that occurred every year, and I was just a participant who had signed up for it alongside many others, I suspect my mindset would have been different – there would have been the conversation going on in my head that if it didn't work this year, it would be good preparation for next year. It's a bit like the saying in sport, "You have to lose a grand final to know how to win one". But there wasn't ever going to be a second grand final to win if I lost this one. There would be no second opportunity. There was so much invested in *this* run that it just had to succeed. I had spoken publicly about it for a year, the team had flown to Thailand, we had personally invested so much – it just had to work.

If my mindset was focused on success – and I think it is fair to say now that it was – equally important to achieving that success, if not more so, was the contribution of the team. We spent a month on the road in a foreign country, away from all the creature comforts of home, moving every day from hotel to hotel, starting at 4.30 a.m. and finishing around 10 p.m., sometimes later, all in service and support of one thing: getting me to the finish line. Think about the dynamic that creates when you bring 11 people together, not all of whom knew each other, and immerse them in those conditions. It was an act of complete selflessness on their behalf to be there and support me in the choice that I had made to run 1400 kilometres over 26 days. An undeniably massive part of my success was their commitment to the mission I had chosen and their service above self. Whatever went on within the crew – the tears, the words exchanged – was kept from me, and even today, months after finishing the run, I am oblivious to so much. Perhaps it is up to them to write their own story.

28

Every day is a gift

The work that I was involved in for 23 years while employed by the New South Wales Police certainly exposed me to the worst of human behaviour, and the work that I have done since with Hands Across the Water has given me an insight into the best that humanity has to offer. The tragedies I have witnessed have left an impact on me on a molecular level, there is no doubt about that. You don't carry the bodies of dead children in your arms and just get to move on; that shit stays with you, like it or not. I have watched on as many mates I worked with during my forensic days were overcome by post-traumatic stress disorder that they continue to suffer from today, decades on. As I have come to understand from one mate, you're not cured, you just learn to manage it. For some reason I avoided the clinical signs of PTSD, and I now like to view those years as a lesson that each day is a gift. The fact that we are here today is a gift. The friends and family in our lives, they too are a gift.

My time on the road during December 2024 was a gift, the impact of which I will never be able to adequately convey in words. Some things are meant to be hard, and in doing hard things, we grow.

In 2023, I released my third book, *Leadership Matters*. I wrote that book while planning the run, and in it I wrote about the value of doing hard things. I discussed how, from where I sit, many of the problems that exist in society, including the rise in childhood obesity and mental health struggles, are connected to our reduced physical activity, particularly outdoors, and hardship. We build resilience by facing challenges. We develop the ability to make difficult decisions by facing hard times. However, as a society, we continually look to remove risk. We lock our kids inside because of unfounded fears about what will become of them if they are out adventuring on their own or with their mates. We live comfortable lives, but to find growth we have to leave comfort behind.

In embracing the run, I had to embrace the lack of certainty that I would complete it. In fact, failure was at least as likely as success. While my mind was fixed on finishing on 26 December, will alone wouldn't get me there, and that was what made it so special.

I know that finishing the run made me physically harder, mentally tougher and sounder on some spiritual level. The needle has shifted, and I don't know that it will ever return to where it was. My definition of "hard" has changed. My limits have changed. With this new perspective, though, comes the responsibility not to impose it on others.

The first time I recognised this was between tours of Thailand back in 2005. A violent storm had passed through our suburb, and as it moved on and the rain eased, the neighbours came out onto the cul-de-sac to assess the damage. Our neighbours two doors up had a three-storey house with a very steep pitched roof, and a branch from a massive gum tree had broken off during the storm and gone through the roof, leaving a large hole and an entry point for the rain that continued to fall. The assembled neighbours were concerned that the rain would ruin the furniture of our neighbours, who were away at the time, and that we should do something. I told them not to worry, noting that the height and pitch of the roof meant nobody was climbing it in the dry, let alone the rain. "But the rain will ruin the carpet and Angie's bed," said one of the neighbours, to which I responded, "Don't worry, that's what insurance is for". My wife then said, "Just because there aren't thousands of people dead doesn't mean this isn't important". She was right, it was important, and it would be devastating to the family when they arrived home, but perspective is a funny thing.

Riding in January with 50 other riders, I needed to remember, particularly for first-time riders who were scared shitless about what lay ahead, that for some, the ride they were about to embark on would be the hardest thing they would ever do, and I couldn't take that away from them by comparing it to the run. They hardest thing you will do is the hardest thing you will do.

During the reflection session that we hold with the riders at Wat Yan Yao before we ride into Baan Tharn Namchai, we invite the riders to share their "high, low and what they are grateful for". It's a beautiful time when each rider takes their turn to share. There are always tears, and there are always lessons. At one of the corporate rides I participated in shortly after the run, one of the riders said, "My high was having Peter join us for the ride; it was unexpected and such a privilege". Looking at me, she said, "I have been watching you on this ride and I am just amazed at how calm you are about everything. Nothing seems to faze you". What she was witnessing was the new perspective through which I was viewing things. The run, in all its messiness and beauty, has given me so much. Physically, I am unlikely to take on anything anywhere near the size and scale of the Run to Remember ever again. However, whatever I do from this point forward, I know my physical limitations are well beyond what I thought they were. I know I am capable of more than I believed, and mentally I have risen up when I could have stayed down.

So, what's next?

It's an interesting question that people often ask after hearing the story of the run. Is it an assessment that what I've done isn't big enough, that I can't be satisfied with the run, that I must do more? Is it a reflection that we can never be satisfied with what we have or have done? Does it come from an expectation that we should always be looking for "what's next"? Or, am I overthinking it, and it is just similar to a greeting like, "G'day, how are you going?" Interestingly, nobody had ever asked me that question until after I had completed the run, and now it's a common question I'm asked.

So, what *is* next?

Well, nothing.

Nothing that will rival the Run to Remember, that's for sure. I guess some people take on runs like what I did in Thailand because they love the challenge of doing something massive. They love the thought of chasing a goal: to be the fastest across a known distance or the first to run an epic route, to go alone, to go further, to go where no one has gone before. Since my run I have become more aware of these amazing athletes, and I guess that's where the assumption comes from that there will be a "next", because for these people it is about the pursuit – I assume.

I can't know, as that's not my reason. My reason for the run was to acknowledge the 20-year anniversary of the Boxing Day tsunami and the massive impact it had on my life. There was, of course, the chance to raise money and awareness of Hands, but not for one minute have I pretended there wasn't something hugely personal about this run. But it was never about the speed, the distance or any other metric. The distance, 1400 kilometres, just happened to be the distance from Baan Home Hug to Baan Tharn Namchai, and as I have said, if I could have found a shorter route, I would have taken it.

Is the fact that I have no grand plans to take on something equal or bigger than the run a reflection of the experience? Well, no. The Run to Remember was, for me, a time and place. The time was the 20-year anniversary, and of course the place was Thailand, and Baan Tharn Namchai specifically. How could I possibly recreate the meaning behind that? Perhaps the reason I never considered not finishing was the time and place: this was a one-time opportunity. Now, my focus lies in other areas.

If you want to gain an insight into the experience of the run and what it meant to me, a better question might be, "Would you do it again?" My answer to this question has never changed: "In a heartbeat". It was, hands down, the best experience of my life. Being on the road with those who matter most in my life was an experience that I just can't imagine ever being surpassed. The memories of the experience are only growing stronger, and months on from the run I still feel a level of fragility when I speak about the experience, such was its depth and the change it has brought to my life. And I know it has impacted others as well. Every now and then CT will text me, "I miss the run". I never could have predicted the positive impact the experience would have. It confirms for me that the purest of rewards lies at the end of sacrifice and struggle. The bigger the sacrifice, the greater the struggle, the deeper the reward.

I have mentioned how the last ten kilometres of each day was always the fastest. I should have been at my sorest and weakest coming to the end of another 60 kilometres on the road, but instead I was at my strongest. At the end of each day on the road, I was full of extreme gratitude: for those who had chosen to be there in support of my run, for the strength and good fortune that had allowed me to complete another day and for being another day closer to completing this journey. Each day, as I crossed the imaginary finish line, I would be greeted by each of the nine members of the team for a sweaty but enduring hug, the type that squeezes a little bit of breath out of you, the type that says, "I've got you, I feel you". The type of hug that says, "Together we can; together we will; together we did".

I play that song "Rise Up" as part of the backing track to a video in my new keynote, and for that moment when I am on stage, I am taken back to the time on the road, and it is such a precious and personal time. I also play it when I want a moment of deep reflection, and whenever I hear it, I can feel CT's arms wrap around me. I can feel her love in that hug, and I feel like the luckiest man alive to have had this experience with those who chose to share it with me, either on the road, watching and cheering on from home, or just holding me in their thoughts. To these people: thank you for being part of the Run to Remember, because I felt your presence throughout the journey.

29

The moments – oh, so many moments

The run was the best thing I have ever done in my life. Without question. I miss it every day and continue to grieve the loss of the time on the road, and if I could return and do it all again tomorrow, I would be there.

Since finishing the run, I have been asked many times in conversations, on podcasts and in interviews on stage for my top ten moments of the run. Well, here they are.

1. The strength of the relationships

I knew from previous experiences that relationships have a way of going to a new level when adversity is faced. I returned from the run having never felt closer to CT, Chris, Wendy and, indeed, the entire team. We shared experiences that no one else can ever understand. It was a privilege and a gift. However, it wasn't just me who benefited from this – connections also formed within our Thai crew, between Squid and Mother, Am and everyone, and Bew and Claire. One of the most unlikely relationships that I took great pleasure in watching grow was between Mae Thiew and Rod Reid, who joined us for the final five days as part of the film crew. At every stop you would see the two of them sitting on the grass on the side of the road in deep conversation. She has such depth to her, and when people immerse themselves in that, it brings me joy.

2. The hugs

I've always been a hugger; I consider it a demonstration of connection and love. But the sweaty hugs at the end of each day of the run just said so much more. Jules was an outstanding hugger, as was CT, but from a "right time, right place" perspective the hug from Chris at the end of day 14 tops them all.

3. The "this is Thailand" moments

One of the strangest moments of the run had to be when Greg, Alison and I ran straight through the middle of an active mine site. The road that served as the perimeter of the mine site was too narrow and busy to entertain running on. As we headed into the mine site, it got more and more bizarre that nobody stopped us. The security guards took their handheld radios from their holsters and called back to command, but either they didn't know what to do with us or didn't care. We were sure we would be turned around and sent back to where we had come from until suddenly we were out the other side. Only in Thailand.

4. The end of each day (not for obvious reasons)

I didn't necessarily enjoy the end of each day because it meant I no longer had to run; it was about the process. It was seeing Squid standing on the road in his Run to Remember shirt (I never saw him without one on) to welcome us in with a high five. It was the sight of the Mothership and the crew, Wendy holding the camera to capture us, and then the sound of Andra Day singing "Rise Up". And, of course, it was the hugs. I loved and appreciated what unfolded each evening. Everyone knew their tasks, and the rush of the day was gone. Bew would come to me and help me remove my stinking shoes and socks, Squid would prepare the ice bath, and Claire would coach me through a reflection session as I washed away the pain and grit of the day. One of the things I loved most was watching the crew all share a Leo beer together. Has there ever been a more deserved ice-cold beer? I think not.

5. The support from back home

The Oscar goes to Kelsey Baines, who put together a mini-series of videos to be released on Netflix. CT knew when to pull them out – it was often at lunch or morning tea, when I was pretty low, and the encouragement from home meant the world. The messages on Instagram and Facebook, the personal text messages – I read and responded to as many as I could, and each of them gave me the energy to continue.

6. The team dinners

How Am found some of the places where we ate still boggles the mind, but find them she did. I loved coming together at the end of the day for good, often great food. The crew would have another beer or two while I settled for a coconut or watermelon shake. We laughed, we relived the good, the bad and the ugly of the day, and we set ourselves up to do it all again the next day.

7. Day 14

When I encountered shin splints, the end was uncertain. The pain that I experienced that day was probably an eight out of ten, but continuing to run with that pain for hours took me to newfound territory. Yet, enduring it and rising above it to run along the foreshore and down the driveway of the hotel to complete the day made it the best day on tour. The response from the crew and the hug from Chris that day made it one of the absolute highlights of the entire tour.

8. Witnessing the joy that CT took from her running

Each day when she completed her running, CT would stop, pause her Garmin, take a photo and hug me, and as her distances increased, so too did her strength and enjoyment. I loved what the run gave her, given just how much she was giving to me and everyone else.

9. The finish on day 23

Day 14 delivered a memorable experience that in some way defined the run, but the finish on day 23 was of equal significance. Arriving at the Cliff & River Jungle Resort and walking through the archway, I felt like I was home, and the run felt like it was done. It felt like it couldn't have gotten any better, and yet it did. Surfacing from the pool to see Jack and Kels bolting across the lawn was an experience that I will never forget. It was the ultimate food for my soul, and I would do it all again just to recreate that moment with my kids.

10. The deep personal satisfaction

It was a bloody long way.

Behind every step: a crew's-eye view

CT, Hands CEO, problem-solver, wife

How do you fit a month like that – one of the most defining experiences of your life – into a few thousand words?

What we did in December 2024 was nothing short of epic. The magnitude of it still hits me like a tonne of bricks some days. The emotional and physical weight is hard to describe. The highs. The lows. The exhaustion. The pride. The sense of accomplishment.

But more than anything, it's the ache of wanting to go back. To be there again, in that bubble, with our crew, living some of the best days of our lives.

So, here it is – my reflection. A little messy, full of feeling and written with deep gratitude.

Highs and heartbeats

I am in awe of what Pete achieved over those 26 days. In fact, I'm in awe of his commitment and dedication ever since "that conversation" in September 2022. What an honour to have witnessed such an incredible feat, to have been part of the crew, and to have walked alongside and supported my person to achieve something so great.

What a privilege.

It's a word we would repeatedly chant during the tougher moments on the run, when we needed to remind ourselves why we were there: this adventure was an absolute *privilege*. It really was a once-in-a-lifetime experience.

The standard things people say after something like this are, "I don't know how you could even do that," and, "How did he get through each day?" What people don't ask is, "What were the moments that became the heartbeat of 26 days on the road?"

For me, there are so many moments. There were the simple joys. Dry laundry at the end of the day. A conversation with Pete's coach, Matty, who was analysing the data with me and telling me we were doing a good job. A hotel finish where everyone could cheer Pete in. A quiet moment to myself before Pete finished for the day. Community support as we ran through the towns. Video messages from home (a special shout out to Kelsey's video series!). Discovering Coca-Cola Calippos at the 7/11s. Turning up at the morning tea stop with power, because that meant a proper "hot" coffee. Spending time with Mum and Am in the Mothership, talking, laughing and dozing. Learning, laughing and sobbing with Jules. We all lifted each other in the moments when it felt a bit tough.

But above all of that was the simple joy of watching Pete bounce back with energy at the end of each day. Some days, I had the privilege of riding beside him as we navigated our way through cities and into the hotel. Other days, I would be preparing things back at the hotel for his arrival, and I would hear the stories and receive texts from Dad telling me about the struggle but also the determination in his whole demeanour to get home that day. On those days, I could feel the last bit of strength melt away as he walked up from the car and into my arms.

His hugs said, "Today is done, but I am not done. Tomorrow is a new day, and I will be ready for it".

There were so many highs and heartbeats, I could write a whole book about them, but one that comes to mind happened at the end of day 10.

We had left a water stop, and Pete's words to me as he sat on his stool at the side of the road were, "I'm cooked. Stick a fork in me. I'm done". We sat there staring down the barrel of the last five kilometres of a 55-kilometre day. It would be one of the rare times that I would finish beside him instead of going ahead to the hotel to prepare.

We were weaving through a busy town, and in the chaos of city traffic we lost the support car. I was on the bike, not just to guide Pete but to be beside him, to help him find his way to the finish. It had been a tough day, as we had unfortunately lost Greg to injury the day before, so while he was still there in spirit and the first to welcome Pete in that day, physically Pete was so alone.

As we turned into the driveway of the resort, my internet had dropped out, so instead of jumping on Facebook Live to share this moment with the community, I switched to video to capture the final stretch to share later, because the community loved a hotel finish. There was something about this stretch that felt momentous. The hotel driveway was a good kilometre long (and felt like ten kilometres), so I waffled my way through, but what a moment to witness. I watched the determination written across his face, in his eyes, etched into every step of his stride. He was digging so deep. He was spent, absolutely running on empty, but he kept going. Because that's who he is. And in that moment, I knew that he was going to do this. My belief in him was stronger than ever.

We reached the end of the day to meet the high fives and warm hugs from our incredible support crew. As we sat quietly on a bench outside the hotel, the recovery phase of the day looming, Pete was motionless. I could see him retreating into himself.

Then, in a broken whisper, he said, "I'm just… empty. Every. Day".

And then… silence. No words, just the heavy weight of it all pressing down.

And the crew, well, they just came in around him.

Greg stepped forward with quiet words of encouragement.

Jules arrived with her signature smile and the biggest hug.

Bew knelt down and gently removed Pete's shoes and socks.

Mum wrapped him in a hug before disappearing to make his recovery smoothie.

Dad gave him a strong pat on the back, then got to work prepping his beloved Ranger for the next day.

Am hurried off to sort out the hotel check-in and get dinner organised.

Squid filled the ice bath and stood nearby, his end-of-day beer already in hand.

Nurse Claire waited patiently, ready to guide him through his end-of-day meditation ritual.

Mae Thiew quietly retreated to her room to rest, ready to take on another day of supporting him from the bike.

And I sat there holding him, watching the team move around us, tears silently falling, wishing with everything in me that I could just carry the weight for him, to take the pain, the exhaustion, the burden. But I couldn't. He still had 16 days to go. And all I could do was be there, beside him, holding space, whispering back, "I've got you".

And really, that's all any of us could do.

The weight of dual roles

Going into this, I never could have imagined the weight of the roles I would carry or how they would collide.

There was never a choice. I was the CEO of Hands. I was Peter's wife. I was the logistics and event lead. I was the marketer. There was no one else. We run a lean team at Hands, and the show had to go on.

Thank goodness for the crew around me. They lifted me just as much as they lifted Pete. They saw the cracks, understood my frustrations and held no grudges. They let me be grumpy, hugged me when I cried and stood beside me when I couldn't stand alone. We looked out for each other. That kind of care is rare.

Having Mum and Dad there was a godsend, not just for Pete but for me. What a privilege – yes, that word again – to spend that time with my aging parents, to share that experience with them. When we started pulling the crew together, there was never a question about asking them to be part of it. They are the bedrock of our village. We hoped they would say yes, and we were stoked when they did.

Before the run, I met with Kirrily Dear, who had completed her own epic journey from Broken Hill to Bondi. I wanted to learn what I could. One of her biggest pieces of advice was to find someone to be Pete's person. The one to have the hard conversations, to communicate decisions, to look after him. Because as his wife, I'd be too emotional. I'd try to take his pain away. He would see it in my eyes. And she was right. Together, we decided that person would be Dad. He gave the tough love safely and lovingly. And Mum, well, she became my support. So, even within our bigger team, we were a team of our own before the run even started.

Still, I had a lot to juggle. As event lead, people looked to me for answers. The crew needed guidance. As a leader, I had to show up for them, even as I felt myself cracking. Letting go of control isn't easy for me, and I am terrible at asking for help, but I'm grateful to every single crew member who said, "Leave that to me, I've got it". And they did.

As CEO of Hands, I had a job to do. We had committed to raising $1 million. With no marketing manager, I had to step into that role too, running communications for both the run and our work back in Australia. I had incredible support in the execution and will be forever grateful to my team in the Philippines, who really stepped up during that time. The work demands came at a cost, though, and if I had to name the hardest part of the whole journey for me, this was it.

I carried the weight of keeping our community connected to the journey – the stories, the socials, the updates – knowing people back home were waking each day to check how the run had ended, waiting for progress updates. I loved sharing it. But behind the scenes, I was torn. Sometimes, I just wanted to soak in the moment. To hold the hug a little longer. To sit in the silence rather than fill it with jobs.

I was consumed by work: falling asleep at the computer mid copywriting when I should've been resting or being present for our crew; writing emails or managing socials while Pete was running into lunch, sometimes looking for me. His person. And I wasn't there. Sometimes, I didn't even know he had arrived; I was so fixated on getting that brief done, or sending that email, or posting that call-out for fundraising. Closing off my work block for that day. That breaks my heart.

I know I did the best I could with what I had. But as a wife, I wish I could have been more present for Pete.

I remember when he hit 1000 kilometres. Wife CT wanted to jump up and down, to fist-pump and scream with joy, because that moment, well, that was once in a lifetime. But CEO/Marketing CT had a job to do. So, I pulled out my phone, and in doing so, the moment slipped away, captured for others but not lived by me. There were many of those moments during our time on the road, and that's OK – I did the best I could with what I had.

My biggest lesson in all of this? Find time to pause. Choose what matters most. And for me, that is best represented by a moment on day 22. We'd been driving for hours, trying to find the perfect lunch stop: shade, toilets, power, safety. We finally found a community fire shed which was perfect. Simple joys. Fist-pump moments. The team was setting up.

Then Dad called. He didn't sound happy. He asked me to move the stop. I was frustrated; we were ready for them. But the tone in his voice told me everything.

I asked, "Is Pete OK?"

His short reply was, "He just needs a hug from you right now".

And I knew he wasn't OK. He'd been battling the shin splints that would later turn into a stress fracture, the heat of the day was sucking the life out of him, and we were so close yet so far from the finish. We were in the third quadrant of the crisis clock. The wheels were wobbly, but I'd be damned if they fell off. Not on my watch.

In that moment, I had to step out of logistics mode and take my CEO hat off. I had to pause. I had to be present for what really mattered. I had to tell the team, who were so proud of finding the "perfect" stop, that we had to move. Twenty-two days in, we were all tired, so that was hard. But we did it. No complaints, we just did it.

And I stood there, waiting for him to come in, arms wide open. Waiting to hug him and lay next to him, wipe away the sweat and remind him that I believed in him.

That the end was near. Just hang in there.

I wish that lesson had landed earlier. Yes, there were plenty of moments in the days before when I paused and was present, don't get me wrong, but the lightbulb moment came right then.

To choose presence over perfection.

To choose love over performance.

To choose to be his person in that moment.

If lying next to him in the hard moments was choosing presence over perfection, then that is what I would do time and time again.

From A to B – the power of purpose in motion

When people ask me about the run, I usually start with this: "Never in my life have I felt purpose more than I did during December".

We hear the word "purpose" thrown around all the time – on stages, in books and in boardrooms. But what does purpose actually look like, not in theory but in motion?

For me, it looked like this: getting Pete from A to B. From Baan Home Hug in Yasothon to Baan Tharn Namchai in Takua Pa.

That was the job. That was the mission. That was the purpose.

Yes, the run was to raise $1 million for the kids we support, and that's what most people connect it to. And of course, that was a key driver. But for me personally, during those 26 days, it was simpler than that. My sole purpose was to get Pete to the finish line.

What that looked like, I had no idea.

I'm an event gal at heart. I knew it would involve logistics, planning and a very big spreadsheet. But this was a whole new playing field. I had never led a multi-day endurance running event in my life. It was daunting and exhilarating. And I was committed to doing it the best way I possibly could.

So, I did what I know how to do: I listened, and I learned.

I met with people. I asked questions. I soaked up advice from legends like Greg, Jules, Kirrily and Matty. I built standard operating procedures and mapped out scenarios with Pete – everything from who could pull him off the road to how to respond when he was exhausted or frustrated. I captured it all and shared it with the crew so we weren't making big decisions under pressure.

With Greg's help, I built detailed risk management plans, and I listened to the wise counsel from both him and Jules about their lessons learned running multi-day running events. And then it was time to get to know the crew. What would they need in tough moments? How could I support them? Surveys, chats, check-ins – we left no stone unturned.

Getting the nutrition right was also a big focus for me. Many times, I had seen Pete go for training runs and come back bonking out. I knew the signs. I knew that if we didn't get his fuelling right, it could be our undoing. We met with Matty Abel in the days following Nedd Brockmann's run. We listened. We learned. We got to work.

With guidance from Kirrily, we created what became our golden solution to nutrition: the bento box. At every stop – and there were up to 12 a day – Pete didn't need a question, he needed a choice. Our job was to take the thinking away. The bento box had eight compartments full of options. Mum was a star here: from pikelets and jelly cups to air-fried creations I didn't even know were possible, she nailed it. We stocked up on favourites from home: Zooper Doopers, Aussie peanut butter, energy bars, coffee pods... whatever it took to get Pete from A to B.

During the run, Matty and I checked in daily. Alongside Nurse Claire, we tracked everything: every bite Pete ate, every electrolyte he took, every toilet stop. If he wasn't drinking enough, we course-corrected. If his salt intake was low, we got creative (although, let's be honest, the salted cheese wraps were not my finest moment... sorry).

Even though Matty was watching from afar, he became part of our crew. I felt like he was right there with me in the Mothership each day when it was time to look at the data. The trust I had in him to guide me, day after day, moment after moment, was immense. I knew that if I ever felt unsure, he would help steer us back on course. He became an anchor for me, and his support was a crucial part of getting Pete from A to B.

And the gear – my goodness, the gear. Medicine kits, blister kits, massage guns, ice packs, cooling towels, head torches, bento boxes. Shopping was half strategy, half therapy. And honestly, some of the last-minute Amazon cart throw-ins turned out to be our most used tools. You're welcome, PB.

On the ground at the start of the run, the pressure built. Pete flew in later, so I was there setting everything up, leading the team, managing logistics. I remember one afternoon Greg asking, "Do you think he'll make it? Do you have a plan B?"

I didn't hesitate. "I'm not entertaining a plan B. We won't need it."

It wasn't naive. It was belief. I knew Pete. I knew what lived inside him. Even on day 14, when shin splints hit hard, I still believed.

So, how did we do it? We relied on routine. It kept us grounded. It kept me from unravelling.

Every day was broken into three blocks:

1. Rise early and run or ride alongside Pete.
2. Work from the Mothership – emails, updates, life admin.
3. Bike the final ten kilometres, prep at the hotel and start recovery.

Eat. Sleep. Repeat.

Without that rhythm, I could feel my wheels falling off. And if I fell apart, Pete would feel it. The team would feel it. That wasn't an option.

For me – and, I believe, for all of us – our purpose was clear: get this man from A to B. One job. No grey lines. And within that, there were many moving parts, each crew member playing a meaningful role. Everyone was "gainfully employed"; everyone was contributing.

For 16 out of every 24 hours, for 26 days straight, I was focused on one thing: getting Pete through today. And by day three, even through the chaos of learning on the go, I trusted the team, the plan and the process. I knew we had it in us to do this.

It might have been Pete running the 1400 kilometres, but it was belief, structure, and the right people in the right roles that got us from A to B. Purpose is powerful, but only when it's backed by planning, belief and the willingness to show up for each other every single day.

351/1400

Hand on heart, the best part of my day was always the mornings, those quiet hours spent running alongside Pete. The world felt still. No emails, no questions, no pressure, just one foot in front of the other, moving together, as I worked toward a challenge I'd quietly set for myself.

In the lead-up to December, I'd hoped to train more, but as Pete's mileage increased, so did my responsibilities at work and home. I took on more so he could focus, and in doing so, my own training slipped away. I felt disappointed, as I had wanted to run beside him, to share that experience. But I knew I could support him on the bike, and that became the plan.

Still, as the start line drew closer, something stirred in me. I wanted to push myself too. So, I committed to a cumulative run: Day one, I'd run one kilometre, day two, two kilometres, all the way to 26 kilometres on day 26 – a nod to the 1400-kilometre journey Pete was undertaking and a challenge that would quietly become my lifeline.

It gave me an individual goal to work towards. It gave me space. It became my oxygen mask.

The running turned into meditation. It was my therapy, my anchor, my moment of peace each day. And while I wasn't sure I could do it, every morning I laced up anyway and put my head torch on, my legs a little sore, my mind a little quieter.

Pete, Greg, and I ran together each morning, a little trio moving in sync. Some days we chatted, filling the air with light conversation and laughter. Other days, we ran in silence, each of us lost in our own rhythm. When Pete needed solitude, Greg and I instinctively adjusted to give him space while never being far behind. There was an unspoken understanding between us. We were just there, together. Steady. Supportive. Side by side.

My runs ended far earlier than Pete's, and every day I felt guilty for that. But as the kilometres added up, so did my pride. Fifteen. Eighteen. A half-marathon, then back-to-back half-marathons. Who even was I?

And I loved it. Every single step of it.

At the end of each run, I'd stop in the middle of the road, press "stop" on my watch, take a breath, take a photo of the distance marked on my watch, kiss my husband, snap a selfie, give him a cheeky pat on the bum as he ran on, then hop in the car, ready to shift into block two of the day.

I never imagined I'd run 351 kilometres. It's an achievement I hadn't really processed until I heard Pete sharing it in conversations after the run. It was epic. It was personal. It was mine: a milestone I didn't chase for anyone else.

I did it for love – and, let's be honest, just a little bit for my sanity.

The moments that mattered most

In all the time we shared in Thailand, there are moments that will stay with me forever. The kind that stop you in your tracks when you think about them, that bring a lump to your throat and a quiet tear to your eye.

There was watching Am rise into a role she'd never done before, stepping into chaos with that beautiful smile and calm composure. I've watched her grow from a child at Baan Home Hug into an extraordinary young woman with a bright future. Her strength, her joy, her presence – she is one of the reasons I fight for the work that we do. It was never a question – Am had to be part of this. She belongs with us. I'll never forget the sound of her voice gently calming Bew over the phone, or the pride in her eyes, arms raised, front and centre, as we crossed that final finish line. I get goosebumps just thinking about it.

There was Pete bowing to Mae Thiew at the end of day six, a moment so full of reverence, humility and love. As he invited her to cross off the day on our shared calendar, his words caught in his throat. He couldn't hug her as she's a monk, but he knelt to the floor and paid respect the only way he knew how, gratitude etched in every movement. Love without words.

There was the arrival of the Baines family, Kels and Jack diving into the pool on day 23 after a brutal stretch, Pete standing on shaky legs and beaming because his people had arrived. The tears, the laughter, the shared experience – no one can ever take that away. In the days that followed, we ran together, cried together and found joy in the hardest of places. The experience will bind us for life.

There was Nicole, in a moment of grace, joining us for the final days. When we invited the kids to Thailand, there was never a doubt that Nicole should be there. I knew it might be hard for her – Thailand holds a complicated place in her heart – but she came. And when we stood at Wat Yan Yao, in the temple where her husband first arrived in the aftermath of the tsunami, she wrapped me in a hug and whispered, "Thank you for bringing my family back together". That moment will stay with me always. Her grace. Her strength. Her love. Our family.

There was Jules, my partner in rants, in laughter, in tears, teaching me how to be a runner's wife. There were days she lifted me and days where I lifted her, but definitely more of the former, and for that I am grateful. We sat on the side of the road, laughing, crying, swearing, surviving. I don't know what I would've done without her strength, her honesty and her care. And despite her deep aversion to feet (and I mean deep), she still showed up for Pete's every single day. That, to me, is love in its truest form.

There was the time with my parents, the quiet afternoon chats, beers at the end of the day, a hug when words weren't needed. At 70, they lived big, long days with us: 16 hours on the road, no complaints. I'm proud of them. I'm grateful they said yes, that they chose to share this with us.

There was the bond between Dad and Pete. I joke that I'm the daughter-in-law, because sometimes it feels like Pete is the son Dad never had. That quiet desire to make him proud, something I know all too well, was visible in Pete, too. And when Dad whispered words of pride, you could see it shift something in Pete. He was enough. He always has been.

There was the final team moment, because the real victory wasn't in the distance covered but in what we achieved together. I watched as our crew of ten crossed the finish line side by side, arms around each other, huddled like a team that had just won the grand final. For someone who grew up in the pool, always swimming solo, the overwhelming feeling of team hit me hard and beautifully. I didn't want the moment to end. Confetti rained around us. The world fell quiet except for the sound of our crew, voices full of pride, shouting, "Together we can!" and just as powerfully, "Together we did!"

And ultimately, there was Pete, from day one to day 26, from Yasothon to Takua Pa. Crossing the physical finish line was monumental, but the final steps into Wat Yan Yao – what would become the finish line to us – were everything. Two years of planning, dreaming, fundraising, believing, culminating in a moment we will never forget.

There were so many moments. I could go on. And on.

The private jokes. The looks. The one-liners. The memories that belong only to us.

Life passes by so quickly. Five weeks in Thailand, and just like that, we were landing at Sydney Airport.

But the moments that mattered? They'll stay with me. Forever.

Together we can

We rose before the sun,
He ran through the days.
One foot in front of the other,
Fuelled by purpose, not praise.

I ran alongside,
Not just with my feet on road
But heart in hand,
Balancing love and leadership,
Emails and exhaustion,
Hugs and heartbreak.

We held each other in the silence,
When there were no right words.
When legs ached,
And the spirit was broken,
We wrapped him up with belief and love
And sent him back out.

Together, we carried weight.
That was never ours alone.
Every message from home,
Every water stop with power,
Every five-kilometre stretch completed
Was a victory for us all.

Some days, I missed him.
Not the runner but
The man. My Husband.

Crew's-eye view

And I missed me too
As I juggled CEO and wife.
But I showed up
In the best way I knew how.

Through grit,
Through tears,
Through stretches of road that made us
And moments that broke us
We moved forward.

From A to B,
From belief to knowing,
From Yasothon to Takua Pa.
Together, we did not just run.
We laughed.
We cried.
We shared.
And boy, did we live.

And though 351 was my number,
And 1400 was his,
It was never about the count.
It was about the *we*.

Because…

Together we can.
And together,
WE DID.

Acknowledgements
Without you, it doesn't happen

The title of the book, *Together We Can*, was as obvious as it is fitting. From the moment I uttered those words, standing on the steps of the Green Park Hotel in Yasothon at 4.30 a.m. on 1 December 2024, that was how the run would be identified by those of us on the road, because what *we* achieved on the roads of Thailand in December 2024 was the result of our combined efforts.

CT, from the moment I shared the concept with you, you have believed in me, and as the start of the run got closer your support grew and grew. I started the run with the honest belief that I had never been supported by one person in anything before to the level that you have supported me. Our time on the road was nothing short of a gift. In the months leading up to the run, we questioned if it was indeed achievable for you to be there for the entire journey. How could we both step away from our full responsibilities at home, knowing also that we would be back in Thailand for two weeks in January with the annual Hands bike ride? Now, I can't for the life of me think how either of us could have imagined you not being there for every minute. It blows my mind to think now, knowing what you contributed to each and every day, how I could possibly have imagined succeeding without you, and nor would I have wanted to spend a day there without you. From that 4.30 a.m. alarm each morning until our heads hit the pillow at night, you took care of everything. Thank you for sticking needles in my feet, washing my running gear every day, keeping the outside noise away and allowing me to focus on one thing: running. Some of my fondest memories of the run are of the moments we shared together on the road, with you running or riding beside me, sometimes in conversation and sometimes just being present. Thank you for holding me when I needed to be held, and thank you for bringing our family together on this incredible journey.

Chris, you are the father that I aspire to be. Seeing your face every five kilometres as you waited patiently for me to arrive was always a highlight. I never felt anything other than unconditional support and encouragement from you, and you always knew what to say and when to say it. On many occasions I would leave a water stop and spend the next 35 to 40 minutes until we saw one another again reflecting on your words. Out of everything you did for me over that month – and there was oh so much – the one moment I will cherish most was your embrace at the conclusion of day 14. What a day.

Wendy, you did what you do best: you held the family together during the most trying of times, and you kept everyone fed – not just the runners but the entire crew and any visitors who came to join us for a day or more. The hotel finishes were highlights, and seeing you with phone out to record the finish and then open your arms for a sweaty hug was how I wish every day could have ended. Despite all the hard work you had to do, seldom was there a day that I didn't round out a day on the road to be met with the smiling face and warm embrace of Mother. I thank both you and Chris for the love and support you give CT and me.

Greg, you said "yes" at the mention of a crazy idea without even knowing what it was. I needn't have worried about your approach to the run and the difference in our abilities. The wisdom you brought to the run and the unrelenting desire to serve me in my efforts made it achievable and enjoyable. But your support wasn't limited to me – the entire team benefited from your wisdom, years of experience, compassion and patience of a saint. When things went sideways and you could have easily abandoned the tour, you just dug deeper, and that is the sign of true character.

Jules, it became clear from the minute we hit the road that you were all in on supporting me as much as Greg. More than once, you would tell Greg to be quiet as he enthusiastically shared his opinions. You were the one gently encouraging me to eat in a way that I found it difficult to refuse at each water stop: "Just have a small bite of this sandwich... that's the way... now another". I found myself eating more than I wanted because I found it difficult to look at your smiling face and say no. You totally understood the role of the support team was to patch 'em up and push 'em back out. It was exactly the mindset needed by the team to create the best chance of success. But while you brought wisdom and deep knowledge to the run, the greatest gift you brought was yourself. Yours was such a calm and beautiful presence, not just for Greg and I running but for CT and the entire team. As many litres of sweat were left on the road you matched in tears of emotion, usually reserved for the end of each day. It became a daily ritual that no matter how dripping wet I was at the end of each day's run, you would welcome a hug to signal another day's victory on the road. I will cherish the memories we created.

Claire, I have described you (in the nicest possible way) as our insurance policy: I didn't ever want to need your expertise, but I wouldn't have contemplated doing the run without you. We never had to call upon your professional skills, and for that I am thankful, but you stepped forward and performed many other roles which were of equal importance to the team and in the execution of each day. You kept me fed with your gentle encouragement of "one more bite" even when I didn't want it, and I take it as a sign of your diligence that I ran 1400 kilometres over 26 days and did not experience a single cramp or dehydration headache. Thank you for your sacrifice and support over the entire month.

Our Thai team came without an insight into what to expect – but then, who of us did have a realistic understanding of what a month on the road meant? I think when they saw the hours and the effort the entire team was committing, which was all to support Thai kids and communities, it enriched their experience and their connection. Their presence and contribution to the run was beyond what they will ever understand or appreciate. They became more than part of the support team – they were already friends, but they left as family.

Am, no doubt there was so much more you did in support of the team beyond booking the hotels and dinners that I was never aware of, but I will always be grateful for the personality and care that you brought to the entire experience. We all enjoyed and benefited from your smiling face and positive demeanour on tour. You found your place in HET, but your coming of age was the integral role you performed on the Run to Remember. CT and I reflect like proud parents on your growth and development and the place you have arrived at in your life – you have truly found yourself and, dare I say it, happiness in life. Our pride in you is only matched by Mae Thiew.

Acknowledgements

Squid, it really was a highlight of the tour to watch you integrate into the team. You joined as a driver and valued staff member of HET but left as a rock-solid member of the Hands family. The bond you formed with Mother over those 26 days on the road as you travelled together from one water stop to the next was beautiful to witness. Did the experience leave an impression on you? Well, the fact that you had the Run to Remember logo tattooed on your forearm would suggest it did!

Bew, a memory we will all take of you is when you stepped up at the end of dinner to practice your English and order dessert for the ten of us: we ordered an assortment of banana splits with various flavours of ice cream, only to be told there was no banana and no ice cream. It will mean little to anyone other than those of us who were there. Just like Am and Squid, your integration into the team and your connection to the cause was a gift to all of us on the road.

Mae Thiew, I have written extensively about your commitment to the run and the lessons I took from your presence. I have learned and grown through my time with you, and feel I always take more from our encounters than I could ever give.

Kels and Jack, it wasn't just the fact that you accepted the invitation to come to Thailand for the end of the run but the enthusiasm in how you embraced the run that mattered most. You both trained like never before so that you could run with us. It wasn't a token effort – it was 100 kilometres in three days. That is serious running. You won't understand the depth of gratitude that I have in sharing that time with you on the road and my enormous, gut-bursting pride. Thank you for creating and sharing the absolute highlight of my life.

Josh and Jords, you both got to experience Hands and Thailand and understand the impact it has on us all. Thank you,

Josh, for driving behind Kels, and keeping her safe from the wild dogs, chasing emus and being her support person as she trained as you travelled around Australia. Jords, I'm not sure climbing a four-kilometre hill in Thailand was part of your life plan, but you did it with a smile. Kels and Jack are lucky to have you both, as is the rest of the Baines family.

Nic, when I first spoke with you about you potentially coming to the end of the run, you didn't blink and you didn't hesitate. While we couldn't get all the kids there, having you there meant a lot to me, and I know it meant a massive amount to Jack, Kels and CT. It was so good for you to experience what Hands does and the roads the kids have been riding since they were teenagers and which have been a big part of their lives over the last 20 years. I hope it was as meaningful for you to be there as it was for us to have you there.

Kay Spencer, I started Hands, but it is thanks to you that it has grown into what it is today. Our partnership has just passed 18 years, and it is remarkable to think what we have achieved during that time for the children and communities of Thailand. As the largest donor to the run through NARTA, you were with me and supporting me from the moment I shared the vision. However, it is the unquestionable support you have given me and my family that I cherish most. I cherish you and I love you for all you are and do.

Garry Browne, I sought your counsel as to how to make the run a success given the admiration I have for you and the work you do to support so many in this rich country of ours. When I face a problem or seek direction in the work I take on with Hands, you are one of the first people I reach out to, and your advice is always so sound. When I spoke of the run, you gently asked if I would consider you joining me on the road for a day.

Acknowledgements

You ran day 11 with me and CT, and you raised $100,000 for the privilege of running on the road. It goes without saying that your fundraising was deeply appreciated, but if it was topped by anything, it would be the conversations we shared that day. It was fitting that we would finish our time on the road together at a monumental point of the run.

Ali Flemming, it was always fitting that you would arrive to join me on day seven and step out of the car proudly wearing your "finisher" T-shirt from your latest marathon. I thought the fact that you ran the 60 kilometres that day with your marathon medal around your neck was a bit of a stretch, but you do you. Your response to the invitation to join the run was a bit like Greg and Jules's: "Yes, I'm in. What have I committed to, and how long can I stay?" You flew all the way from Sydney just to run a day or two with us, and I very much looked forward to it. You were due to leave the morning of day nine, the day Greg went down injured, and I know in my heart you were a breath away from ringing work to advise them you'd missed your flight and the next one would be on 28 December. Thanks, Al, for being part of everything we do.

Steph Ellis, your day running with me was never a certainty given the injury you carried into it. Each five-kilometre leg was an accomplishment, and before long you had completed the 60 kilometres, leading us into the hotel with Mae Thiew at the halfway point. Thanks for coming over and running with me on my birthday. It's one I won't forget, that's for sure.

Matty Abel, I simply hadn't contemplated using a coach before I signed up with you, not because I was arrogant and thought I could do it myself, but more because I just didn't appreciate the experience and wisdom you would bring. For six months you developed a weekly plan for me and then painstakingly analysed what I did, and called me out when I missed a session. You responded to my crazy travel schedule, and you started from a very low base to get this 57-year-old body into the best condition possible. I guess it was always going to be easy to see improvement. Matty, while your coaching in the lead-up positioned me for success, it was your work that no one saw during the run that mattered most. Every day, CT would be in contact with you, sharing how I was going, what I was eating and drinking, my mood and my niggles, and you developed a plan to help me respond: "Get more salt into him", "Give him coffee shots", "Tell him to run on the other side of the road", "He needs to eat more cheeseburgers", "Tell him he is doing awesome and I am so bloody proud of him." Not only was your advice solid based on experience and wisdom, but it was so reassuring to CT. Thank you, mate – you are a gift to all those trying their hardest, and I hope, as one of your students, I did you proud.

Dom, if ever there was a meant-to-be connection, ours was it. The V8 Supercars – what a random place to meet you. Once I had Matty on board, the only obvious gap I saw was getting my headspace right. Again, to state the obvious, running 1400 kilometres over 26 days was something I had never done before and would present me with challenges I had never faced before. The time we spent in the lead-up on Zoom discussing the various scenarios calmed my mind, and I have no doubt your words and advice were a massive part of what got me through the darkest and toughest days on the road. What a joy it was to then have you ride with us in January to live at least part of the run.

Hana and Nat from The Stretch Lab at Terrigal, you joined our team to get my body into the best condition it could, but you went so far beyond and embraced the Run to Remember, hosting your own fundraising event. Thank you for the support and belief, and

Acknowledgements

most of all the friendship we developed during my time on your massage bench.

There is a long list of sponsors who contributed to the run financially to help us get to $670,000, as well as those who contributed goods and services that made it achievable. As with everything we do at Hands, the first to step forward were our wonderful friends at NARTA. Without their contribution and support, nothing we do would reach the heights we achieve. Thanks to Ford Thailand for the loan of the support vehicles; Hoka Thailand for the shoes, which worked an absolute treat; Thai Life Insurance, Thaivivat Insurance, Robinson Khao Lak, Injinji, Ratch Group Foundation and AIA Insurance from Thailand for their financial contributions; and Paul Reid at Panasonic for the very generous donation. A huge shout out to the team at Marketing Bear for supporting our endeavours to make people aware of what we are doing for the kids and communities of Thailand.

This list of acknowledgements has been really confined to the Run. If I wanted to acknowledge all those who have contributed to Hands, it would be as long again. Hands Across the Water is only as strong as it is because of people such as Dale and Katherine Beaumont from Business Blueprint, Steve Carroll from Digital Live and the very long list of those who choose to support our kids in Thailand. Thank you.

To Lesley Williams from Major Street Publishing, thank you for embracing *Together We Can*. It has been such a joy to write this book and a delight to work with you in getting it out there so others can feel what it was like on the road.

Will Allen, my editor, thank you mate for bringing clarity and simplicity to my words. The readers of this book and I thank you for your contribution.

About the author

Peter Baines OAM is one of Australia's most respected voices on leadership, purpose-driven work, and navigating crisis.

With a career forged in some of the world's most challenging environments, Peter spent 22 years with the NSW Police, including time leading international disaster response teams across Southeast Asia. He played a key role in the forensic response to the 2002 Bali bombings and was deployed to Thailand after the Boxing Day Tsunami of 2004, where he led multiple rotations of international teams working to identify thousands of victims. These experiences tested his leadership at every turn and ultimately shaped his philosophy that true leadership is found not in titles, but in action.

It was that same sense of responsibility that led Peter to establish Hands Across the Water in 2005, a charity born from the devastation of the Boxing Day tsunami and a promise to help the children left behind. Since then, Hands has raised over

AU$40 million and continues to support hundreds of children across Thailand through education, housing and pathways to independence. At the heart of its success is a model built on shared experiences – most powerfully through the multi-day charity bike rides Peter still leads each year. Looking ahead, Hands is focused on creating a sustainable future by growing its social enterprise, expanding vocational opportunities and building a model where charity and business work together to deliver long-term impact without reliance on traditional donations.

In the final chapter of his policing career, Peter was seconded to the National Institute of Forensic Science, where he led national and international projects focused on building leadership capability and strengthening counter-terrorism strategies. His expertise was sought by global agencies including Interpol in France and the United Nations Office on Drugs and Crime in Southeast Asia. Following devastating floods in Jeddah, he was invited by the Saudi Arabian government to assess their emergency response and provide strategic advice on crisis leadership. In 2011, he was deployed to Japan to assist following the catastrophic tsunami that claimed thousands of lives.

Peter's insights have earned him national and international recognition. He was awarded the Order of Australia Medal in 2014 for his humanitarian work and was the first Australian to receive the Rotary International Professional Excellence Award. In 2016, the King of Thailand honoured him with the Fifth Class of the Most Admirable Order of the Direkgunabhorn. In recognition of his long-standing contributions to Thailand, Peter was named one of the five most influential Australians working in the region in 2025.

Peter is also an accomplished author and sought-after speaker. *Together We Can* is his fourth book, following the release of

About the author

Hands Across the Water (2011), *Doing Good by Doing Good* (2014), and *Leadership Matters* (2023). His keynotes connect deeply with audiences – from corporate leaders to change-makers – offering powerful lessons in resilience, values-based leadership and creating legacy through service.

When he's not writing, speaking or leading charity rides, Peter lives with his wife Claire on a rural property in New South Wales where they run a glamping business called Wildnest. A qualified helicopter pilot and ultra-marathon runner, Peter marked the 20th anniversary of the Boxing Day Tsunami by running 1,400 kilometres across Thailand in just 26 days – equivalent to 33 marathons – raising funds and awareness for the next generation of leaders supported by Hands.

Appendix

The numbers as they stack up

Date	Distance (km)	Elevation (m)	Pace (min/km)	Calories	Cum. distance (km)
1 Dec	59.67	356	8.15	4144	59.67
2 Dec	60.12	381	9.06	4044	119.79
3 Dec	60.52	464	9.15	4189	180.31
4 Dec	57.55	403	9.06	3941	237.86
5 Dec	59.31	384	8.41	4048	297.17
6 Dec	59.00	427	8.24	3925	356.17
7 Dec	58.64	1101	8.32	3569	414.81
8 Dec	55.56	499	7.56	3112	470.37
9 Dec	55.97	237	7.37	3597	526.34
10 Dec	52.82	206	7.44	3364	579.16

Date	Distance (km)	Elevation (m)	Pace (min/km)	Calories	Cum. distance (km)
11 Dec	57.73	387	8.12	3384	636.89
12 Dec	60.84	288	8.05	3637	697.73
13 Dec	57.43	396	7.37	3277	755.16
14 Dec	51.08	214	7.56	3121	806.24
15 Dec	31.37	166	7.15	1771	837.61
16 Dec	64.41	485	7.35	4576	902.02
17 Dec	57.35	246	7.24	4092	959.37
18 Dec	61.65	462	7.38	4276	1021.02
19 Dec	50.46	264	7.55	3190	1071.48
20 Dec	55.73	365	8.23	3688	1127.21
21 Dec	57.21	206	8.18	3884	1184.42
22 Dec	55.31	329	7.55	3674	1239.73
23 Dec	55.31	329	7.55	3674	1295.04
24 Dec	47.29	329	7.36	3674	1342.53
25 Dec	25.2	323	7.21	1765	1367.73
26 Dec	24.94	117	7.30	1738	1392.67*

---

* The km readings were taken from my Strava. CT's Strava recording showed a slightly higher daily distance.

Fun facts

Hottest day: 39°C (without consideration of radiant heat from the road)

Total rainfall: 0mm

Number of shoes: four pairs on rotation: 2 × Hoka Bondi and 2 × Hoka Clifton

Longest day: 64.4km

Shortest day: 25.2km (Christmas Day)

Most elevation in one day: 1101m

Most calories burnt in a day: 4576

Fluid intake: 15–20 litres per day

Kilos lost between morning and night: 2–3kg per day (regained 2–2.5kg overnight)

Favourite meal: Mother's pikelets or the 7/11 microwaved cheeseburger

Total net weight loss: 7kg

Dehydration headaches or cramps: nil

"The hardest part about the Hands ride
is not the training or the fundraising,
it is leaving everyone when
the ride is over."

Garry Browne AM

To view a gallery of behind the scenes video and photos from the run, along with a detailed daily diary visit:

peterbaines.com.au/exclusive-content

A portion of the profits from the sales of this book is donated by Peter to Hands Across the Water.

You can contact him at:

peter@peterbaines.com.au
linkedin.com/in/peterbainesconsulting
instagram.com/peterbaines

TOGETHER WE KEEP GOING

This book may be coming to a close, but the story of *Together We Can* continues – in the lives changed, the communities built, and the futures still being shaped.

What began as a response to tragedy has grown into something lasting. Hands Across the Water exists because of people who believe that every child should have the chance to grow up safe, supported, and able to choose their own path in life.

Now, we invite you to be part of what comes next.

Consider the following two ways to stay connected, create impact, and continue the story.

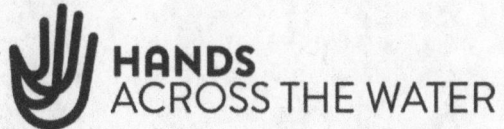

JOIN A RIDE

There's something life-changing about getting on a bike with strangers and finishing with friends. Our charity rides through Thailand aren't just about fundraising for the kids, they're about connection, perspective, and doing something meaningful for yourself.

www.handsacrossthewater.org.au/experiences

"I looked around at the start of the ride and thought, I am not a real bike rider. But by the end of the first day I knew I was part of a family."

SPONSOR A CHILD

Child sponsorship is one of the most powerful ways you can help to build bright futures. It's a monthly commitment that helps to ensure education, safety, and opportunity for a child in our care.

Shared experiences bring us closer – to each other, to our purpose, and to the legacy we want to leave. Just as Peter ran across Thailand with nothing more than a goal and a community behind him, you too can take the next step in building bright futures.

Because this story was never about one person – it's about all of us.

www.handsacrossthewater.org.au/sponsor-a-child

"I started sponsoring a child to make a difference in their life but I didn't realise how much it would change mine. It is a daily reminder that even from across the world, you can be part of someone's story."

Let's continue the journey, together.

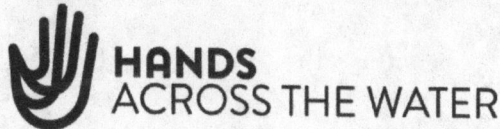

handsacrossthewater.org.au

Be better with business books

MAJOR STREET

We hope you enjoy reading this book. We'd love you to post a review on social media or your favourite bookseller site. Please include the hashtag #majorstreetpublishing.

Major Street Publishing specialises in business, leadership, personal finance and motivational non-fiction books. If you'd like to receive regular updates about new Major Street books, email info@majorstreet.com.au and ask to be added to our mailing list.

Visit majorstreet.com.au to find out more about our books (print, audio and ebooks), and read news and reviews.

We'd love you to follow us on social media.

- linkedin.com/company/major-street-publishing
- facebook.com/MajorStreetPublishing
- instagram.com/majorstreetpublishing
- @MajorStreetPub

www.ingramcontent.com/pod-product-compliance
Lightning Source LLC
Chambersburg PA
CBHW011944150426
43192CB00016B/2773